Th

Helping athletes to learn and develop – and so improve their performance – is the essence of sports coaching. However, coach education has not traditionally focused on educational theories to achieve this.

The Sports Coach as Educator expands on traditional conceptualisations of coaching, encouraging a view of coaches as professionals with a primary role as educators. The text shows how both established and leading-edge educational theories can enrich the practice of coaches and coach educators, opening up opportunities to approach the coaching process in new and inventive ways.

With contributions from leading international scholars in coaching and education, *The Sports Coach as Educator* provides a clear and accessible introduction to how key concepts from pedagogical theory can assist sports coaching. These include:

- viewing the coach as an expert guide to the learning process
- reflective practice and mentoring
- the viability of 'empowering' athletes
- coaching communities and the social process
- professional development and expert coaching
- future directions in professional sports coaching.

The Sports Coach as Educator will provide students and practising coaches with fresh insight into this exciting profession.

Robyn L. Jones is a Reader in the School of Sport, Physical Education and Recreation at the University of Wales Institute, Cardiff.

The Sports Coach as Educator

Re-conceptualising sports coaching

Edited by
Robyn L. Jones

Routledge
Taylor & Francis Group

LONDON AND NEW YORK

First published 2006
by Routledge
2 Park Square, Milton Park, Abingdon, Oxon OX14 4RN

Simultaneously published in the USA and Canada
by Routledge
270 Madison Ave, New York, NY 10016

Reprinted 2007, twice

Routledge is an imprint of the Taylor & Francis Group, an informa business

British Library Cataloguing in Publication Data
A catalogue record for this book is available
from the British Library

Library of Congress Cataloging in Publication Data
A catalog record for this book has been requested

ISBN 10: 0–415–36759–X (hbk)
ISBN 10: 0–415–36760–3 (pbk)
ISBN 10: 0–203–02007–3 (ebk)

ISBN 13: 978–0–415–36759–2 (hbk)
ISBN 13: 978–0–415–36760–8 (pbk)
ISBN 13: 978–0–203–02007–4 (ebk)

To my wife Theresa

Ei hynni, a'i dylanwad anhygoel,
ei neges a'i chennad;
Yn ei geiriau, hen gariad;
Yn ei rhoi mae pob parhad.
                                        Ynyr

And, as always,
to our daughters
Savanna, Seren and Siân

Contents

Illustrations

Notes on contributors

Kate Bullock is a Senior Lecturer in the Department of Education at the University of Bath. Formerly a teacher of science, she has worked in Higher Education for over 20 years. Her recent publications include co-authorship with Felicity Wikeley of *Whose learning?* (Open University Press). Her research focuses on student learning which has led to an interest in the nature of educational relationships and the ways in which they support it.

Dr Tania Cassidy is a Lecturer in the School of Physical Education at the University of Otago, Dunedin, New Zealand. Her research interest focuses on the pedagogy of tertiary physical education programmes and coach education courses. She is the co-author with Robyn Jones and Paul Potrac of *Understanding sports coaching: The social, cultural and pedagogical foundations of coaching practice* (Routledge). Another recent publication, co-authored with Professor Richard Tinning, considers the usefulness of knowledge-ability in understanding the possibilities for teacher education (*Teaching Education Journal*).

Dr Diane M. Culver completed her Ph.D. in 2004 at the Faculty of Education, University of Ottawa, Canada. Her scholarly interests are coaches' development and qualitative research. She has been a national ski team coach and coach trainer in Canada and New Zealand, as well as a consultant for athletes and coaches. Dr Culver is currently managing a research project at the University of Ottawa that is integrating a physical activity counsellor with a family medicine practice to motivate inactive patients to exercise.

Dr Chris Cushion is a Research Lecturer in Sports Coaching at Brunel University, where he is course leader of the undergraduate coaching degree. He also teaches on the Master's programme in Sports Coaching. He has published in a range of peer-reviewed journals, books and professional publications on issues pertaining to the coaching process, coach education and development. He is currently on the editorial board of

'Physical Education and Sport Pedagogy', serves as a 'coaching' reviewer for 'Psychology of Sport and Exercise', in addition to being a founder member of the British Association of Sport and Exercise Sciences' Coaching Special Interest Group.

James Galipeau received his Master's degree in sport psychology in 2002, and is now completing his Ph.D. in the Faculty of Education at the University of Ottawa, Canada. His research interests focus on social learning processes through the development of a community of practice among students in a Master's level sport psychology programme. James has five years of experience as a sport psychology consultant with a number of university and military teams, as well as individual athletes and teams from the local to international level of sport.

Dr Wade Gilbert is the graduate sport psychology coordinator and an Assistant Professor of sport psychology and physical education in the Department of Kinesiology at California State University, Fresno. Prior to arriving at Fresno State, Dr Gilbert was a Postdoctoral Fellow at the International Center for Talent Development at the University of California, Los Angeles. Dr Gilbert's areas of research and teaching include coaching science, talent development, measurement and evaluation, and qualitative research methodology.

Dr Robyn L. Jones is a Reader in the School of Sport, Physical Education and Recreation at the University of Wales Institute, Cardiff, UK. His research area comprises a critical sociology of coaching in respect of examining the dynamism and complexity of the inter-active coaching context and how practitioners manage the inevitable dilemmas that arise. He has published in many leading journals including *Quest*, *Sport, Education and Society*, *The Sport Psychologist* and the *Sociology of Sport Journal* among others. To date, he has authored and co-authored/edited four research-based books and a practical handbook on pedagogy and coaching.

Dr Bryan McCullick is an Associate Professor at the Department of Kinesiology at the University of Georgia. To keep his feet firmly planted in the realities of contemporary public schools, he regularly teaches 'Personal and Social Responsibility through Physical Activity' at Barnett Shoals Elementary School in Athens, Georgia. Stemming from his commitment and concern for quality physical education instruction, his research interests are germane to teacher/coach education and teaching/coaching expertise. He has published widely on participants' views of teacher/coach education programmes while his current research includes a study of children's perceptions of student teacher effectiveness as well as an analysis of expert sport instructors' working memory.

Ilse Sannen Mason received her BS in Physical Education from the Katholieke Universiteit Leuven in Belgium and her MEd in Adapted Physical Education at the University of Georgia. She is currently a full-time Lecturer in the administrative foundations of coaching and physical education methods at the Kinesiology Department at the University of Georgia. Her research interests include coaching, expertise and pedagogy.

Dr Dawn Penney is a Senior Lecturer in the School of Education at Edith Cowan University, Australia. Prior to this appointment, she was a Senior Research Fellow at Loughborough University, UK and Research Fellow at the University of Queensland, Australia. Dawn has been involved in policy and curriculum research at national, state and school levels in the UK and Australia, focusing upon development in Health and Physical Education. Her publications include *Politics, policy and practice in physical education*, co-authored with John Evans (1999, Routledge) and *Gender and physical education: Contemporary issues and future directions* (2002, Routledge). Her most recent work has focused on the development of Specialist Schools in the UK and collaborative research with teachers engaged in curriculum development.

Dr Paul Potrac was formerly at the University Otago, New Zealand, and is now a Lecturer in Sports Coaching at Brunel University. His research interests principally focus on the interaction between coach and athlete in top-level sport. In conjunction with colleagues in the UK and New Zealand, he has co-authored *Sports coaching cultures: From practice to theory* (Routledge) and *Understanding sports coaching: The social, cultural and pedagogical foundations of coaching practice* (Routledge). He has also published in journals such as *Quest, Sport, Education and Society* and the *International Review for the Sociology of Sport*.

Dr Paul G. Schempp is currently a Professor in the Department of Physical Education and Sport Studies, University of Georgia where he currently serves as the Director of the Sport Instruction Research Laboratory and Head of Department. He is also President of Performance Matters, Inc. a private consulting corporation specializing in enhancing sport performance. He is a former recipient of a Senior Fulbright Research Scholar at the University of Frankfurt, Germany where he studied the role of social theory in the analysis of sport instruction. His research has focused on teacher development and instructional expertise. Most recently, Dr. Schempp has been engaged in a series of studies on the characteristics and practices of expert teachers of sport and physical activity. This work has emerged through numerous edited and authored books (e.g. *Scientific Development of Sport Pedagogy, Learning to teach* and *Teaching sport and physical activity*) and peer-reviewed journals (e.g. *American Educational Research Journal, Journal of Teaching Physical Education, Research Quarterly for*

Exercise and Sport, and the *Journal of Research and Development in Education* among others). Dr. Schempp also serves on the National Education Program staff of the Ladies Professional Golf Association and as a technical consultant for the Swedish National Golf team and *Golf Magazine*.

Dr Martyn Standage is a Lecturer in Sport and Exercise Psychology in the School for Health at the University of Bath. Primarily, his research examines the motivational mechanisms that account for variations in cognitive, behavioural and affective responses of individuals engaged in physical activity settings. His research has been published in journals such as the *Journal of Educational Psychology*, *Journal of Sport & Exercise Psychology*, *Journal of Sports Sciences* and the *British Journal of Educational Psychology*.

Professor Pierre Trudel received his Ph.D. in 1986 at Laval University, Canada. He is a full professor at the School of Human Kinetics, University of Ottawa, Canada. In the last 15 years his research group has been funded by the Social Sciences and Humanities Research Council of Canada to conduct research on coaching and coach education. Over 65 articles have been published in a variety of journals and books. Professor Trudel has been a consultant for many sport organisations, developing programmes and supervising coaches.

Mike Wallace is a Professor of Education at the University of Bath. He researches the management of complex change. He is currently co-directing research on effective professional learning communities in schools, funded by the DfES, NCSL and GTCE. He also holds an ESRC AIM (Advanced Institute for Management Research) Senior Public Services Fellowship, investigating the management of complex and programmatic change in education and health. He has written a practical handbook, *School centred management training* (1991), and four books reporting his research: (with A. McMahon) *Planning for change in turbulent times: The case of multiracial primary schools* (1994); (with V. Hall) *Inside the SMT: Teamwork in secondary school management* (1994); (with L. Huckman) *Senior management teams in primary schools: The quest for synergy* (1999); and (with K. Pocklington) *Managing complex educational change: Large scale reorganisation of schools* (2002).

Dr Felicity Wikeley is a Senior Lecturer and currently Director of Studies for Research, in the Department of Education at the University of Bath. Her main research interests are educational relationships and the contextual nature of school effectiveness and improvement. Her most recent publication *Whose learning?* (Open University Press) with Kate Bullock looks at the relationship between tutors and students in schools and colleges.

Preface

Aim

Despite becoming a common area of academic study, our understanding of sports coaching remains scant. This, in large part, has been due to the limited perspectives employed to analyse it. The aim of this book is to expand current conceptualisations of the coaching role and, subsequently, coach education. The case is made that coaches should be considered as educators and coaching as a complex pedagogical process. Hence, coach education programmes should be structured along lines that develop related competencies. In supporting this position, examples from educational theory are cited that can directly enhance our understanding of coaching and how to go about it. The purpose then, is to provide fresh, new ways to look at coaching, thus building on the current framework of analysis. It is based on the premise that coaching is fundamentally intertwined with teaching and learning within given situational constraints. In this respect, it takes coaching back to its problematic teaching roots, emphasising that many of the dilemmas and complexities inherent within coaching closely mirror those in teaching. Through the writings of leading international scholars in the fields of sports coaching and education, the case is made that drawing theoretical concepts from a critical pedagogical paradigm can enrich the practices of coaches and coach educators by giving them increased access and opportunities to reflect upon coaching practice in previously untried, inventive ways. Indeed, with increasing investment in coaching from centralised initiatives (Sports Coach UK 2002, 2004), now would appear to be the opportune time to re-evaluate our traditional understanding and conceptualisation of coaching and coach education, which has been recently criticised by coaches as being unrealistic (Saury and Durand 1998, Jones et al. 2004).

Content

In relation to its content, the book is divided into three parts. The first (Chapters 1–3) makes the case for a re-conceptualisation of coaching as an educational endeavour. The second (Chapters 4–7) deals with this proposed change in terms of the coach's role, while the third (Chapters 8–11) examines it in relation to coach education. More specifically, Chapter 1 by Jones serves as a general introduction to the book, in contending that current conceptualisations of coaching, that is, what coaches do, need to be expanded and refined. Drawing on recent work, it argues that coaches should be viewed as more akin to social pedagogues, with their effectiveness being highly dependent on the relationships established with athletes.

Chapter 2, by Wikeley and Bullock, builds on this foundation by discussing the nature of such educational relationships, before illustrating how associated theories can inform our understanding of sports coaching. The final chapter in the section (Chapter 3) by Penney highlights the current relevance of viewing the coach as a pedagogue both through UK stated policy and Australian practice at an Aboriginal Sports College. Here, the responsibilities and roles of teachers and coaches are firmly linked. The remainder of the book is concerned with elaborating on the case made in this section, so as to make it more understandable and operational for scholars, coaches and coach educators.

Chapter 4 by Potrac and Cassidy borrows from the work of Vygotsky (1978) in arguing that our comprehension of the coaching role can be enhanced if the coach is viewed as a 'more capable other'. The following chapter (Chapter 5) by Jones and Wallace makes a similar claim for considering the coach as an 'orchestrator'. In Chapter 6, Jones and Standage critically examine the current tendency towards empowering athletes, before discussing the role of the coach within such athlete-centred pedagogies. Here, the concept of shared leadership is examined as both a desirable and workable entity. This theme is continued in Chapter 7 by Galipeau and Trudel who further question and explore the nature of the coaching role in terms of athletes' communities of practice and the learning that takes place within them (Lave and Wenger 1991).

In moving to examine how pedagogical theories can contribute to more critical and contextual coach education programmes, Culver and Trudel initially discuss the value of cultivating coaches' communities of practice (Chapter 8). In Chapter 9, Gilbert and Trudel, borrowing from the work of Schön (1987), argue that coaches should be reflective practitioners in order to further generate knowledge, while in the following chapter (Chapter 10) Cushion cites several educational theorists in contending that critical mentoring should be an integral aspect of coach education. Finally, Schempp, McCullick and Mason (Chapter 11) examine the development of expertise in coaching through Berliner's (1994) four-phase model, which incorporates the stages of (1) beginner, (2) competent, (3) proficient and (4) expert.

Although the book is divided into distinct parts, several points of commonality emerge in the chapters. This is particularly so in terms of the reference made to certain theoretical viewpoints (e.g. the work of Lave and Wenger is referred to in many chapters). This further highlights the integrated nature of coaching and how differing theoretical viewpoints can inform different areas and conceptions of it. Although at one level, then, the reader may get a certain sense of overlap, the point to remember here is the necessity to draw upon various aspects of many positions as the situation demands in order to better understand the complex pedagogical nature of coaching.

Who is the book for?

The book is primarily aimed at final year undergraduate and postgraduate students of coaching. It is anticipated that such an audience would already have some knowledge and/or experience of traditional coaching principles. It therefore aims to build on this knowledge as it seeks to develop in readers an appreciation that coaching can be viewed and interpreted in a number of ways, thus increasing our theoretical understanding of it. As such students are often, or are soon to be, coaches, the text also has direct relevance for practitioners. To accentuate this, the chapters, although theoretical, are written in a reader-friendly fashion that allows the concepts presented to be easily linked to practice. The book can also be useful for coach educators as they increasingly seek to engage coaches with the complex and multifaceted nature of the work, and how to manage it better. Consequently, the book speaks to both practical and academic cultures with the theory presented being a thought-provoking pre-requisite to experimentation, innovation and progress in coaches' practice. Finally, the book can also serve as a reference text for those who wish to be, or who are currently, involved in doing research on coaching, as it provides several alternative viewpoints through which to analyse findings. In this way, it can be seen as an attempt to inform more realistic and reliable evaluation of coaching practice, thus increasing our understanding of it.

RJ

Acknowledgements

In the production of this book I have incurred many debts. Special thanks go to the contributing authors, for their insightful work and good humour as the project unfolded; to Human Kinetics for permission to use copyright material from W. D. Gilbert and P. Trudel, 'Learning to Coach Through Experience: Reflection in Model Youth Sport Coaches', *Journal of Teaching in Physical Education*, (2001), 21(1): 23, Figure 1; and to colleagues at Routledge, in particular Kate Manson and Samantha Grant, who seemed to believe in the project from the first word. I'm additionally grateful to Ynyr, for words far more meaningful than mine, and to my ever supportive parents, who believed before any words were written. My most special thanks, however, go to Theresa, my wife, to whom the book is primarily dedicated and to our wonderful daughters, Savanna, Seren and Siân, who truly make my 'blood sing'.

Part I

Introduction

Coaching as an educational enterprise

Chapter 1

How can educational concepts inform sports coaching?

Robyn L. Jones

Introduction, aim and content

Despite a recent upsurge in scholarly interest, coaching remains an ill-defined and under-theorised field. Indeed, it has been argued that no conceptual framework currently exists which adequately deals with the complex reality within which coaches work and how they can better manage it (Jones 2000, Gilbert and Trudel 2004b). It is a situation that has contributed to the dissatisfaction of many coaches with professional development programmes. The advice given is simply not considered actionable as it ignores the many tensions and social dilemmas that characterise their practice (Saury and Durand 1998, Cushion *et al.* 2003, Jones *et al.* 2004). Consequently, although there is increasing realisation of the value to coach in a more holistic, contextually sensitive fashion, the predominant theoretical discourse continues to constrain professional development as it is perceived by practitioners as lacking relevancy. Similarly, the strong thread of time-honoured beliefs seen running through coaching, provides a compelling argument that coach education programmes are having a very limited impact on practice (Cushion *et al.* 2003, Gilbert and Trudel 1999a). This leads us to question current conceptions of coaches, coaching and coach education.

The aim of this book is to present a re-conceptualisation of coaching. It marks an attempt to widen and enrich the theoretical lens through which the coaching role and how coaches are prepared for it can be viewed. It is based on the notion that at the heart of coaching lies the teaching and learning interface, and the myriad ways through which coaches influence athletes to develop and improve. The concepts discussed within the book come from the field of pedagogy, which, in turn, is viewed as a social process. They rest on a different set of assumptions about the nature of coaching and the coach's role than currently operate. These include that coaching, like teaching, is an inherently non-routine, problematic and complex endeavour; that a great deal of untapped, tacit knowledge already exists in athletes and coaches; that coaching is an activity primarily based on social interaction and power; and that, like teachers, the challenges that coaches face are partly localised and need to be addressed on the ground (Toole and Seashore Louis 2002). It therefore embraces the belief that coaching is not limited to styles of delivery, sport-specific knowledge and sequential management of a set procedure, but is also infused with the dynamic rings of invisible social contexts that surround the coach–athlete relationship (McLaughlin and Talbert 1993).

The theoretical notions presented within this book are an attempt to expose some of these invisible contexts, so we can better manage them (Toole and Seashore Louis 2002). The goal is to enable and to encourage us to look at coaching through fresh eyes (Duckworth 1997), thus breaking free from the cramped confines of the familiar. The concepts aim to inform an enhanced understanding and refinement of the role of the coach and how to teach it through developing more discerning strategies to deal with the complexity and constraints inherent within both. In this way, it is hoped that improved conceptual insight and clarity will lead to increased knowledge and understanding of coaching and how to do it well. It builds on earlier published work by Jones et al. (2004) and Cassidy et al. (2004) among others in problematising sports coaching, thus further developing the critical tradition currently lacking in the area. By doing so, it pushes the case for coaches, like teachers, to be recognised (and educated) as professionals who constantly need to make decisions in the interests of their charges based on astute contextual considerations (Toole and Seashore Louis 2002). The purpose then, rather than providing a set of ready-made answers, is to make coaches and coach educators reflective of previously unconsidered theoretical notions, thus giving them the options to think in different ways about their practice and its consequences. Ultimately, it is to improve coaches' understanding and discretion, to provoke thought, questions and discussion among them as to why they coach as they do.

The text is largely in response to recent calls to widen the search beyond the usual suspects of content knowledge that has traditionally informed coach education programmes if imaginative, dynamic yet thoughtful practitioners are to be developed (Cushion et al. 2003). If the challenge is ignored, we run the risk of getting a souped-up version of the same coach education fare, which has been criticised by coaches and some scholars alike as being fine in theory but divorced from reality (Jones et al. 2004, Gilbert and Trudel 1999a, Saury and Durand 1998, among others). Consequently, in going beyond the known to new theoretical horizons, the book is concerned with developing more realistic analyses and understandings of what coaches actually do while suggesting ways to do, and teach, it better.

Following a brief illustration of the traditional teaching–coaching divide and the current inability of theoretical concepts to cross it, this chapter questions the necessity for such a situation. It makes the case that there are many more similarities than differences between teaching and coaching, particularly with regard to their complex leader–follower natures; a complexity that precludes any paint-by-number plans that practitioners can easily stick to (Toole and Seashore Louis 2002). Drawing predominantly on the work of Armour (Jones *et al.* 2004) and Bergmann Drewe (2000a) it views coaches as social pedagogues and argues for expanding the conceptualisation of coaching to include attributes that have been traditionally viewed as having to do with the educational enterprise (Bergmann Drewe 2000a, Jones 2004). Hence, it both problematises the coaching context as a learning environment, while emphasising the need to coach holistically if the potential of athletes is to be fully realised. Finally, it frames the theories presented in the book as threshold concepts (Toole and Seashore Louis 2002), which can act as signposts to new ways of seeing and understanding.

Before embarking on the discussion, however, definitional clarity is required in relation to the term 'teaching'. Here, as opposed to the narrow instructional act, it is taken as being akin to educating; as a holistic developmental activity connected with a wider set of beliefs about social learning (Bergmann Drewe 2000a). Consequently, although Garforth's point about the elusive nature of teaching or educating is well taken, in the context of this book, both terms are viewed synonymously as a 'deliberate process of manipulating the environment by a variety of means in order to influence, modify and improve human beings' (Garforth 1985: 21).

The traditional teaching–coaching divide: a forced separation?

Elsewhere, I have argued the case that the bio-scientific assumptions on which dominant conceptions of the coaching process lie have limited potential for either a theoretical understanding of coaching or for guiding practitioners (Jones and Wallace 2005, Jones 2000). The tendency to view coaching from a rationalistic perspective reflects the assumption that it is feasible to establish a clear and uncontroversial set of fully attainable goals, whose achievement can be unequivocally measured. Such an approach is flawed because the complex and dynamic nature of the coaching context itself doesn't allow for such clean treatments (Cassidy *et al.* 2004). The many diagrammatic models that characterise coaching literature can similarly be criticised for unproblematically representing complex dealings (Jones and Wallace 2005, Meyer and Land 2003). Such models allow students to plot hierarchical relationships and interactions without generating an understanding of the functional complexity that lies behind and between them. It is a perception that has not only simplified a very intricate process, but has also restricted a more complete conceptual understanding of coaching through its marginalisation of more critical analytical paradigms.

Conversely, research indicates the coaching context to be multifaceted, constantly in a state of flux, where coaches must continually make decisions in a variety of contingent situations, which themselves are influenced by any number of factors to varying degrees (e.g. Saury and Durand 1998, Jones *et al.* 2002, Potrac *et al.* 2002). Such work highlights the nature of coaching expertise as requiring the flexible adaptation to relationship-imposed constraints, as the actual immediate task of a coach cannot be 'totally defined or specified in advance' (Côté *et al.* 1995: 255). Such arguments closely mirror those made in relation to teaching. Indeed, recent studies have confirmed that coaches view their work, not as physical trainers, but as educators or guides in developing and growing athletes (Jones *et al.* 2004). This begs the question of whether pedagogic concepts should take a more central role in coaching analysis and coach preparation than is currently the case. Let us examine some of the reasons why so far they haven't.

It can be argued that the division between teaching and coaching has been developed and accentuated by the dominant discourses used in the perceived parental disciplines of education and sport science. Specifically, as physiology, psychology and biomechanics have dominated sports coaching literature, coaching itself has come to be associated with training. Demand has thus been placed on the 'specialist knowledge of the coach to provide technical direction and proper sequence'. It is a discourse that 'privileges factual knowledge over interpretation' (Prain and Hickey 1995: 79). This is at odds with the more holistic and problematic emphasis often given to teaching through its strong connection with education. Lee (1988) clarified the effect of these differing associations in concluding that while teaching or educating is seen to be more about an individual's total development, coaching has been viewed as the sequential attainment of physical skills and their testing in competition. The distinction has been further emphasised in studies on teacher–coach role conflict (e.g. Chelladurai and Kuga 1996, Staffo 1992), which have underlined the perception that differing skills and knowledges are needed in the differing domains (Bergmann Drewe 2000a). Teaching, and the pedagogical theory that informs it therefore, has tended to lie outside traditional conceptualisations of coaching.

Despite this division, a pedagogic function to the coach's role has been acknowledged (e.g. Martens 1997), although it has been varied and scant in nature. The reasons for this marginalisation are many. They include the traditional conception of psychology and physiology in particular as coaching's guiding disciplines, the absence of a definitive coaching role frame, that is, a consensus about what the job ought to entail (Gilbert and Trudel 2004b), and a limited interpretation within coaching literature of the term 'teaching'. In respect of the latter, teaching appears to have been narrowly conceived as being synonymous with direct instruction. For example, in searching for conceptual clarity for the coach's role, Lyle (2002) stated that coaching is, above all, a process, with any teaching within it confined to participation or recreative coaches as manifest in the episodic act of developing a motor skill in others. Consequently, teaching is judged to be largely absent from performance or higher-level competitive sport.

Teaching and coaching, then, are pretty much viewed as distinct entities. This divide is presented as being so definitive, that Lyle doubts if there is enough commonality of purpose between practitioners who operate in both sporting domains to justify one form of membership of a professional body. It is a belief somewhat reflected by coaches themselves, who have been found to bracket their role and what it entails according to the competitive level of their athletes (Gilbert and Trudel 2004b). Clearly, in making this distinction, the notion of pedagogy as the essence of coaching gets limited appreciation.

This dichotomy, fuelled by different discourses and competing interests, which has grown up to distinguish teaching from coaching, has had a negative influence on both fields (Prain and Hickey 1995). This has been particularly so on coaching, as educators have not seen it as their territory, while coaches have not looked to educational theory to inform their practice. The situation has retarded an adequate conceptualisation of coaching particularly in relation to acknowledging it as a pedagogic and educational endeavour. Regardless of common ancestry, then, in terms of improving the performance of learners, it seems that coaching and teaching have been talking *past*, as opposed *to*, one another (Cassidy *et al.* 2004).

Coaching as pedagogy

Despite this separation, some scholars, while acknowledging that both activities are sometimes driven by distinct goals, consider that the line of demarcation between teaching and coaching is not so obvious or, indeed, necessary. For example, Bergmann Drewe (2000a), while agreeing that many participation-level coaches are obviously involved in acts of didactic teaching, concluded that just because performance 'coaches work with fewer people and at a higher skill level, does not negate the fact they (too) are involved in teaching – teaching their athletes skills, technique and strategy' (p. 81). Perhaps the point to remember is that there are many ways to teach and things to learn, even at the highest level. For example, sensitively facilitating a small innovation in a high-jumper's technique, or proactively introducing new lines of defensive organisation through guided discovery in a team invasion game, can easily be interpreted as pedagogical or educational acts. Similarly, so can attempts to cultivate athletes' responsibility and creative engagement with game-related problems, or to generate greater fortitude in them to cope with anxiety-provoking situations.

This was reinforced by the recent work of Potrac (2000) and Jones *et al.* (2004) among others, who found that both instruction and facilitation loomed large even in the practice of top-level coaches. In other words, the pedagogic role, including that of pastoral care and mentorship, was an important one in the make-up of these coaches' personas. Indeed, Graham Taylor, the former coach of the English national football team and one of the coaches interviewed in this body of work, went so far as to proclaim that 'coaching really is a form of teaching' in that it primarily involves communicating, learning and maintaining positive relationships with those being taught (Jones et al. 2004: 21). Even Sir Clive Woodward, the victorious coach of England's 2003 World Cup winning rugby union team, was recently quoted on the issue as stating that '[t]he best coaches are good teachers' (Cain 2004). It is a view that has been constantly emphasised in the multitude of coach behaviour research carried out over the past two decades, which has been unequivocal in reporting instruction as the dominant act engaged in by coaches at all levels while coaching (e.g. Potrac 2000, Hodges and Franks 2002). It also echoes the recent work of Corlett (1996), who argued that the supportive pedagogical component in the athlete–mentor (coach) relationship is vital in allowing performances of courage, originality and even genius to occur. On closer inspection then, perhaps the constructed divide between teaching and coaching is not so wide or deep as we have imagined it to be.

In analysing interview data from several top-level coaches, Armour (in Jones et al. 2004) concluded that the practitioners under study could be viewed as modern-day pedagogues and, hence, that coaching has much to learn from pedagogical concepts. It is a position that places the wider notion of athlete learning as opposed to mechanistic performance at the heart of coaching practice, and is based on the belief that the coaching role involves more than knowledge of method and content. Indeed, the coaches interviewed considered that caring for their athletes was a crucial component of their practice, as was the establishment of a positive and supportive working climate. They likened it to a holistic and realistic philosophy of athlete development. Such a view echoes the work of Day (1999) in education, who concluded that caring for and about pupils in a broad sense was central to good teaching practice. Similarly, the educational philosopher Vygotsky's belief that individual development is linked to contextually sensitive guided practice scaffolded by more capable others (Beltman 2003), resonates clearly with how these coaches perceived their roles.

Additionally, it appears that, like teachers, the coaches studied by Armour (Jones et al. 2004) based much of their practice on folk pedagogies (Bruner 1999), which consist of a set of beliefs about what and how people learn best. Far from being rational, such theories are based on individual perceptions of the learner, the context and constant reflection on, and refinement of, experience and knowledge. This is supported by the work of Saury and Durand (1998) who found that elite sailing coaches' knowledge was highly personal through being tightly linked to experience, involved much context-based opportunist improvisations and was difficult to verbalise. They concluded that, like expert teachers (Berliner 1988), such coaches' knowledge was shaped by previous behaviours and stored in contextualised directories of related actions. The results provide further support for recognition of a common ground between teachers' and coaches' work and how they go about it.

Other studies (e.g. Gilbert and Trudel 2001) have also found that good coaches, like good teachers, constantly engage in much reflection, not only on what they do but why they do it. Such a process is akin to that of peda-gogical reasoning (Shulman 1999), which involves a progressive spiral of comprehension, adaptation, evaluation, reflection and new comprehension. However, lest we are tempted to place these stages into a model of successful coaching, Shulman is quick to point out that these stages often overlap, in no particular order, and can happen at different times. Pedagogy is just not that easy. Furthermore, such critical educational concepts as mentoring, observing and socialisation within cultural communities of practice echo the ways that coaches learn how to coach, underlining their relevancy to better understanding coaching knowledge and to possible coach education (Cushion 2001). Indeed, unlike the rational coaching process depicted in much current literature, the learning that occurs in such contexts is anything but sequential. On the contrary, it is multifaceted, social, fluid and highly personal. Consequently, for Armour, the key to understanding coaching, like teaching, lies in appreciating the articulations and connections between all the human interactive elements that comprise it (Jones 2004). To better analyse and comprehend coaching, then, we need a far more complex, problematic and pedagogically orientated conceptual lens than we have so far used.

Undoubtedly over recent years, the call to coach in a more holistic fashion has gained credence. Such a stance recognises, to varying degrees, the social nature of coaching and the need to ensure the rounded development of athletes. The parallels with educating, as opposed to training, the whole person are obvious (Bergmann Drewe 2000a). For example, Lyle's (2002: 44) definition of coaching as a 'period of social activity [involving degrees of] commitment, success and failure, emotional highs and lows, personal ambition and status', endorse the thoughts of an increasing number of theor-ists that it is a complex pursuit and, hence, needs to be treated as such. Similarly, others have lamented the tendency in coaching to develop a high degree of athlete dependency (see for example Kidman 2001). This is where athletes are heavily reliant on the coach in terms of their decision making. The link to poor on-field performance is clear as such athletes can't cogni-tively adapt to the dynamic live environment. Despite this rhetoric, the means and accompanying discourse of exactly how to coach in a more holistic fashion has not developed (Cassidy et al. 2004). Consequently, although the recognition that coaching may have much in common with education, in so far as both should develop the totality of the individual, has surfaced, the link towards seeing pedagogic theory as a means to inform coaching has remained undiscovered.

What's the value of a book like this?

The significance of this book lies in provoking thought about how we should view the nature of coaching. This is particularly so in respect of the role of the coach and how coaches should be prepared for it. Its importance then, lies not in asking if coaches and coach educators 'know their stuff', as many clearly do, but rather in questioning the kind of 'stuff' they know (Stones 1998). It is also based on the premise that we need to know more 'stuff' than we currently do and how to systematically order it, so that we can think responsibly and maturely about the coaching role and how to be good at it. In other words we need more, and more appropriate, theory in relation to coaching.

It is hoped that the theoretical concepts contained within the book will rouse many pedagogical, interactional and social sensitivities that have been purged from the scientific discourse of too many coaches. It is anticipated that they will stretch coaches in ways they are meant to be stretched. Through such an awakening, coaches can engage in a level of creative thought and experiment with novel strategies that the current standard coaching model doesn't allow (Gilbert and Trudel 2001). Furthermore, as the study of coaching is evolving in depth and sensitivity, with recent research highlighting its complex, flexible and contextual nature, problematic questions such as 'why coach that way?' and 'what kind of learning is taking place?' and even 'what is coaching?' are now appearing of prime importance. In response, it is crucial that the coaching role is equally reconceptualised to take account of these changes, and for practitioners to learn a new grammar of coaching to adequately address them (Toole and Seashore Louis 2002).

The concepts presented here are offered as signposts towards this grammar as they illustrate ways how to form and manage this changing appreciation of coaching. Indeed, based on the assumption that professional coaching knowledge is largely tacit and difficult to verbalise (Gilbert and Trudel 2001), the concepts and associated metaphors discussed can provide insight and clarity into it, so that its component ideas can be better understood (Jones and Wallace 2005). In this way, they can raise some of this know-how to consciousness so that it can be further developed. Additionally, through their explicit presentation, it is hoped that the concepts will enable coaches to resist the pressures to focus solely on the technical, surface features of coaching and to have the confidence to examine the underlying pedagogic process and the human aspects of being a coach in the quest for improvement. They also have the potential for coaches to better critique their own and others' practice while helping them to deal better with the integrated socio-pedagogic nature of their work.

Such an altered perception of coaching can make a significant contribution to the on-going struggle to have it viewed as a legitimate profession.

According to Shulman (1999), a basic criterion for being viewed as a profession is that of becoming a scholarly community. This includes the need for members not only to have detailed information on particular content but also 'a broad education that facilitates new understandings' that is also 'flexible, adaptable and open to new interpretations' (Jones et al. 2004: 103–104). It is to be able to see underlying principles and perceive relationships, in addition to possessing worthwhile subject matter knowledge. Shulman's criteria for a profession also include the necessity for a formal body of research, which encompasses the study of philosophical and ethical issues, in addition to those of the wisdom and practice of the most able practitioners.

Similarly, borrowing from the work of Leach and Moon (1999), Armour (Jones et al. 2004) believes that if coaching is to be regarded as a profession it must be intellectualised. This refers to developing theory that better encompasses the complex factors that influence athlete development, while appreciating the need to grow the necessary quality of mind in coaches through habits of reflection, questioning and critique. The establishment of degree courses within coaching goes some way to address the issue of a broad education, but doubts persist about the current depth of critical scholarship that both underpins such programmes and supports coaching's claims to be a profession (Jones et al. 2004). The theories presented in this book, which situate coaching in a pedagogic setting, have the potential to address these concerns by providing some of the means through which the criteria for professional status can be achieved. For example, they encourage coaches to seek and reflect on new interpretations of coaching, while continually reminding them of the need for contextual flexibility in practice. They also provide new ways through which coaching can be analysed, thus leading to a better conceptualisation of, and direction for, its study.

The significance of the text is also grounded in the need to develop more realistic preparation programmes for coaches that mirror the complex reality of their work. Many of the concepts presented then could act as continuing professional development (CPD) catalysts in providing alternative ways to think about coaching and how to go about it. In this way, they can encourage coaches and coach educators to see themselves as theorists as opposed to merely practitioners, thus becoming better aware of the suppositions that underlie their practice and how to use them. Again, this mirrors current thought in education where similar developmental activities are structured around critical and reflective discussion with peers and appropriate experts within a shared professional culture (Loughran and Gunstone 1997). Crucially, as pointed out by Armour (Jones et al. 2004), it should be remembered that such programmes cannot be delivered but are about working with professionals, to ensure that they are viewed as investments in personal growth (Loughran and Gunstone 1997). Indeed, unless their perspectives are expanded, it is likely that future practitioners will emerge from coach education courses with a narrow and shallow conceptualisation of the coaching role, thus being ill-equipped to deal with the complex pedagogical and social nature of their work.

Conclusion: new knowledge and threshold concepts

According to Meyer and Land (2003) such theoretical notions as presented in this book can be seen as threshold concepts. These can be considered portals, enabling us to see and think about things in new ways. However, due to their often critical, post-structuralist nature, such concepts may lead to what Perkins (1999) describes as troublesome knowledge. This is because they have the capacity to undermine previous beliefs 'in so far as they uncover the limits of rationality and truth claims' (Meyer and Land 2003: 3). Such revelations can be disturbing to learners as they are forced outside their traditional cognitive comfort zones to deal with the messy and problematic reality of knowledge in the social world we inhabit. For some, then, the contents of this book on first reading may be troublesome, as previously familiar concepts are rendered strange. However, while every effort is made to present them in a reader-friendly fashion, and their link and relevancy to coaching practice is continually emphasised, no apology is made for this. This is because coaching itself is difficult, problematic and troublesome. To present it otherwise would be to fall into the trap of earlier work, which has tended to dumb down a multifaceted, intricate and complex endeavour. As Armour states, the challenge is daunting yet exhilarating, but if we are to progress 'the complexity must be faced and ways of grasping it must be found' (Jones et al. 2004: 108).

Despite having the potential to be troublesome and for generating resistance among some, once grasped and embraced, the concepts presented are capable of shifting perception and developing insight. In this way, they can lead to a 'transformed view of the subject matter and landscape' as they can fundamentally alter how a person perceives the subject, in terms of what they look for within it (Meyer and Land 2003: 1). They thus have the capacity to open up an enhanced understanding of the nature of coaching and the relationships that comprise it. They also have the potential to make connections between what are conceptually difficult topics, for example, between discourse, ethics and context, and practice. This credible link to practice is crucial, as one of the problems with coaching knowledge so far is that it has not adequately engaged with such problematic topics in ways that are accessible to coaches.

Finally, I willingly acknowledge that the claims made in terms of the theoretical concepts discussed in the following chapters need qualification. First, there is no assertion that the field of education has somehow got it right, and that coaching therefore ought to unquestioningly copy it. Rather, recognising that coaching and teaching are perhaps not so conceptually far apart as previously considered, and that education continues to be theorised to a much greater degree than coaching, it appears appropriate to short-circuit some of the growing pains experienced by teaching by using some of its concepts to better interpret coaching. Second, the concepts presented in the book only represent a few examples of pedagogic theory that can contribute to re-conceptualising and further informing quality practice in coaching and coach education. There are others that can equally assist in the process. Nevertheless, as a collective group of scholars we consider these particular concepts as important in enabling us to view coaching and coach education through new insights, thus providing productive future directions for further developing our understanding of both coaching theory and practice.

Chapter 2

Coaching as an educational relationship

Felicity Wikeley and Kate Bullock

Introduction

In this chapter, we specifically address the element of a coach's work that is concerned with helping groups or individuals to learn. The chapter builds on the case made in Chapter 1 that coaching can, and should, be viewed as an educational endeavour, the success of which depends on the relationship between coach and athlete. To support this claim, we scrutinise some accepted theories of learning and reconstruct them to be more appropriate for coaching. Our preferred model of learning is founded on that of an educational relationship. We explore the conceptual framework for this model and discuss how the associated theories can inform our understanding of sports coaching.

Models of learning

Coaches are educators in that their role is to work with one or more athletes[1] in order to move the latter's performance to an improved level. Coaching is a process akin to teaching, tutoring or mentoring. It requires an understanding of the complex business of how people learn and develop as well as knowledge and skill in the discipline or field (Parsloe and Wray 2000). The quest for a universally accepted theory of learning has engaged educational researchers, psychologists and practitioners but most models remain inadequate. It could be argued that this is, *inter alia*, because of the restricted theoretical perspectives employed in the scrutiny. For example, learning appears to have been investigated either from the perspective of the teacher (pedagogical strategies – see Clarke 2000, Collins and Cook 2001), the activities of the learner (learning styles – see Marton and Säljö 1984, Sadler-Smith 2001, Klein 2003), theories of cognition (learning development –

---

1 For the purposes of this chapter, we will use the word 'athlete' to denote any learner when participating in a sporting activity.

see Wood 1998) or the content (disciplinary knowledge – see Bishop and Denley 1997, Mercer 2000), but the transference of issues across these major perspectives appears to have been under-explored.

There is some agreement however (Kolb 1984, Riding and Rayner 1998, Sfard 1998), that learning requires both acquisition of skills or knowledge and internalisation of these into individual learner identities. This would appear to resonate strongly with the aims of coaching to improve athlete performance to a level where preferred actions are habitual; by which we mean they evoke an immediate response rather than involving a process of slow, conscious problem solving or decision making. Some researchers have viewed these two essential steps of learning – acquisition and internalisation – as distinct continuums of practice, with a learner's preferred approach to learning distributed between two diametrical ways of gaining and using information or skills. Rayner and Riding (1996), for example, identify the dimensions as Wholist-Analytic and Verbal-Imagery styles. By this they mean that when presented with a piece of information some learners have a preference for grasping it as a whole concept, while others favour an atomistic, step-by-step approach. At the stage of internalisation, some will use words to accommodate the new knowledge into their existing understanding while others prefer images or pictures. In coaching, the internalisation stage of learning may be afforded more emphasis than in other forms of teaching with 'visualising success' regularly employed as a coaching tool. While it may not be necessary to know whether individual athletes prefer verbal or image-related messages in the coaching context, it is likely that using both approaches will lead to more effective learning outcomes.

One of the most documented, and adapted, models of learning is that of Kolb (1984). Kolb's theory of experiential learning may be of particular interest to coaches and trainers. He suggested that effective learning results from a cycle of: experience, reflection, conceptualisation and testing those concepts in new situations. Kolb saw experience and conceptualisation as the polar extremes of the acquisition stage of learning. He argued that we gather knowledge either by living the experience or by being told about it. Internalisation of knowledge is achieved either through reflection or active testing. Kolb believed that few people have equal skill in all four areas and, hence, individuals develop an orientation towards one of the poles in each dimension. This he called their preferred learning styles. The Kolb model is set out in Figure 2.1.

There have been efforts to categorise learners into preferred learning types, and to link these particular styles of learning, such as that which balances experiencing and conceptualising, with the quality of learning outcomes in different contexts (see Heffler 2001, Mainemelis et al. 2002). It may be more useful, however, for coaches and teachers to see the acquisition of new knowledge or skills as a process that needs to encompass all segments from the cycle. Where the cycle begins depends on the learning context.

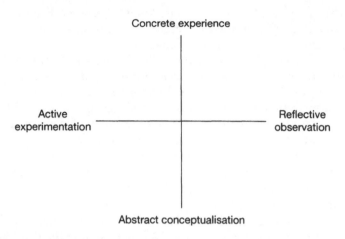

Figure 2.1 Kolb's learning cycle

From Kolb, David, *Experiential learning: Experience as the source of learning,* © 1984, p. 215. Adapted with the permission of Pearson Education, Inc., Upper Saddle River, NJ.

On the other hand, many educators question the trustworthiness of learning style categorisations (Duffy and Duffy 2002, Garner 2000, Henson and Hwang 2002, Swailes and Senior 1999) and challenge the belief that learning styles should be matched by curricular or pedagogic modifications (Klein 2003). Klein points out that learning styles are usually assessed through a range of perceptions and skills, including cognitive style, which concerns central processes such as reasoning and memory. Most students indicate mixed and inconsistent preferences and he argues that almost all learning activities require different quantities of a variety of skills. Swailes and Senior (1999) observe that analyses of learning style profiles in academic settings reveal a dominance of the Reflector/Theorist traits. Their findings do not support the four categories of learning style and they observe a more generic structure of learning, indicative of a three-stage cycle of Action, Reflection and Planning (Figure 2.2). We could speculate that a similar analysis of preferred learning styles in any sporting or physical context might tend towards experience and experiment but that the three-stage model could also apply here.

If, however, we accept Kolb's argument that people are not equally proficient at all these learning tasks, and that it is worthwhile to identify a preferred style, we can return to an adapted version of the Kolb model that might be useful in the coaching arena. It seems sensible to separate initial experience or activity from the practice or experiment that is congruent with developing sporting skills and to present them as the polar extremes of reflection and planning. The four categories in the coaching learning cycle can then be set out as shown in Figure 2.3.

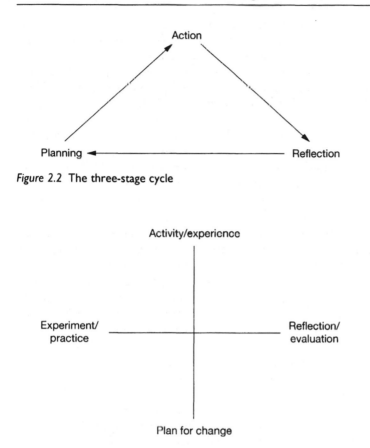

Figure 2.2 The three-stage cycle

Figure 2.3 Learning cycle for coaching

Another view of learning that we feel might have relevance to the field of coaching is Alexander's (2003) Model of Domain Learning (MDL). This is based on the inter-relationship of knowledge, strategic processing and interest as a participant moves from novice through competence to expert within any particular field. Alexander argues that the three components configure differently as learners reach improved levels of expertise, with interest or motivation increasing along with proficiency. For many situations, competence – rather than expertise – is sufficient. For example, Alexander would argue that school learning is more about competence than expertise. For coaches, however, understanding how to enhance athletes' interest, in order to progress them to the expert (elite) level, could necessitate consideration of the reasons why individuals participate in their sport; what constitutes participants' view of achievement; and the motivational impact of enhanced knowledge and strategic skills.

The interaction of motivation and learning that can be recognised by most is explored in the concepts of deep and surface learning. The theory suggests that learners can take either a deep approach or a surface approach depending on their motivation or level of interest in the subject. The model was originally developed from empirical research by Marton and Säljö (1976) and has since been expanded by many others including Entwistle (1981). Deep learning is viewed as better as it involves an understanding and engagement with the subject matter rather than a purely instrumental approach. The predictor of deep or surface learning lies with the motivation to be involved in the learning experience. Motivation will vary with individuals, their self-confidence in the field and their level of expertise. Coaches, working with a range of athletes from novice to elite, will therefore need to know and build on the athletes' pre-existing skills and self-esteem in order to increase motivation. At the beginning of an athlete's career, surface learning, fuelled by the need for recognition or the accolade of prizes, may suffice. However, this is unlikely to be sufficient for those whose learner identity is interlinked with their identity as a sportsperson. At the elite level, coaches will work with sportspeople who are more capable and motivated than themselves. Deep learning that addresses individual inspirations, responses and preferences should, therefore, be a fundamental part of the coach's work.

Entwistle's development of this work (Entwistle and Smith 2002) creates a more intricate model of learning that takes heed of a distinction between *target understanding* of the subject content interpreted by the teacher, and the *personal understanding* that is obtained by the learner. The remit of the coach (teacher, mentor) is to work with athletes (students, colleagues) to close the gap between target and personal understanding. The provision of feedback on performance is essential to build up the necessary skills and learning (Heylings and Tariq 2001). Improvement derives from reasoned judgements of previous performance. Feedback on these will instigate reflection and explanations and develop clear goals. But to be effective, feedback must be timely and challenging, and knowing how to make it so will depend on the educational relationship between the coach and the athlete.

At this stage in our argument it can be seen that approaching learning purely from either the perspective of the teacher or from that of the learner is not enough. While the interpretations of cognitive behaviours of teacher and learner are useful and informative, it is the interaction between them that, we believe, brings about learning. Learning interactions begin from the personal and contextual stances of both learner and teacher. The gap can only be bridged by the reciprocal educational interactions through which they develop a common language and a shared understanding of tasks.

While we recognise the two essential steps of learning – acquisition and internalisation – we believe there is a more useful development of this theory; the socio-constructivist view (Vygotsky 1978).

Educational relationships

Society is based on social relationships. It is these relationships that shape our values, influence our choices and mould our experiences. As they mature, children embrace different social groups. The first they encounter are 'at home' but these are soon extended by their interaction with a number of different constituencies 'in school', and even more within the wider community. The socio-constructivist theory of learning (Vygotsky 1978, Bruner 1977, Forman and Cazden 1998) argues that learning occurs in these social groups through the ongoing interactions between people.

The contexts in which young people interact with others have specific characteristics with socially constructed rules and expectations guiding behaviour within the setting and, therefore, conditioning the ways in which they learn. In this respect, identity (Mead 1934), and particularly learner identity, will be influenced by factors such as parental expectations, school experiences and social confidence. These, in turn, cannot be divorced from characteristics such as gender, class and economic circumstance, each of which is associated with particular cultural and material resources (Bourdieu and Passeron 1990), and with particular patterns of behaviour and belief that impinge on individuals through their relationships with others. Relationships that are wholly educational are not confined to formal educational settings although they are, perhaps, less explicit in the wider world which contains many learning contexts (home, school, college, workplace, leisure and sports clubs and the like) with a variety of teachers both real and virtual (Renshaw 2003). Such educational relationships tend to be hierarchical in nature (Edwards 2001), fashioned by the cultures of the context and dependent on communication. Indeed, it is the interactions, both implicit and explicit, between learners and a more capable other that form the basis of the educational relationship. How young people understand these relationships and operate within them has a profound impact on their lifelong dispositions to learning.

Another way of viewing these learning groups is as a 'community of practice' (Lave and Wenger 1998), and this may have real relevance to the field of coaching. Such communities operate within a sport and can be seen as a formal arrangement with boundaries, rules and expectations on both sides of the teaching and learning experience. Whatever the sport, the novice sportsperson will enter the field on the periphery of its community of practice and rely on the coach to initiate them into its culture, rules and practices. As their skills grow, participants will move towards the centre of the sporting community gradually adopting the persona of the sportsperson (e.g. cricketer, runner . . .). However, the sporting persona comprises skills, beliefs and values constructed from both formal and informal learning experiences. Learning is fashioned not only by individual characteristics and preferred practices but also by the various contexts of social practice that the learner encounters (Lave and Wenger 1998, Dreier 1999). An example might be how competitive a novice sportsperson is, or the persistence with which they are willing to improve their skills. Bourdieu and Passeron's (1990) notion of dispositions for learning which are nurtured in a variety of inter-actions in local social contexts and are acted out and extended throughout a life course may be helpful here. In any situation, individuals (teachers and learners) both create and draw on the culture of the group to develop personal stances within that particular social context and to decide the extent and quality of their participation. Within this socio-constructivist view of learning it is the interaction between the actors and the agency of the learner that is important.

In our observations of learning (Bullock and Wikeley 2004) constructed over the past decade from a range of empirical research projects, we have developed a view of learning that has some reality for those working in posi-tions that support the learning of others. In this, we have taken account of the theoretical frameworks discussed above. We conceptualise learning as active, unique to the individual and socially constructed, but increasingly we have come to see the most important element in learning to be the educational relationship between the actors. This relationship, we believe, has to take account of:

1   the content of the subject to be learned;
2   the resources and strategies available to the individuals involved in the learning task; and
3   the skills of personal understanding that need to be developed in both the learner and teacher.

If we examine these three fundamental requirements for learning in terms of the educational relationship between the coach and an athlete, we might explain the first as 'knowing what'. A coach must be an established member of the community or network of practice who holds the knowledge of skills, practices, beliefs and values inherent within that group. Without this profi-ciency (sought by the novice athlete) the coach could not retain credibility in that role. But, as we have already argued, coaching must be more than facilitating acquisition. Taking Engestrom's (2005) concept of 'learning by expanding', aspiring athletes need to use the knowledge and operate in a context of criticism in order to develop and own their individual ways of doing things. Drawing on the expertise of the coach, they need to critique and engage with taught practice in the light of their own experiences in order to enhance their own skills or performance. This will be particularly applicable to the elite or professional athlete whose relationship with his or her coach will be affected by the athlete's superior performance.

The second requirement for learning is procedural knowledge or knowing how. Bereiter and Scardamalia (in Engestrom 2005) see effective learners as always working on the edge of one's competence while Lave and Wenger's (1998) community of practice is essentially concerned with understanding the position of that edge of competence within the local community or wider network of participants. As an established member of the community, a coach should have that overview. How good is the athlete now? What must they do to raise his or her potential? How far can they go? Sharing that view with athletes gives them a choice of whether or not they wish to move closer to the hub of the community.

In knowing how, a shared understanding of what contributes to 'good performance' needs to be established between the coach and athlete. Any longstanding group holds cultural values and tacit knowledge that are not routinely shared within or beyond the community. The discourse between coach and athlete should not only address the skills, activities and tacit procedures underpinning the sport, but also examine the strategies needed to apply them. These strategies are not guided by explicit rules and propositional knowledge but, rather, are used and developed as preferred and consistent practices that might, or might not, change as skills and knowledge grow.

Our third strand is 'knowing self'. In our book (Bullock and Wikeley 2004) on the role of the personal tutor in schools and colleges we focus on the need for students to know themselves, not just in their preferred styles of learning, but also knowing how they transfer knowledge; what motivates them and the extent of their resourcefulness (Carr and Claxton 2004). Our argument is that this knowledge enables students to engage with their tutors in such a way as to take back some control of the relationship. In a coach–athlete(s) relationship some of these issues should already be explicit. Athletes should have a very clear understanding of their aims – to play/ perform their sport better. This is obviously a very simplistic perspective in that many athletes in the early stages of their careers will have had their sport, and their attendance at coaching sessions, chosen for them by well meaning parents or teachers, but the involvement of a coach would indicate that there is some intention to improve performance.

Implications of a relationship

We have argued that it is the educational relationship between the coach and the athlete that is the key to effective learning. But in any relationship there are issues of customary procedures and the power inherent in them. This, we believe, gives rise to some important considerations.

Relationships are often built on sets of assumptions that guide the actors' interpretations of their dialogue. Any educational relationship always operates not only within the context of the situation – in this case sport and the particular sport – but also within the culture of the actors – the coach and the athlete. Both will bring to the relationship baggage from previous educational interactions, contexts and lives. Their behaviours will not be independent of their learning histories. In our considerations of educational relationships, we are beginning to think that there is a fourth strand that needs to be explored. This is 'knowing who'. For any learner it is important to know who might be a preferred role model who can make connections and engage you personally. From the athlete's point of view it is not just a matter of knowing yourself as a learner but also knowing what makes your coach tick and how that relates to your own model of learning. Similarly, beliefs about athletes and sport could affect the way coaches interpret and respond to the athletes' behaviour. There is a need for these values, on both sides, to be made explicit and to have a degree of congruence in order that progress can be made. It may be that choosing which coach you work with is an important aspect of a successful relationship.

Writers such as Free and Sabini (1985) and Leont'ev (1981) (in Gauvin 1998: 71) have argued that the 'purpose for conducting an activity may influence how the activity is organised which in turn may influence the learning'. They suggest that how the learner sees the activity, what he/she thinks is its purpose and his/her background, will affect his/her learning. Engestrom (2004) captures this in the equation, 'will capital' = human initiative + intentionality. This is an interesting concept in a coaching situation as it embraces both the need for content (the sport) and commitment to succeed in that sport; a recognisable combination at the competent and elite level. However, a school coach may be working with students who have no desire to participate in the sport, in which case 'will capital' might be very low. In such cases, coaches may have to manufacture a substitute for intrinsic interest with advice and feedback related to the ancillary benefits and generic skills that may be derived from participation in the activity (Sloboda 2001).

The balance of power in any relationship will change over time. At the start of a novice athlete's career, it is the coach whose knowledge and skills have importance and legitimacy. It is the role of the coach to present legitimate knowledge in such a way that the athlete can access it. This knowledge or skill then needs to be integrated into the consciousness, practice or identity of the learner. Only the learners themselves can make this step. Thus, independent activity is a key stage in the process of learning (Wood 1998). An educational relationship, therefore, needs to move between an interaction that facilitates access to new information and one that encourages self-determination to enable the learner to absorb the new knowledge or skill. Bruner (1977) identified this move as a point of handover from the teacher to the learner. The concept of handover, however, also highlights the complexity of the concept of independence. The essential activity of working alone is only a small part in a sequence of activities where the responsibility for the learning process moves back and forth from teacher to learner in the appropriate context. Tharp and Gallimore (1991) show

how this sequence can be viewed as part of a cycle where handover takes the learner from dependency on the teacher to a stage of self-monitoring within what Vygotsky termed the zone of proximal development (ZPD):

> Indeed, by asking questions and adopting other sub-routines of the adult's assistance, children gradually take over the actual structuring of the task and thereby acquire not only the performance but also the process of transfer of performance.
>
> (Tharp and Gallimore 1991: 51)

Within the learning process, from this perspective, learners are not entirely dependent on the teacher; there are stages when they have to be left alone (Mercer *et al.* 1999). For example, athletes will need time to reflect on performance and to practise new ways of doing things. The coach may still be responsible for the learning process but the dependency of the athlete increases and decreases as the coach intervenes and steps away. The learning process can, therefore, be seen as a sequence of episodes in which the learners work with the support of the teacher to identify and assimilate knowledge (scaffolding) followed by episodes of working independently to analyse (think about) and evaluate the learning (self-monitoring). In this phase of independent working, values and judgements will be informed by the context in the community of practice. Learners have independence during the episodes of individual activity by taking responsibility for the task. Their shared understanding of the task does not reduce this responsibility and the coach may continue to have authority over, rather than direct control of, the learning process. It is at this stage that the coaching relationship is perhaps more akin to that of a parent, whose major task is bringing their children to complete independence while maintaining an influence and acting as a support in their lives.

This cycle of scaffolding–handover–self-monitoring is seen by many researchers as the basis for the development of 'meta-cognitive' skills (Flavell 1977, Bruner 1996, Gipps and MacGilchrist 1999) or understanding your own learning. Metacognition implies that the learner is aware of, and takes responsibility for, his or her own learning, selecting appropriate practices and thinking strategies, and monitoring these processes. Self-monitoring requires a learner to distinguish between the support they are given by the more capable other and their own efforts, and also to assess their performance during the task (Broadfoot 2001). Metacognition prevents a learner from becoming passive, entirely dependent on the teaching which, paradoxically, can also happen in situations where learners spend much of their time working alone (Gipps *et al.* 1999, Galton *et al.* 1999). Within many of the studies on children's learning it was found that although they spent the majority of their time working alone, the dependency of the learner on the teacher prevented their activity being described as independent.

Working alone is not synonymous with independent learning and coaches need to recognise this. Effective coaches will, themselves, learn from their educational relationships with their athletes and recognise points where feedback and advice and new plans are required. In fact, Jones *et al.* (2004) suggest that any coach–athlete relationship may have a 'use by' date as athletes outgrow the knowledge and skills of the coach and the balance of power shifts. However, we would argue that if the relationship is truly educational then the shift of power can lead to a more equitable interaction that is equally productive.

In this way the role of the coach shifts from being the knowledge expert to that of the learning manager (Carnell and Lodge 2002). The relationship has to move from being one of dependence to one of interdependence (often seen in the behaviour of elite coaches of established athletes) which at its best gives meaning to the collaborative nature of the interaction. It becomes 'promotive interaction' (Abrami *et al.* 1995 in Carnell 2000) in which communication is effective because the interdependence is seen as positive, involving mutual help, trust and the successful management of conflict.

Conclusion

Our main argument is, therefore, that coaching needs to be seen as an educational relationship with the emphasis being on the relationship. Unlike a purely social relationship there need to be agreed and clearly understood parameters but the investment in making the relationship work needs to be equally as strong. Positions of power will shift as the relationship develops but that shift will not always be in one direction. The creation of the independent athlete will not always mean that he or she moves on beyond the influence of the coach but that a different set of strategies and resources and needs come into play. These will relate to both the coach and athlete. Responding to the needs of the other will bring a dynamism to the process and enables both to feel equal partners in what can only be described as an educational endeavour.

Chapter 3

Coaching as teaching

New acknowledgements in practice

Dawn Penney

Introduction

In 1998 Tom Bentley stressed that education

> must be able to use human, financial, social, cultural and informational
> resources from the whole of society to stimulate and develop young
> people's ability to learn and understand for themselves. This learning
> will not take place only inside schools and colleges, but in commun-
> ities, workplaces and families. It requires a shift in our thinking about
> the fundamental organisational unit of education, from the school, an
> institution where learning is organised, defined and contained, to the
> learner, an intelligent agent with the potential to learn from any and
> all of her encounters with the world around her.
>
> (Bentley 1998: 1)

As a profession and an activity, coaching captures the scope for learning
to occur outside of formal education systems and structures. Furthermore, a
commitment to learning and learners has increasingly been recognised as
fundamental to 'good coaching'. Lynn Kidman's (2005) recent book entitled *Athlete-centred coaching* and many of the chapters in this collection are
testimony to that. As someone with passionate interests in the sociology
of education I have been increasingly struck by the similarity of the discourses that are now taking centre stage in coaching and coach education/
development and those being pursued in teaching and teacher educa-
tion/development. If it was directed to a different audience and featured
stories from teachers rather than coaches, Lynn's book could easily have
been called *Student-centred teaching*. At another level we can reflect that the
above quotation and the key points within it are as pertinent to coaching
as they are to teaching. If we have interests in enabling people to reach
their potential, we clearly need to make use of the many resources at our
disposal that influence learning and learners, and recognise the merits
of connecting with learning opportunities and experiences in other parts of
learners' (athletes') lives.

Pursuing those themes, this chapter addresses commonalities and linkages between coaching and teaching at a number of levels. One perspective arguably provides all the justification needed for adopting the stance and focus that I do in this chapter – namely, the perspective of the young people whose learning and lives we are concerned with. The individuals who are considered students in one context and athletes in another will be all too aware that many people contribute towards the realisation of their potential, and that advances in their learning are made in both school and non-school contexts. Teachers and coaches will undoubtedly agree that if anyone's true potential in sport is to be realised, a team approach and, furthermore, a coherent team approach, is essential. As other chapters reaffirm, coaching emerges as an undeniably pedagogical enterprise, the success of which relies not least upon the development of productive pedagogical relationships with athletes but also with other members of their 'learning community'. Below, I explore the notions of learning communities and networks. With others (see for example Chapters 7, 8 and 10) I see merits in drawing upon Lave and Wenger's (1991) work and, specifically, suggest that there is a need for greater acknowledgement of teachers' and coaches' shared interests in facilitating 'legitimate peripheral participation' in sport and physical activity as 'communities of practice'.

Before progressing, however, it is important to acknowledge a somewhat different stance on the issues being addressed. As Kidman (2005) has pointed out: 'The media rarely portray a successful coach as an educator. Nevertheless, one of the biggest jobs in coaching is to educate athletes, preparing them physically, psychologically and socially' (p. 28).

We need go no further than the matter of terminology to be reminded that distinctions between teaching and coaching contexts and the professionals associated with them continue to be reproduced and reaffirmed by people with interests in teaching or coaching. The dilemmas that I face in writing about 'coaching as teaching' are already evident. Talk of either 'students' or 'athletes' seems inherently problematic, destined to merely reaffirm differing perspectives and interests in young people who, instead, we should be seeing as exactly that, young people whose lives can be enriched and advanced by teachers and coaches. In actively seeking to bring together what have often been presented as two sets of discourses and two arenas, each with its own set of professionals and professional skills, this book and, more specifically, this chapter will undoubtedly be seen by some as controversial and, possibly, unwelcome. As Young (1998) has discussed, inherent in established stratification of knowledge (in this case, that associated with teaching and that associated with coaching) are understandings about what each of these activities is and the basis of established professional identities and power-relations in educational and sporting arenas. The prospect of resistance and/or uncertainty from some quarters should not, however, dissuade us from debate. By focusing on a number of challenges that have been posed for education and educationalists in the twenty-first century, I will argue that more than at any time in history, coaching and teaching can now be viewed as more similar than different and, furthermore, *as in need of closer connection.* I will describe aspects of education policy and practice associated with the development of Specialist Sports Schools in the United Kingdom (UK) and Specialist Sports Academies in Western Australia (WA) that have prompted and supported enhanced alignment of teaching and coaching, teachers and coaches. Internationally, Specialist Sports Schools have been developed in different ways, with various intended outcomes in mind. But while priorities have differed, a point of commonality is that developments have repeatedly sought to combine sport development and educational agendas. In both the UK and WA this dual commitment is very apparent, as is the blurring of boundaries and closer connections between teaching and coaching within the schools concerned. Young people emerge very clearly as the 'point' of connection. Throughout the remainder of the chapter I draw upon research projects undertaken in the UK and in WA to describe some key aspects of that connection in policy and practice.

Putting the young person first

In drawing attention to the importance of a learning orientation in teaching, Deakin Crick *et al.* (2004) speak of 'the complex mixture of experience, motivation, intelligences and dispositions that any particular learning opportunity evokes' (p. 247) and call for a shift in focus to *'what learners themselves bring to the learning situation* rather than on the content that the teacher is seeking to deliver' (p. 267, my emphasis). Their comments are directed to teachers and teacher educators but could as easily have been directed to coaches and coach educators. The challenge posed is not insignificant. A cultural as well as pedagogical shift is involved – to first and foremost consider young people as individuals who are differently positioned in terms of their ability to engage with and benefit from whatever it is we might have in mind that a lesson/session is going to address. In the UK, the stated government commitment to 'personalisation' as a 'central characteristic' of an education system that 'fits the individual rather than the individual having to fit the system' (Clarke, in DfES 2005: 4) is to be applauded and could usefully also be adopted in sporting contexts and by coaches. Yet, the challenges of realising such visions should not be underestimated. From the perspective of the individual coach, planning from what Kidman (2005) terms an 'athlete centred approach' is a complex task. Coaching is acknowledged as fundamentally a relational activity and, furthermore, requiring the development of different sorts of relationships to those that some coaches (and also athletes) may be familiar with. The emphasis is upon 'facilitation' rather than 'control', a *sharing* of responsibility for learning within a partnership, an approach that 'encourages athletes to become self-aware and self-sufficient, allows them to make informed decisions and emphasises individual growth and change' (Kidman 2005: 17) and that also acknowledges the individuality of each athlete. Hodgkinson (2005) has provided a reminder of the consequences of that individuality in a learning/teaching/coaching setting, explaining that:

> no single person is synonymous with their learning or teaching context, even though they are a part of it. Each of us has to live outside of our current site of learning . . . Furthermore, the ways in which one person is part of a learning context may be very different from the ways in which another person is part of even the same learning context.
>
> (p. 112)

Significantly, the growth and change that Kidman refers to relates to more than performance. It is about lives; the 'holistic development of the athlete' (Kidman 2005: 25). As soon as we accept that orientation we cannot escape the need to be considering 'whole lives', the varying potential that they hold to support learning and performance development, and the scope to enhance that development by devoting greater attention to establishing coherent learning networks for young people. Such networks have been a central focus in the development of Specialist Sports Colleges in England and, similarly, Specialist Sport Academies in WA. Joint investment has been sought to establish structures and programmes that enable schools to be simultaneously sites of learning and performance development, and to connect directly school and community-based learning, participation and performance.

Learner-focused networks

In 2003 David Hargreaves stressed that meeting public need in the twenty-first century required 'resilient institutions to interact far more creatively with the resources – social, economic, cultural and knowledge-based – that surround them in local communities' (p. 11). He also identified that: 'A key to transformation is for the teaching profession to establish innovative networks that capture the spirit and culture of internet hackers – the passion, the can-do, the collective sharing' (p. 56).

Once again, the challenges being posed in educational arenas, and for educators, are ones that coaches as educators and innovators will relate to. In some respects there seems nothing new in talk of 'partnerships' in contexts of education and sport. Cynics might well brand it with the label of 'more good rhetoric'. Yet, the talk of partnerships that has come to the fore in recent education policy in the UK particularly, which schools, teachers and others have been challenged to take forward in practice, is arguably of a new order and orientation. Setting out its vision for the transformation of secondary education, the Secretary of State for Education and Skills identified the creation of 'partnerships beyond the classroom' as a key strategy for the government (Clarke, in DfES 2003: 3). Planning and providing for learning was formally appropriately acknowledged as a collective and community endeavour: 'Helping children to learn is not a job for schools and teachers alone' (DfES 2003: 35). Nowhere is this more evident than in contexts of physical education and school sport, where the role of parents, siblings, peers, coaches and others in advancing learning becomes vividly apparent to teachers. Flintoff (2003) recently highlighted that for many young people and perhaps particularly many young women, 'the school may not be the primary context for meaningful learning' (p. 247) and stressed the importance of identifying 'contexts beyond the school and its immediate setting that can provide positive learning environments for different youngsters' (p. 247).

But at the heart of the Specialist Sports College initiative in England is also a realisation of the role that sport can play in helping children learn many and varied things. Specialist Sports Colleges have sought to demonstrate the rich potential that sport presents as the focus of learning networks or communities. They are a part of the Specialist Schools programme that has grown in size and diversity during the Blair government's term in office. The specialist route has been formally established as the expected development path for *all* state secondary schools to take. It now includes ten specialisms: arts, business and enterprise, engineering, humanities, language, mathematics and computing, music, science, sports and technology and enables schools to combine any two specialisms (DfES 2004). Specialist Sports Colleges stand out as of interest not just to the Department for Education and Skill (DfES) but also to the Department of Culture, Media and Sport (DCMS). They are positioned centrally in the transformation of education and, simultaneously, the transformation of the sporting infrastructure in England. They are concerned with excellence in education *and* in the provision of sport for young people in England (DCMS 2001, Penney and Houlihan 2001, Youth Sport Trust 2002).

Recent policy statements have added important clarity to the focus sought in the ongoing development and expansion of the Specialist Schools programme. Notably, the emphasis is upon coherency from the young person's perspective, with parts of the system 'interlinked and interdependent' in 'creative and dynamic ways' (Clarke, in DfES 2005: 5), such that the services 'are more than the sum of their parts' (DfES 2005: 19). Coaches, working collaboratively with teachers and, increasingly, working within Specialist Sports Colleges (during and/or outside of core curriculum time) and/or their local network of primary and secondary schools, are playing a key role in efforts to realise these visions. With coaches working in direct partnership with teachers in schools and/or employed in a teaching capacity, the prospects are of enhanced continuity in young people's experiences of physical education,

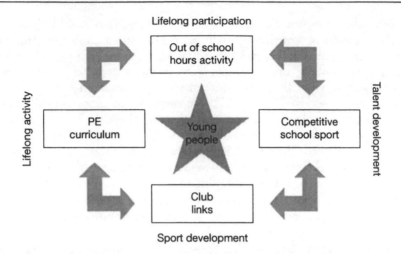

Figure 3.1 Putting young people first. Connecting physical education and school sport
From Teachernet, 2005.

school and community-based sport. As Figure 3.1 illustrates, perhaps for the first time young people seem to be being positioned centrally in planning informed by collaboration between education and sport in government arenas. The government's five-year strategy recently reaffirmed its commitment to the development of partnerships focusing upon expansion of opportunities for children to participate and compete in sport (DfES 2005). Sport was identified as a central facet in plans for 'extended schools' offering opportunities for participation in sport before and after school and at lunchtimes, and community use of school facilities. Information from the Qualifications and Curriculum Authority (QCA) addressing the question 'What do teachers and coaches need to do to achieve high quality school sport?' captured the shift in thinking about who can and/or should play a role in supporting learning. The QCA explained that their guidance was 'for anyone who helps to provide school sport, including teachers, qualified coaches, dance teachers, classroom assistants, midday supervisors, sport development officers, young leaders and volunteers. All are included here under the umbrella term "teachers and coaches"' (QCA 2005).

On the other side of the world, in the metropolitan area of Perth, Clontarf Aboriginal College (CAC) is run by the Catholic Education Office, for students in years 10–12 of schooling, aged 15–18 years of age. The college has an explicit community orientation. It operates as a community and simultaneously seeks to connect with communities and enhance students' life prospects in contemporary Australian society. The focus is on enabling Aboriginal and Torres Strait Islander Australians 'to access opportunities for spiritual, educational, cultural and social renewal that will enhance their future lives' (CAC 2003: 4). As I explain below, a key vehicle for this is Australian Rules Football. Coaches at the Clontarf Football Academy, then, are concerned with far more than performance in sport. They vividly demonstrate the wide scope of learning that coaches can facilitate and that 'putting the young person first' demands that we engage with those young people as unique individuals, each with their own complex identities and lives beyond sport.

Providing for *all* learners: learners, lives and identities

In March 2005 Brendon Nelson, the Federal Minister for Education, Science and Training in Australia, stressed 'that every young Australian should be encouraged to find and achieve their own potential – whatever that is' (Nelson 2005: 7). Education and sport, teachers and coaches, are charged with ensuring equity and inclusivity, enabling diverse individuals to pursue different interests and realise wide-ranging potential. Hargreaves (2003) identified that if the goal of education systems is 'equity as well as excellence', a key challenge emerges, namely 'to learn how to meet the needs of people they have never successfully served, as well as to operate at the leading edge of pedagogical and organisational innovation' (pp. 13–14). That challenge has been, and remains, one that has particular currency in physical education and sport. In neither arena can we escape the harsh reality that while some people are 'successfully served', others are marginalised in, or excluded from, learning and participation opportunities. Variously, ability, body shape and size, gender, ethnicity, class or perceptions (one's own and others') about any or all of these things feature in the processes via which individuals will either feel that they have a place, or, in contrast, have no place in physical education and sport. At a more systemic level, we can reflect that the UK government's open acknowledgement that in education 'we have not yet broken the link between social class and achievement' (DfES 2005: 6) might well be echoed in relation to sport.

Coaches, as teachers, consciously or inadvertently either challenge or reaffirm stereotypical views about who has the potential (and right) to participate in particular activities and take on various roles within them. In arenas of physical education and sport 'informal' learning is undoubtedly as powerful and meaningful in lives as the formal instruction. This is learning that may not be on a teacher's or a coach's agenda but is still destined to happen. Perhaps most obviously, an inevitable part of a young person's learning experience will be learning about belonging (or not) in the community of practice; learning whether or not I have a hope of legitimate peripheral participation (LPP) in that community of practice (Lave and Wenger 1991). Belonging is key to LPP. As Lave and Wenger (1991) explain: 'The processes, relationships and experiences which constitute the participant's sense of belonging underpin the nature and extent of subsequent learning' (p. 51). Thus, doors to learning can either be opened up or prematurely closed not only by what coaches say and do in their direct communication with an athlete, but also by their management and nurturing of peer relations in coaching settings. Establishing a 'quality team culture', characterised by mutual respect and trust among athletes as well as between them and a coach, is identified by Kidman (2005) as a core component of the 'athlete-centred approach'. Sport Education (Siedentop 1994) is well suited to a focus on 'team culture' and enhanced appreciation of individual abilities. In the UK it is being developed across Specialist Sports Colleges and their local school networks, as a means of facilitating citizenship and leadership. With students taking on the role of peer coaches, coaching simultaneously becomes a matter of 'learning and teaching' in physical education. Furthermore, Sport Education offers clear potential for teachers and students to positively engage with inclusivity in physical education and sport in schools. Teachers and coaches adopting the model can use it to prompt recognition of a broader role of skills and knowledge than may otherwise be the case (see Penney and Clarke 2005).

To further illustrate inclusivity as a principle underpinning and informing developments that connect teaching and coaching, I will, however, return to Clontarf Aboriginal College and Football Academy. As indicated above, Clontarf has been established with the explicit agenda of reducing social disadvantage for the young indigenous people who are enrolled at the College and Academy. The Football Academy was established by Gerard Neesham, an experienced Australian Rules Football player and coach, with the aim of making a difference to the lives of young Aboriginal men. It became operational on-site at Clontarf Aboriginal College in January 2000. Australian Rules Football presents a 'vehicle' and learning context via which an attempt is made to reverse an anticipated downward spiral that it is recognised may otherwise come to characterise many students' lives; of non-attendance at school, lack of qualifications, skills and experience for employment, increased risks of developing unhealthy lifestyles characterised by a lack of regular physical exercise, poor diet, drug use and involvement in crime (Penney et al. 2004). The Clontarf Foundation's 2004 Memorandum explained that:

> Methods are based on the premise that many Aboriginal youths fail to experience achievement in their formative years and hence lack self-esteem. This coupled, with a position of under privilege, often leads to alienation, anger, a feeling of hopelessness and worse. In order to break this downward spiral and as a prelude to tackling issues such as education, employment and lifestyle, the Foundation provides an opportunity for them to succeed using Australian Rules Football as the vehicle.
>
> (Clontarf Foundation, cited in Penney et al. 2004: 10)

As I explain below, 'success' here extends well beyond improved performance in football.

Coaching as teaching: sport skills, life skills and life chances

In exploring the athlete-centred approach to coaching, Kidman draws attention to international rugby coach Wayne Smith's philosophical stance, captured in the comment 'I believe coaching is all about trying to develop better people, not just better players' (Smith, cited in Kidman 2005: 26). This is clearly the ethos at Clontarf. The Academy staff have a coaching role that is explicitly educational, encouraging the development of skills, attitudes and behaviours that will make a difference in students' lives beyond school. Football skills are recognised as, ultimately, just one aspect of a bigger picture. The programme at the Academy is designed to achieve healthy lifestyles, enhanced self-esteem, sustained educational attendance and achievement (through to completion of year 12), post-school employment, life skills and leadership, as well as the development of football skills. The Academy coaches provide significant personal support to students and endeavour to get to know, understand and develop them as individual young people with, often, very difficult home lives (Penney et al. 2004). As one of the coaching staff explained:

> I have had kids who go home, family would come from other areas, lob in their house, parties, cards all night, nowhere to sleep, nowhere to do homework, clothes not getting washed, not getting a decent feed.
> (Staff interview C, cited in Penney et al. 2004)

Another member of staff also drew attention to ways in which poor home environments will impact upon the prospects for learning and participation, saying that:

> Quite often they don't engage or attach themselves to community football because ... they got to buy a pair of boots, got to find 50 bucks to become a member, you've got to have someone who'll get you out of bed on a Sunday morning to take you, the person's got to have a car to travel around ...
> (Staff interview B, cited in Penney et al. 2004)

The Blair government's five-year strategy for children and learning has highlighted the importance of precisely the skills and attitudes that the staff at Clontarf are endeavouring to develop in students:

> To succeed in the contemporary work environment, young people must be able to handle uncertainty and respond positively to change, to create

and implement new ideas, to have the capacity to solve problems and make sound decisions on the basis of evidence, and to be self-reliant and motivated.

(DfES 2005: 73)

At Clontarf 'coaching as teaching' in the context of Australian Rules Football provides a prompt and means via which to address the aim of success in contemporary work environments for students who may have no direct experience of it. The Clontarf Foundation and the Academy staff would certainly share the view that

> [w]hatever their talents and aspirations all young people should have choices that interest them from 14, should be equipped with the skills critical for success in employment, should have a realistic, stretching goal to aim for by the age of 18, and should have the advice and support to achieve it
>
> (DfES 2005: 71)

and would identify themselves as key providers of that advice and support.

In many respects, much of the educational interest in sport relates to the notion of transfer of learning from physical education or sport to other learning and other life contexts. Undoubtedly, the ability to think laterally and to use existing knowledge and experiences to effectively engage with new contexts and challenges within them is a great asset in sport but also in life. In a world in which the need for young people to continue their learning beyond school and school years is very evident, Quicke (1999) has identified the teacher's aim as 'to encourage pupils to make use of existing concepts, knowledge and experience when tackling a new problem and to create a readiness to see connections between apparently discrete frames of reference' (p. 39). The alignment of those comments to statements made about Teaching Games for Understanding (TGfU, Thorpe *et al.* 1986), or 'Game Sense' approaches to teaching/coaching (see Kidman 2005, Light 2004) is striking. The approaches represent an extremely powerful point of connection between teaching and coaching and, also, between physical education and sport and other areas of education. The emphasis upon learning in and through authentic situations and environments, of developing understandings that will inform actions in various contexts and the encouragement of creative thinking are all characteristics of these approaches, and are also prominent agendas for teaching and learning in contemporary education policy internationally.

Technology, teaching and coaching

Governments and educators worldwide are also recognising that new technology is a potentially rich resource to utilise in efforts to widen access to learning opportunities and enhance progress and achievements. Notably, the UK government's emphasis has been upon the potential that technology presents for more personalised learning, for learners to have greater ownership of their learning and for learning to extend beyond the classroom (DfES 2003). Once again, the push has been for Specialist Schools as the hubs of learning networks to lead innovative developments in teaching and learning. Specialist Sports Colleges need look no further than sport coaching to see the potential of new technologies and, in particular, digital video, movement analysis and game analysis software, to engage learners and accelerate learning. But perhaps even more significantly, these technological developments also provide a prospective focus for teachers, coaches and students/athletes to better share responsibility for learning and to enjoy enhanced communication and collaboration. Coaching and coaches have been at the fore of innovative application of digital video and movement analysis and game analysis software. Looking to the future, technology, perhaps more than anything, may facilitate the connection between school and non-school experiences that, for many young people, has been lacking in the past. The sharing of video clips of a student/athlete's participation/performance across teaching and coaching contexts may be a powerful tool in the transformation of relations and deconstruction of professional boundaries.

Coaching as teaching: a life of learning

> The continual deepening of knowledge and skills is an integral part of the development of any professional working in any profession.
> (Boyle et al. 2004: 46)

This final section acknowledges that, in order to be effective, coaches, as teachers (in both senses of that phrase), have to be open and committed to lifelong learning. For many it will be an entirely natural orientation. Self-reflection, evaluation and refinement of pedagogical plans and practices are inherent characteristics of quality coaching/coaches and teaching/teachers. To keep abreast of developments in knowledge relating to athletic performance, training practices, coaching techniques and the technology one might employ to enhance one's own and an athlete's understandings is no mean feat. But research and developments in education have also highlighted the need for a shift in thinking about professional development in terms of what it involves and when it occurs. While there may still be a tendency towards thinking of professional development as occurring on particular days and involving attendance at organised courses, in educational arenas the emphasis is now upon engagement in a professional learning process that is ongoing and an integral element of one's professional work. Undoubtedly, 'Action Learning' and/or 'Action Research' approaches to professional development are as applicable and appropriate to teachers as they are to coaches. Many coaches who are already keeping and routinely evaluating data that they have collected at sessions and using this to inform their work are already working within these frameworks.

But professional development (and Action Learning as a professional development model) is not just about oneself. Rather, it needs to be a collaborative endeavour and core activity within the sorts of learning communities/networks that Specialist Sports Colleges or Academies are set. Coaches, particularly in these school network contexts, are uniquely placed to support the professional development of others. Their teaching role can very effectively be one of teaching teachers, providing much needed support and encouragement to people concerned to provide quality learning experiences for young people, but possibly not secure in how to do so.

Conclusion

> Some speak of a gap between educators and coaches but, in reality, many of us are trying to get rid of this perceived gap. Educators and coaches can learn from each other; educators and coaches can learn from athletes (and students). The athletes are the ones to benefit from this sharing of ideas ... No one has all the answers, but through conversations and observations we can learn from each other.
>
> (Kidman 2005: 286)

In this chapter I have sought to direct attention to arenas where the gap that Kidman refers to seems to be rapidly narrowing and increasingly problematic to sustain. Problematic that is, in a conceptual sense, but also if we think first and foremost of the young people whose interests we claim to be concerned with.

Part II

Re-conceptualising the role of the coach

Chapter 4

The coach as a 'more capable other'

Paul Potrac and Tania Cassidy

Introduction

The Tuesday evening coaching session at the Erewhon City Football Club Centre for Excellence for players aged 11–16 had come to a close. Having cleared away the balls, training bibs and cones, the coaches gathered in the club lounge for some refreshments. As was usual on these occasions, the coaches enthusiastically engaged in conversations about the technical and tactical content that they had addressed within their respective sessions, what aspects they thought had gone well and not so well, and what drills and practices they would use in the forthcoming Thursday night session. Inevitably, their discussions turned to focus on the performances of individual players within their coaching groups. In this respect, several expressed great frustration at the failure of certain players 'to do what I told them to do' or 'make the right decision under pressure'. Indeed, the coaches appeared to be mystified as to why some players could not grasp concepts that to them were so straightforward. In attempting to explain why certain players were underperforming, their comments tended to focus on the shortcomings and inadequacies of the players themselves, with certain players being considered to be uncoachable or lacking the attention, motivation or the 'nous' needed to succeed.

The vignette above is based upon the lead author's experience of coaching youth soccer in the United Kingdom, United States of America and New Zealand. A common feature of these coaching experiences has been the reactions of surprise and frustration from some coaches who cannot understand why the players in their charge fail to readily understand concepts that have been accurately explained to them. When an athlete persistently fails to grasp concepts that the coach presents, the lack of understanding is often attributed to the former's insufficient motivation, attention levels or some other innate attribute (Floden 1989, Horn *et al.* 2001). Consequently, it has not been uncommon for some coaches to suggest that: 'Some people just aren't good at soccer. It doesn't matter how many times you go over things. They just don't understand what I want them to do.' We are sure that readers of this book can relate to the issues described above in the context of their own sporting experiences.

What we find interesting in the above scenario is that often it is the athlete who is blamed for any failure to learn rather than the coach coming under scrutiny for how he or she attempts to stimulate athlete learning or how the content makes sense to athletes. In drawing upon the work of Floden (1989) in education, we suggest that one of the weaknesses of existing coach education provision has been its failure to provide coaches with the opportunity to explore how their instruction looks to athletes, how athletes perceive what they are learning and how athletes learn content that is in some way new or foreign to them. Indeed, as has been argued in the opening chapter of this book and elsewhere (e.g. Jones 2004), the educational function and role of the coach has been largely ignored.

The purpose of this chapter is to present the argument that if coaches are to develop knowledgeable athletes, who are capable of performing well when not under the direct influence of the coach, then the coaching role requires more than either the one-directional transmission of knowledge from coach to athlete or the total ownership by athletes for their own development. In order to achieve such a complex aim, we suggest that coaches may benefit from viewing themselves as *more capable others* (Vygotsky 1978). This conceptualisation of the teaching and learning nexus of the coaching role highlights the need for coaches to engage in contextual collaborative and learning relationships with athletes if the psychological functions required for maximal sporting performance are to be fully developed. Towards this end, this chapter will initially introduce Vygotsky's writings on the zone of proximal development (ZPD) and more capable others, before discussing the potential implications of these concepts for coaching practice. In this respect, it should be noted that the chapter does not intend to provide a detailed discussion of Vygotsky's work (for comprehensive overviews in this regard see Kozulin *et al.* 2003, Wink and Putney 2002, Moll 1990, Daniels 2001), nor does it aim to provide prescriptions as to what coaches ought to do. Instead, the intention here is to stimulate debate and discussion regarding the educational role of the coach.

Lev Vygotsky: 'the zone of proximal development' and 'more capable others'

Much of Vygotsky's original research and theorising focused on the cognitive development and learning of children (see Wink and Putney 2002, Moll 1990, Daniels 2001). More recently, as a consequence of his work being translated, scholars from the English-speaking world have begun to apply his concepts and findings to enhance the educational development of adults in a variety of settings (e.g. Cassidy *et al.* 2004, Dunphy and Dunphy 2003, Reiman 1999, among others). At the heart of Vygotsky's writings was the view that cognitive development is a social, historical and cultural process and, as such, 'action is mediated and cannot be separated from the milieu in which it is carried out' (Wertsch 1991: 18). Vygotsky (1978) thus contended that our higher mental functions (such as problem solving, reasoning, planning and communication) develop through interaction and collaboration with others. Here, he argued:

> Every function in the child's development appears twice: first, on the social level, and later, on the individual level; first between people (interpsychological), and then inside the child (intrapsychological). This applies equally to voluntary attention, to logical memory, and the formation of concepts. All the higher functions originate as actual relations between human individuals.
>
> (1978: 57)

Vygotsky (1978: 86) further suggested that the development of our higher mental functions takes place within what he termed the zone of proximal development, which he defined as:

> The distance between the actual developmental level as determined by independent problem solving and the level of potential development as determined through problem solving under adult guidance or in collaboration with more capable peers [others].

The concept of ZPD suggests that after the learner receives instructional support or tutelage from someone who happens to be more capable in that particular context, the learner internalises the new idea and, as a consequence, will be more likely to perform independently in the next similar problem-solving situation (Wink and Putney 2002).

Wink and Putney (2002) suggest that Vygotsky's experiences as a teacher and researcher led him to recognise that children were able to solve problems beyond their predicted development level if they were provided with guidance in the form of leading questions or prompts from somebody who was more knowledgeable and capable. This more knowledgeable person, who Vygotsky termed the more capable other or the more capable peer, could be a teacher, coach, parent, caregiver, or another student or athlete (Wink and Putney 2002, Chaiklin 2003). Undoubtedly, Vygotsky's writings suggest that the more capable other has a significant role to play in the learner's transition from other-assistance to self-assistance (Daniels 2001, Bullock and Wikeley 2004). The ZPD can be thought of as comprising three inter-related phases. These are (1) assistance by others, (2) transition from other-assistance to self-assistance and (3) assistance by the self; stages that can be pictorially represented as a staircase (Dunphy and Dunphy 2003, Tangaere 1997). In this respect, 'the learner's independent development of achievement can be conceived as the stair upon which the learner is standing, having successfully climbed the other stairs' (Cassidy et al. 2004: 74).

In the quest to facilitate a learner's progression through the three phases of the zone of proximal development, Vygotsky insisted on the development of collaborative and co-operative instructional practices between the more competent other and the learner (Daniels 2001). In this respect, he advocated the use of instructional strategies such as demonstrations, asking leading and open-ended questions, and introducing the solution to the initial elements of a task. He went on to say that the nature and frequency of these strategies or forms of assistance are dependent on the learner's level of performance and perceived needs (Dunphy and Dunphy 2003, Moll 1990). For example, during the early phases of the learner's development the assistance provided by the more capable other may be frequent and elaborate, as the learner may have a limited understanding of the situation, task, or the goal to be achieved. At this level, the more capable other may organise activities and facilitate learning by regulating the difficulty of tasks and modelling mature performance through joint participation with the learner (Lyons 1999, Gallimore and Tharp 1990). However, as the learner's understanding of a concept develops, the assistance provided by the more capable other may become less frequent and truncated.

In addition to emphasising co-operation and collaboration to facilitate a learner's progression, Vygotsky (1987, cited in Daniels 2001: 54) was also very critical of the use of direct instruction. He considered that such a strategy often resulted in little more than recitation from the learner as opposed to any genuine cognitive development. Indeed, he noted:

> Pedagogical experience demonstrates that direct instruction in concepts is impossible. It is pedagogically fruitless. The teacher who attempts to use this approach achieves nothing but mindless learning of words, and empty verbalism that stimulates or imitates the presence of concepts in the child. Under these conditions, the child learns not the concept but the word, and this word is taken over by the child through memory rather than thought. Such knowledge turns out to be inadequate in any meaningful application. This mode of instruction is the basic defect of the purely scholastic verbal modes of teaching which have been universally condemned. It substitutes the learning of the dead and empty verbal schemes for the mastery of the living knowledge.

It is, perhaps, worth noting here that Vygotsky's views on teaching and cognitive development are in contrast to the traditional nature of the teaching and learning environment in many sports, where the orthodoxy has been for coaches to adopt a largely prescriptive approach regarding when and how athletes should perform specified skills or movements (Kidman

2001). Indeed, while Vygotsky's work places considerable emphasis on co-operative and collaborative learning relationships and the use of techniques such as questioning and problem solving, the educational relationship that has traditionally existed between coach and athlete has tended to be largely autocratic and prescriptive in nature (Cassidy et al. 2004, Kidman 2001). In this respect, the coach has been regarded as the sole source of knowledge and has been responsible for the unidirectional transmission of this information to athletes, who have adopted a largely passive role in the teaching and learning process. The problem with such a didactic approach to learning is that the athlete can be dismembered (Smith 1991). Specifically, the utilisation of a pedagogy 'guided primarily by tradition, circumstance, and external authority' (Tinning 1988: 82) could lead to a situation where athletes may feel undervalued due to the lack of opportunity to voice and share their respective ideas and experiences with the coach and other athletes. A potential consequence of feeling undervalued and bored is that the athlete might stop anticipating what is happening next and just do what they are told to do when they are told to do it, with the end result being that athletes adopt a robotic approach to their sporting performances. As such, the sole use of this approach may not only disempower athletes but may also reduce their chances to learn and develop their decision-making, problem-solving and creative skills (Cassidy et al. 2004).

In addition to highlighting the potential pitfalls of exclusively utilising a prescriptive pedagogy in coaching, Vygotsky's work also challenges the notion that athletes are capable of taking total ownership over their own development. In this respect, Butler (1997: 42) suggests that while an athlete's understanding may develop when he or she is active and seeking solutions for themselves, it is possible for them to 'go from one level of being "partly wrong" to another because their construction of understanding is never checked'. As such, it could be suggested that, if athletes are to develop cognitively, the coach has an important role to play in terms of assisting them to not only explore how and why they address the sporting problems that they encounter in the ways that they do, but also in helping them to deconstruct their knowledge in relation to the various aspects of their sporting performances.

Having briefly introduced Vygotsky's concepts of the zone of proximal development and the more capable other, the remainder of this chapter will focus on exploring how these concepts could be applied in a beneficial and productive way to enhance coaching practice. In this respect, it should be noted that Vygotsky never specified the forms of social assistance that a more capable other might provide to a learner (Daniels 2001, Moll 1990). Indeed, while he wrote about collaboration and direction, assisting children by asking leading and open-ended questions, providing demonstrations and by introducing the initial elements of a task's solution, he did not specify beyond these general prescriptions (Moll 1990). As such, the following section represents the authors' interpretations of just some of the ways in which Vygotsky's work might usefully be applied to enhance coaching practice and athlete learning within the context of sport. The following discussion then presents some of the issues that coaches may wish to consider as part of the process of moving towards becoming a more capable other.

The coach as a 'more capable other': implications for coaching practice

In this section we address some of the ways in which a coach, as a more capable other, might support athletes to a position of increased capability in terms of their knowledge, understanding and skills. In drawing upon the work of Bullock and Wikeley (2004) in education, a useful starting point for coaches who want to structure their coaching sessions in a way that would recognise athletes' zone of proximal development and therefore view themselves as a capable other, would be for them to reflect upon the extent to which their pedagogical approaches recognise that learning is both an active and social process; a process that requires athletes to develop their information gathering and processing skills in collaboration with more capable others. One way in which a coach might facilitate such cognitive development in athletes is to incorporate guided discovery, problem solving and 'Game Sense' approaches in practice sessions (Cassidy et al. 2004, Thorpe 1997). Rather than simply telling the athletes what to do, these pedagogical strategies position the coach as a facilitator of learning who, through the use of questioning, prompts and feedback, leads athletes to gradually discover the solutions to various problems related to the technical and tactical aspects of sporting performance (Johnson 1997, Kidman 2001). According to Ainsworth and Fox (1989), such learner-centred approaches are valuable in encouraging athletes to actively engage in, and take responsibility for, their own learning.

With regard to the latter mentioned strategy, Game Sense is a concept that has been introduced to coaches in an effort to encourage them to focus on developing players' capacities to use strategies and tactics and make informed decisions. It was adapted from an educational model known as 'Teaching Games for Understanding' (TGfU) (Bunker and Thorpe 1982). TGfU was designed with the intention of challenging orthodox 'skill-based approaches to games teaching' by integrating 'the players' cognitive appreciation of games simultaneously with their skill development' while retaining 'most of the tactical considerations of adult games' (Tinning et al. 1993: 102). This was illustrated in a developed Game Sense video (Thorpe 1997) where two tennis coaches are depicted, both of whom have the objective of improving a player's ability to attack an opponent's backhand. The coach who adopts an orthodox approach to coaching sets up a drill that requires a player to choose from three different (coach) presented forehand options to hit the ball to the opposition's backhand. The coach also provides the player with a prescribed number of opportunities to practise the drill. Alternatively, the coach who adopts a Game Sense approach to achieving the objective begins by setting the scene and asks the player some questions before a ball gets hit. Here, the coach asks 'quite often in a game situation, when you are playing in a match, your opponent will be weak on the backhand side. How are you going to exploit that?' (Thorpe 1997). Using open-ended questions is useful for educating and guiding players to a predetermined outcome or to invite them to make original contributions to an issue. In responding to the question, the player replies by saying 'you can angle [a shot] across court, or you can hit one to their forehand and then, when they have moved up to the net, lob them or go deep across court again' (Thorpe 1997). Once the player provides the coach with some options, she is encouraged to go onto the court and try to put some of her suggestions into operation. A further example of a Game Sense approach could include a coach researching opponents and setting problems for the athletes that were specific to the forthcoming opposition.

In addition to the use of game-specific activities, the use of questioning lies at the heart of such athlete-centred approaches to learning. In this respect, Kidman (2001) notes that there are a number of different types of questioning available to the coach. These can range from low-order questions, which focus on specific ideas or concepts, to higher-order questions, which tend to be more appropriate to analysing tactics and complex skills and require athletes to engage in higher level or abstract thought processes. Indeed, with regard to the latter she notes that higher-order questions 'challenge athletes to apply, analyse, synthesise and create knowledge' (Kidman 2001: 120).

An issue for coaches to consider in their role as a more capable other with regard to the use of questioning is the design and sequencing of the questions that athletes will be encouraged to find solutions to. In particular, Kidman (2001) suggests that coaches need to pitch, and if necessary redirect and rephrase, questions so that athletes can fully engage with what has been asked of them. In addition, she also notes that a crucial role held by the coach within the questioning process is to be able to listen closely to the responses athletes give, interpret their significance and react appropriately. Indeed, perhaps a key point for coaches to consider in regard to the use of questioning and athlete-centred approaches to learning is that their choice of activities and how they teach the activities should assist an athlete within his or her zone of proximal development. As such, a critical challenge for coaches is to define an athlete's limits in relation to his/her zone of proximal development and to match their support just beyond the athlete's current capabilities (Siraj-Blatchford 1999). It is important to stress that any activities and assistance from a more capable other that lie within an individual's existing capability are wasted, while activities and assistance that go beyond the extremity of the zone of proximal development can be meaningless and potentially damaging to the learner's confidence (Siraj-Blatchford 1999).

In addition to the use of game-specific tasks and a questioning approach that engages athletes in a collaborative exploration of the technical and tactical dimensions of a particular sport, the coach's role as a more capable other might also include being sensitive to the different learning styles of athletes. According to Murrell and Claxton (1987) learning styles can be classified according to personality characteristics, information processing, social interaction and instructional preference. In the following section, we focus on the instructional preferences of athletes. Brunner and Hill (1992) suggested that before a coach attempts to change coaching sessions to cater to athletes' preferences in instructional or coaching styles, it is useful to introduce the ideas to them. In this respect, the coach might wish to share their own preferred learning styles with the athletes. What is more, it is useful to emphasise to the athletes that there is no right or wrong preference; rather, people have various preferences, often dependent on the context. By introducing athletes to these ideas it may mean that they support any innovations that attempt to cater for various preferences that are introduced into the coaching session. Indeed, such an approach might also help athletes to become more self-aware about their respective preferred modes of learning (Bullock and Wikeley 2004).

Another way coaches can cater for an individual preference is to consider redesigning the coaching environment. Brunner and Hill (1992) illustrated the way they had redesigned a practice area in the wrestling room so there were stations for skill learning that reflected different learning preferences. For example, for those wrestlers who had an aural preference an area had been set aside where a skill or move was 'introduced by a tape recording or a discussion led by the coach' (Brunner and Hill 1992: 103). In another area, designated for those wrestlers with a visual preference, there was a collection of books, charts, diagrams and videos. Those wrestlers with a kinaesthetic preference went to the mats and physically practised the skill. Brunner and Hill (1992: 103) argued that by having stations that emphasised different preferences the coach could introduce a new skill via a wrestler's dominant preference, review it via 'the second preference and then reinforce [it] through the individual's third perceptual preference'. While it is not always feasible or appropriate to divide the practice area into different stations or areas, it could be argued that by presenting information and activities in a variety of formats a coach can further facilitate athlete learning and support his/her standing in the eyes of others as a more capable other (Cassidy et al. 2004).

In addition to considering the ways in which material is presented to athletes, a coach could further support the latter's learning preferences by guiding their 'attention and search strategies' in particular directions by providing them with feedback and adopting appropriate teaching methods that do just that (Rovegno and Kirk 1995: 460). For example, coaches could preface their feedback with words that focus athletes' attentions towards specific instructional preferences, as below:

*   for *Visual* learners a coach could say – 'See', 'Watch', 'Look', 'Picture this', 'Focus';
*   for *Auditory* learners a coach could say – 'Hear', 'Listen to the beat', 'Identify the rhythm';
*   for *Kinaesthetic* learners a coach could say – 'Feel', 'Move', 'Demonstrate', 'Practise'.

In addition to basing their feedback around specific learning preferences, the coach as a more capable other might also strive to provide feedback that is challenging, positive and specific (Bullock and Wikeley 2004, Finch 2002, Metzler 2002). In further drawing upon the work of Bullock and Wikeley (2004) it could be suggested that assertations from the coach to 'work harder', 'pay more attention', and 'spend more time on task' are of limited value in stimulating athlete learning. Indeed, it could be suggested that athletes have little more than 'a hazy conception of the reality of these exhortations' (Bullock and Wikeley 2004: 42). For example, what constitutes working harder for one athlete might mean performing tasks at a higher intensity, while for another it could mean spending more time discussing with the coach and other athletes what had been covered in a particular training session in order to make sense of what had been offered (Bullock and Wikeley 2004). As such, athletes might benefit from the provision of more specific and personalised feedback.

Furthermore, the educational relationship that exists between coach and athlete may also stand to benefit from the provision of feedback that is positive in nature and which is delivered in a sensitive manner. Here, Bullock and Wikeley (2004: 54) suggest that 'feedback should not be reduced to negative comparative judgements of performance because levels of confidence, motivation, and enthusiasm will not be boosted by a wholly negative or disappointing one-to-one conversation'. Consequently, as a more capable other, the coach could support athlete learning by highlighting the athlete's strengths in order to allow them to build the confidence required to address their limitations and weaknesses (Bullock and Wikeley 2004, Jones *et al.* 2004).

In addition to considering the nature of the feedback given to athletes, a coach's role as a more capable other might also involve encouraging athletes to adopt a reflective stance in relation to their learning and development. If coaches want athletes to reflect in, and on, their actions and performances, then they may benefit from providing athletes with data upon which to reflect. Some ways a coach could do this would be to provide a video-recording of competitive performances and training sessions or to encourage athletes to keep diaries of their experiences, thoughts and feelings associated with training sessions and competitive performances (Cassidy et al. 2004). Such data could then form the basis for subsequent discussions between the coach and athlete. In particular, the coach could help athletes to explore which aspects of performance or learning they find difficult, avoid, or just do not do. Indeed, the coach as a more capable other could help athletes to explore what it is about themselves that makes particular aspects of sporting performance difficult (Bullock and Wikeley 2004).

A further factor that the coach may wish to consider in relation to his or her role as a more capable other is the nature of the team or group culture and how this might impact upon athlete learning. The notion of team culture is often talked about and valued, at least at the rhetorical level, but developing a positive team culture does not just happen. In this respect, coaches, managers and players alike are all actors in developing the culture (Carron and Dennis 2001, Jones et al. 2004, Kidman 2005). For example, Daryl Gibson (an ex-member of the New Zealand All Blacks national rugby team), speaking from a player's perspective, described how a team culture was established when Wayne Smith coached him at the Canterbury Crusaders. In his own words:

> What happens at the start of the year is that the team sits down and plans the year. At planning we establish our culture which is the values that we share and believe in and that is a team process. We develop a whole list, we brainstorm the things we value, and we put them up on a board. We then rationalise them, cut them down ... We select the ones that [we] look upon as valuable ... The values are always in your mind and being reinforced ... You have to work at it constantly ... people on the team are genuinely fun to be around ... because they have all bought into it.
>
> (Kidman 2001: 103)

In a similar vein, Anna Veronese (an ex-member of New Zealand Silver Ferns national netball team) developed Gibson's point that a team culture has to be constantly worked upon by saying:

> We have a really good culture that has obviously been built up by the coach/coaches over the years and is still continuing to be built up ... I think when you have a directive-style coach, if people disagree or don't like what is going on, rather than talking about it amongst the team, it gets talked about among the players and that creates disharmony, which affects the team culture. But when you have a coach ... where people are open and feel like they can talk about things and you

know what the coach's philosophy is and where you are heading, it does make for a better team culture.

(Kidman 2001: 103–104)

Indeed, the literature (e.g. Kidman 2001, 2005, Poczwardowski *et al.* 2002, Jowett and Cockerill 2003, Jones *et al.* 2004) suggests that a positive team culture can be assisted if players are in an environment where they feel physically and emotionally safe, have some control over their learning, consider that the tasks that they are being asked to perform are meaningful, understand what they are doing, and can ask questions of the coach and other more knowledgeable players. What is perhaps most pertinent from such statements in the context of this chapter is that it is useful to recognise that the attributes of a positive team culture could also be favourable to developing a culture that is conducive to learning from a Vygotskian perspective (Cassidy *et al.* 2004). As such, coaches may wish to give considerable attention to the nature of the working climate that exists between themselves and the athletes in their charge. Moreover, as a part of the process of developing a positive learning environment, we would argue that coaches stand to benefit from recognising and being sensitive to the different motivations, philosophies, values, outlooks and identities that athletes bring to the coaching process in a particular context (Cassidy *et al.* 2004, Potrac *et al.* 2000, Jones *et al.* 2004).

Summary

The purpose of this chapter was to provide some suggestions as to how Vygotsky's notion of a more capable other might provide a useful concept for framing the educational relationship that exists between coach and athlete. In this regard, we believe such a conceptualisation of the coach's role within the teaching and learning nexus provides a valuable perspective for guiding coaches and coach educators in the quest to increase the skills, understanding, knowledge, and decision-making capabilities of athletes (Bullock and Wikeley 2004). Towards this end, we have outlined a number of issues related to coaching methods, learning preferences, the provision of feedback, and the working climate of the learning environment that coaches might wish to think about as a part of the process of developing contextual and collaborative learning relationships with athletes. However, it should be noted that we do not consider these aspects to be definitive, nor are we providing a list of prescriptions as to what coaches should or ought to do. In this respect, we recognise that the same activities are not necessarily effective for all people and that every coaching context has its own unique social and cultural dynamics (Bullock and Wikeley 2004, Cassidy *et al.* 2004). Indeed, it would be naive to believe that coaching practices are neutral and can be transplanted unproblematically to another context, either local or global. That said, we do believe that Vygotsky's work provides a valuable framework for exploring and understanding athlete learning and, thus, could be used by coaches and coach educators to stimulate reflection upon the ways in which we can best facilitate and support athlete learning in sport.

Chapter 5

The coach as 'orchestrator'

More realistically managing the complex coaching context

Robyn L. Jones and Mike Wallace

Introduction

In this chapter we argue that the rationalistic assumptions on which dominant conceptions of the coaching process lie are out of touch with the less tidy reality experienced by coaches on the training ground. Coaching is inherently fluid and multifaceted, militating against 'clean' treatment typified by the pre-specification of a cumulative sequence of precise objectives and monitoring of their achievement (Jones *et al.* 2004, Cassidy *et al.* 2004). Such rationalistic notions, therefore, have limited potential either for understanding coaching or for guiding practitioners. We draw on organisational and educational theory, and on evidence about coaching practice to support our contention that conventional rationalistic assumptions ignore the endemic element of ambiguity in the coaching process.

Our antidote is to consider the metaphor of 'orchestration' (Wallace 2003), derived from research on complex educational change, as one basis for a more realistic representation of coaching. Viewing the coach as an orchestrator provides a new platform for research and theorising about the coach's role aimed at improving the practice of coaching and of coach education. First, we examine what makes the coaching context so difficult to manage. Coaching activity here emerges as inherently problematic because it is characterised by ambiguity: enduring dilemmas for coaches that cannot be resolved thus generating perpetual ambiguity about which way to go. Second, we build on this platform in developing a critique of popular adherence to rationalistic assumptions about coaching, and suggest that practitioners need help in learning how to cope with the intricate and often uncertain nature of the work they do. Third, understanding the inherent complexity of the coaching process is a precursor for presenting some tentative practical themes for operating effectively in such a dynamic environment. The final section illustrates how such thinking could and should be integrated into future coach education programmes.

We recognise that ideas derived from the macro sphere of educational change can apply only loosely at best to the micro context of the individual coaching session. However, as both environments are inherently characterised by dynamism and complexity, the orchestrating metaphor and accompanying analysis presented may have some applicability to both types of setting. This is because both entail continuous decision making, dilemmas and ambiguity requiring iterative planning, observation, evaluation and reactions to 'goings on' (Jones *et al.* 2004).

Our conceptualisation is consistent with the preliminary findings of Saury and Durand (1998) about expert coaches' knowledge, and those of Jones and colleagues (2000, 2004) about the problematic and pedagogical nature of coaching. The findings from these and other related studies (e.g. Côté *et al.* 1995) accord with the premise that coaching expertise requires flexible adaptation to constraints. The coaching task cannot be 'totally defined or specified in advance' and so 'is organised differently from that presented in coaching manuals' (Saury and Durand 1998: 255). For such writers, existing manuals fail to help us grasp the essential nature of coaching as, like teaching, it is characterised by 'multidimensionality, simultaneity, uncertainty, publicity and historicity' (p. 255).

Our account is grounded in ideas about the extent and limits of human action, explaining why the coaching process is ambiguous, while at the same time manageable to some extent. Recognising the nature of this process offers a starting point for coaches to maximise whatever potential they have to choose between alternative courses of action that may work in their contingent circumstances.

The problematic nature of coaching

A speaker at a recent conference began by likening coaching to holding a bird in one's hands. Hold it too tight and it would be crushed, while too loose a grip would see it fly away. The only certainty was that, even if success was achieved in holding the bird comfortably without distress, it was still sure to shit over you! This metaphor illustrates the inherent intractability of coaching. Attempting over-control risks squashing the very talent that the coach is trying to nurture. But a laissez-faire approach risks this talent being dissipated unproductively. Knowing in advance what the best balance will be is not an easy task. And whatever the coach does, there is no guarantee that his or her efforts will be appreciated, let alone acknowledged.

The problem of goals

The goals of coaching are inherently challenging, the variables within the process many and dynamic, and the outcomes always uncertain. Certainly, some limited objectives are achieved, but often, when one considers the longer-term goals that coaches establish for themselves, contradictions, tensions and perceived failures are inevitable and endemic. In other words, an inherent *pathos* or unbridgeable gap exists between the lofty and often contradictory goals inspiring coaches to act, and their capacity to attain all these goals on the ground. Such pathos is an enduring feature of the social and practical world of coaching, and springs from a complexity that precludes any generalised 'paint-by-numbers' plan that practitioners can easily follow.

A principal form of pathos in coaching relates to the fundamental notion of goals (typically formalised as performance targets). It is a term much in play with professionals, managers and coaches. Yet this term is, at best, problematic. In rationalistic management theory, goals are often the starting point for understanding organisations while, similarly, they have come to assume a dominant and foundational role in 'good practice' coaching guidelines (Martens 1997). Seductively, goals appear to offer a means of overcoming the pathos endemic to coaching through giving focus and direction to coaches' intent. But they may actually contribute to that pathos. A key problem is that coaches generally set team goals. It is often difficult to unify a team behind a cohesive strategy to achieve the goals set. Indeed, even the 'consensus' goals, which by definition assume an agreement between coach and athletes, may operate at only a superficial level. The relationship between coach and athletes remains characterised by hierarchy and asymmetry, as was recently confirmed by Jones *et al.* (2004). The researchers found that the democracy of elite coaches stretched only so far as to give their athletes an illusion of empowerment to ensure they 'buy in' to the coaches' agenda. So the official goals of a team are usually the goals of those that hold most authority within the group. These goals are then sometimes overtly or covertly contested by others within the team. It is somewhat stretching credulity that all athletes will share and willingly accept exactly the same goals as their coach.

In theory, collective intentions and activities are likely to coincide to the extent that there is consensus over the goals to be achieved – a situation that is rare in reality. Hence, as goals are often proclaimed by coaches, who make efforts to have them accepted as operational guides, there is potential for considerable slippage between avowed goals and their implementation. The problem of goals thus, is ultimately one of power: whose goals are to count? Uncertainty and pathos are inherent in such contexts, as proclaimed goals are often unattainable for a variety of reasons, which condemns all coaches to be underachievers.

In examining why proclaimed coaching goals are unobtainable in full, a number of characteristics can be noted that point to the difficulty in accepting their rationality:

1   Goals that are capable of being pursued at the same time are diverse. They may range from winning competitive fixtures, through developing sportsmanship and good manners, to promoting enjoyment of participation.

2   Some goals are diffuse in that they are concerned with the develop-
     ment of the whole athlete or child. Such goals are long-term and so
     difficult to assess in the short term.
3   Some goals are inherently incompatible in that players are encouraged
     to be creative but yet are expected to conform to a given norm.
4   Coaching goals are often so diverse, for example those related directly
     to winning as opposed to holistic athlete development, that they cannot
     all be pursued at the same time with the same vigour. Consequently,
     priority is given to some over others, establishing a hierarchy of goals.
5   Goal displacement sometimes occurs when coaching performance
     becomes the goal in itself that consumes the activities of those in
     coaching roles, but it is only loosely linked with the core function of
     the coach to support others' learning.
6   Informal patterns of social interaction taking place within the coaching
     context can precipitate a variety of individual and group social goals.
     Although they are not always oppositional, neither should they be
     regarded as amenable to colonisation by coaches.

When faced by such situations there is a tendency for proclaimed goals
to be substituted by more pragmatic operational goals through everyday practices, precisely because such amended goals are achievable and measurable.
Hence, even where more expressive (process) goals are originally stated, the
nature of a complex environment means that more instrumental (product)
goals are likely to be pursued, such that goals to control the product of
coaching may become substituted for process-learning goals. For example,
structuring a coaching session around a rigid set of progressive practices as
opposed to critically evaluating the learning needed, deciding how best to
go about it while retaining the flexibility to react to analytical observations
regarding the strategy's success.
    We do not abandon the notion of goals altogether. Rather, we suggest
that organisations embody a mix of different types of goals held by different
individuals and groups at all levels of the hierarchy, with different and
changing degrees of intensity. The purpose of our critique is to alert those
who are constantly subject to a dynamic environment that a rationalistic,
consensual goal-orientated model can be no more than an ideal. We wish
to highlight the limitations of the popular assumption that a set of goals
can be universally shared, and point to the validity of diverse explicit and
implicit goals that individuals and groups in coaching settings may pursue.
    A related source of pathos within coaching derives from inherent limits
to effective coordination of organisational activities. There are just too many
variables entailed to achieve very close and enduring coordination. Pathos
occurs as there is a chronic discrepancy between the rational model of
organisation, which holds considerable sway for those who manage, and
the less-than-rational reality of real coaching life. For example, a group of

football players chatting off-task could be perceived as behaving irrationally from a coach's perspective in which rationality is seen as the maximisation of athletic attainment. The players, however, could have other interests and motivations that make their actions very relevant – such as prestige and standing in the peer group, rivalries and jealousies, protecting slight injuries and home life concerns. Within the coaching environment then, there are competing rationalities arising from differences of real or perceived interests.

The endemic ambiguity of coaching

In addition to pathos, the degree of ambiguity or uncertainty that is inherent in sports coaching contributes to its problematic nature (Jones and Wallace 2005). Ambiguity can be attributed to the slack relationship between goals, structures, decision making and decision outcomes. Not only are the goals of coaching multifarious and diffuse but the organisational structure surrounding it is often loose, leaving decisions to be made in a haphazard way, and outcomes, particularly those related to player development, difficult to evaluate in relation to other elements. It is therefore practically important to recognise that a measure of ambiguity is endemic in coaching situations, and so attempts to rationalise coaching can have only moderate impact.

One source of ambiguity is the coach's variable but always limited control over other stakeholders, be they players, other coaches or administrators. Indeed, no one in a social environment can exert absolute control over anyone else. So, even though power relations are almost universally asymmetrical, in that the holder of most formal power exercises greater control over the behaviour of the individual who is subject to that power, the reciprocity of informal influence within a social context is not totally absent. The athlete is never without power in the coach–athlete relationship, which defines it as being interactive in nature (Jones et al. 2004). This is an idea that many coaches appear to find difficult to grasp fully. Consequently, even where coaches force the issue with their athletes that their bidding must be done and the requested task is carried out, it is usually done in the absence of best effort. Associated damage done to the coach–athlete relationship then leaves a legacy to contend with (Potrac et al. 2002).

A second source of ambiguity arises from the individual's equally variable but always limited awareness of what is happening. Hence, a coach cannot know all that is going on in an environment that requires a multiplicity of coaching tasks. Thus, decisions are often made on incomplete information, skewing the coach's perception towards whatever information is available. Similarly, coaches can possess only limited awareness of the totality of the situation beyond the immediate impact of their actions, as with the longer-term outcome of treating an athlete in a particular way and its effect on others whose interests may be affected.

A third source of ambiguity relates to the prevalence of contradictory beliefs and values held by any individual or among different groups involved. For each athlete, belief in stretching oneself in order to excel is likely to be tempered by belief in avoiding serious sports injury. A coach's belief in building a winning team may run counter to team members' pursuit of individual glory. So although coaches may emphasise the need to 'get everybody pointing in the same direction', the environment is actually characterised by a multitude of stakeholders (including coaches, assistants, medical staff, managers, administrators, players) with a range of priorities, perceptions and specialities. Since they hold allegiance to partially conflicting beliefs and values, which cannot easily be transferred to best realising professional and personal goals, control over them must be considered relative. Additionally, as the wider coaching context is an 'ill-defined domain' (Côté et al. 1995: 3) typified by both the face-to-face interaction of training sessions and the mediated interaction of much sports management, ambiguity often results from unintended consequences of actions of which their perpetrators may be unaware.

A constant shift in practice and intuitive learning is required, as any setting at hand will differ in some degree from coaches' past experience. They need to be able rapidly to assess situations that do not wholly fit their mental model of expectations, and make accommodatory changes (Côté et al. 1995). So there is a continual interplay between what they plan to do and how they adapt to what is happening. According to Saury and Durand (1998) this is the very nature of coaches' expertise: a cognitive function that has only limited roots in either planning or reason. Alternatively, they conclude that the actions of expert coaches are 'highly adaptive in nature', with their planning being 'flexible and based on continuous step-by-step tuning to the context' (p. 264).

Dilemmas of coaching

A dilemma implies equally valued alternatives that cannot be permanently resolved into a single course of action. Organisational dilemmas have been well conceptualised in management literature, and parallels may fruitfully be drawn with coaching. Ogawa et al. (1999) offer a typology for educational organisations as follows:

1   Dilemmas over goals, e.g. organisational purposes versus individual needs and interests.
2   Dilemmas of hierarchy, e.g. limited involvement in decision making versus involvement at all levels of the hierarchy.
3   Dilemmas over task-structures, e.g. the extent of enforcing formal structures against allowing the emergence of informal structures.
4   Dilemmas over compliance, e.g. commitment to given goals, and acceptance or resistance to change.

These categories reflect classic dilemmas constantly faced by coaches in their everyday practice. For example, how much emphasis to put on team as opposed to individual development? To empower athletes or not and, if so, how far? To demand strict adherence to given roles or to allow individual creativity? And, finally, how flexible should coaches be to changing circumstances? Such dilemmas within coaching are enduring, and, therefore, are not amenable to final resolution. The real-life constraints within which training sessions and events occur force coaches to act under uncertainty and time pressure, generating or exacerbating dilemmas. One inescapable dilemma relates to the need for a coach to react quickly on the basis of a superficial analysis of events at the risk of making a mistake, or 'to take the time to analyse a situation more thoroughly to find a more appropriate solution, at the risk of acting too late' (Saury and Durand 1998: 263).

Decision making in organisational contexts marked by dilemmas and accompanying ambiguity was famously referred to by March and Olsen (1976) as conforming to a 'garbage can' model. Here, the decided upon outcome is not the result of a logical and rational sequence of decisions but of reactions to a churning up of problems, solutions and ever-changing participants, and choice opportunities. The garbage can model resonates with the micro-coaching experience. Athletes and their coaches act in a relatively unpredictable environment, fraught with dilemmas and iterative decisions. The challenge is to acknowledge such dilemmas, to reflect on them and to consider how best they can be dealt with. In other words learning how to cope better with dilemmas rather than eradicating them.

Moving away from a rationalistic view of coaching and coach education

Coach education has been founded upon, and remains littered with, rationalistic ideas, belying the complexity we have depicted. Despite isolated calls to the contrary over the past twenty years (Martens 1979, 1987, Salmela et al. 1993 among others), oversimplification of coaching in rationalistic 'how to coach' texts (Gervis and Brierley 1999, McConnell 2000) appears not to be losing any momentum. Such texts remain targeted at increasing control and managing effectively the coaching context to achieve unproblematically pre-specified aims.

As a consequence, coaches come to live within a culture of control over which they are presumed to have dominion. It assumes the establishment of a clear set of achievable goals, the availability of all necessary resources, and the unequivocal achievement of successful outcomes. Coaches are similarly encouraged to take charge and control the coaching process and environment over which they preside (Seaborn et al. 1998). It is further assumed that coaches' leadership will create a culture where athletes come to understand, unquestioningly accept and internalise the logic of the goals–outcome linkage. But under this logic, if coaches experience problems it must be their fault, and it is their sole responsibility to rectify the situation. They are therefore encouraged to seek solutions that promise greater control and the certainty it implies. Ideas such as pathos or ambiguity, which suggest that strong control is not possible, are not likely to be bought so easily. Such an approach can be a road to neuroticism, as coaches continually try to reconcile the discrepancy between the ideal world which they carry around in their heads, and the imperfect world of everyday experience. It is a situation that has led to illness for many, as witnessed by the high-profile cases of football coaches Gerard Houllier, Graham Souness, Joe Kinnear, Glen Roeder, Barry Fry and most recently Dario Gradi, among others, all of whom have suffered from apparent stress-related troubles. The source of stress may be the chronic discrepancy between proclaimed goals and coaches' capacity to achieve them (Sandford 2002).

The 'coach as exclusive controller' orthodoxy is now under challenge, with coaching increasingly recognised as an inexact science and therefore vulnerable to social vagaries (Jones 2000, Jones et al. 2002, Schempp 1998). Indeed, the notion of a coach who, when making decisions, knows all the alternatives and their respective outcomes and is able to rank each in an order of preference, is patently unrealistic. Critique of such a rationalistic conception of decision making goes right back to the work in management of March and Simon (1958). They showed how decision makers 'satisfice' by seeking an acceptable course of action, rather than optimise by identifying and weighing up all possible alternatives.

There is a sense in which the orthodoxy rests on an enduring myth – expectations of how coaching ought to be, rather than what it is. Recent work by Potrac et al. (2002) and Jones et al. (2004) highlighted how elite coaches adopted behaviours they perceived gave them authority and the respect of their athletes, because it was what they thought the latter wanted. The behaviours were adopted to satisfy both their own sense of legitimacy and the perceived expectations of others, often without much consideration of sporting effectiveness. Such symbolic actions help perpetuate expectations that coaches should operate rationalistically. The burgeoning field of coaching science has been subject to the acceptance of rationalised myths. These are sets of taken-for-granted assumptions about procedural features that remain largely untested. They often stem from categories created by so-called professionals and relate to what and how to coach, athlete characteristics, methods of testing or assessing improvement, and accreditation. Through the presentation of these categories to the wider sporting and social world, a logic of competence is developed, which ensures the survival of those who adopt it. It is a mode of control rooted in ideology and constructed legitimation (Cassidy et al. 2004, Pitter 1990).

Not only is the coaching process subject to myths about good practice, but the coaching context itself is a social construct. Although it has physical objectivity in terms of, for example, the training ground, club and players, as a social institution it is amenable to competing interpretations, where different groups may 'see' the training and club differently (Cushion 2001). Coaches come to a personalised definition of their role that is shaped by their perception of what it means to be a coach together with the influence of occupational socialisation and subculture which provide a sense of what others expect of them. Of course, we recognise that there are limits to this constructivism, as external factors inescapably impinge upon sporting clubs and the coaches who operate within them. In this respect, it appears that coaches behave both as they choose and how they are influenced to choose (Lemert 1997).

Why have such ideas not been more widely accepted to date? We believe the basic reason to be that they get filtered out by a series of knowledge gatekeepers whose interest in tight coach control is not well served by them:

1   These ideas are perceived not to meet the 'needs' of coaches (e.g. ideas such as ambiguity imply limits to coaches' capacity to control their athletes).
2   They are considered too complex and abstract in and of themselves. As they are not presentable as guaranteeing coaches a high level of certainty over expected outcomes, it is considered that coaches (somewhat ironically) would find them of limited relevance. The elixir of the quick-fix is not provided.
3   They are largely restricted to academic texts and so would require greater promotion at the appropriate pitch for coaches as practitioners.
4   Such concepts run counter to the prevailing 'heroic' orthodoxy in the current literature. The alternative view of coaches learning to cope in conditions of some ambiguity and balancing contradictory pressures is not so attractive.

As a result, coach education practice and research remains dominated by a heavily practical orientation. The imperative to impart skills through training and consultancy directly to improve practice means that the prevailing ideology and its application to the field have been rarely questioned. Yet superficial practicality has been bought at the expense of the deeper understanding that sociological and pedagogical approaches stand to offer, and which might inform the development of more realistic approaches to coach education.

We have noted how research about coaches has begun to reveal the limitations of an overly rational approach to coaching ('fine in theory . . .'). But how can coach education programmes address this most pressing of issues? Certainly pushing for increased rationality and accountability are not the answers. Indeed, how can they be in a coaching context that is constantly in a state of flux, and where coaches must continually be making decisions in a variety of situations which, themselves, are influenced by any number of factors to varying degrees (Jones et al. 2002, Woodman 1993)?

We suggest that a sound starting point for more effective coach education programmes is the assumption that it is beyond the capacity of any coach to achieve fully predictable control over the coaching process, and so effective practice is built on learning to cope with an irreducible degree of ambiguity and pathos that are endemic to the coaching endeavour. Such a strategy is not to admit defeat to the forces of unbridled relativity and anarchy and simply hope for the best. Coaches still have a role in influencing athletes' actions. Some elements of coaching are quite predictable, while others are predictably unpredictable. There are modest possibilities for maximising control within the limits evident, and coaches should focus on them.

Towards effective coping: the coach as 'orchestrator'

It has long been recognised that human agency inevitably operates within structural boundaries (Giddens 1986, Lemert 1997) that are economic, social, political, cultural and ideological. They tend to frame what people entertain as being doable, and even thinkable, leading to rarely questioned assumptions about the legitimacy of the existing social order and constraining thought about the possibility of alternative courses of action. Coaches, however, far from being made aware that their actions are bounded, are constantly encouraged to use their own unconstrained agency – whether to try and channel others' agency in their favoured direction by encouraging them to act in a particular way (the stuff of collaboration), or to command they do (the stuff of monitoring and corrective action). Coaches demonstrably need to rely on their own agency. But, given the complex nature of the evolving environment in which they work, how may they operate successfully in the less than ideal conditions of practice that bound that agency?

The notion of the coach as orchestrator rather than all-powerful leader can help clarify thinking here. The concept of orchestration was recently developed by Wallace and Pocklington (2002) in theorising about the management of complex educational change. While coaching situations are obviously somewhat removed from those entailed in bringing about system-wide educational change, the idea that senior leaders are orchestrators does resonate with the way coaches have to operate in their relatively uncontrollable and ambiguous environment. Just as senior educational leaders have to make the most of their limited agency to achieve their goals with and through others, so do coaches. The metaphor of orchestration, therefore, seems worthy of adaptation as a conceptual basis for theorising coaches' contribution to the coaching process. As applied to coaching, then, orchestration may be defined as:

coordinated activity within set parameters expressed by coaches to instigate, plan, organise, monitor and respond to evolving circumstances in
order to bring about improvement in the individual and collective
performance of those being coached.

Orchestration implies steering, as opposed to controlling, a complex interactive process. It entails instigating, organising and maintaining oversight
of an intricate array of coordinated tasks and coping with the way things
are turning out – often unpredictably – as the process unfolds, while keeping
sight of the objective of the exercise. As opposed to leading from the front,
orchestration is unobtrusive, it is characterised by behind the scenes string
pulling, it is evolutionary, while including great attention to detail. It
contrasts with visionary leadership, which arguably overstates leaders' agency
and underplays factors that limit what leaders can do. Such factors include
the expectations of others, socialisation, and existing professional preparation programmes, in addition to more formalised accountability mechanisms.
Orchestration, then, has potential for coaches in terms of providing realistic practical guidance, as it implies that they should make the most of
their limited agency without expecting to achieve strong directive control.

In many ways, orchestration means less than leadership as the scope for
selecting the content of a vision is generally more restricted than within a
paradigm of visionary or transformational leadership. Orchestrators are more
ready to acknowledge their limitations and not invest as much where efforts
are not likely to bring rewards. Consequently, there is limited scope for,
and reliance on, individual 'charisma', although this is not to say that
coaches may not be charismatic figures. Conversely, the emphasis is on their
need to stimulate and steer the performance and learning of their charges,
to make new things happen and keep them on track. On the other hand,
orchestration means more than leadership. In this regard, it involves detailed
oversight of the minutiae of the coaching situation. It involves constant
analysis, evaluation and monitoring to keep things going, be they established
core or new tasks. Thus, orchestrators attend to maintaining momentum
and making sure the set course, which is carefully planned in advance, is
followed. They monitor in considerable detail and are ready to step in if
tasks are not carried out as specified. In short, the concept can be seen as
straddling both leadership (leaders do the right things) and management
(managers do things right) in making good new things happen while keeping
established good things going.

The detailed planning and coordination functions inherent in orchestration are crucially characterised by flexibility. Such preparation covers what
needs to be done, retaining short-term flexibility through incremental
planning while attempting to retain some coherence through longer-term
planning cycles. Plans are coordinated and frequently updated both informally and formally based on the detailed monitoring and evaluation of

practice. Changes are implemented in a coordinated and definitive manner, informing all relevant personnel of their value and the rationale behind them.

Recent findings on expert coaches indicate that they do use flexible planning strategies within detailed set routines which permit improvised adaptations to the context. Such actions recognise that many principles cannot be applied outright where they have 'contradicted other sets of constraints inherent in coaching situations' (Saury and Durand 1998: 264). However, this does not mean that their actions are totally reactive, thus lacking consistency and coherence. Rather, and in line with orchestration, it reflects awareness of the need to retain short-term adaptability while preserving constancy through longer-term cycles.

Further echoing their roles as orchestrators, the planning undertaken by these coaches reached into the realm of differentiated support, as it entailed carefully considered responses to what different athletes needed and when they needed it. This often took the form of expert tactical or technical help, giving time to listen, counselling, additional training, as well as addressing issues of injury and retirement. Hence, orchestration is also a philosophy of care, tailored where possibly to the specific needs of the individual.

Underlying the original notion of orchestration as applied to complex change is the assumption that most formal power, or authority, lies in the hands of managers in hierarchically ordered organisations. However, other organisational members have recourse to informal power, or influence, which may be used to resist or support managers. Therefore, managers are heavily dependent on winning the acquiescence or more positive endorsement of those who are ultimately responsible for implementing change. Hence, although coaches generally have authority to coach, their effectiveness in maximising their charges' performance depends on the latter being willing to accept this authority, rather than using influence to disrupt or delay proceedings.

In other words, orchestration for coaches implies attention to culture building and communication. Forcing through what they want to happen by overcoming resistance, rather than heading it off by nurturing a culture of acceptance, can never bring more than minimal compliance, hence the need to work with people to overcome their doubts, anxieties and shortcomings. In this respect, orchestration involves the channelling of agency in the desired direction through encouragement and incentives. Tied to this is the recognition of the value of communication to voice consistent messages, in addition to gathering feedback in order to assist coordination and to pre-empt any resistance. To make culture building work, however, coaches need to establish a reputation for open-handedness: to convince their charges that they have their diverse best interests at heart. Such a stance resonates with the recent findings of Jones et al. (2004) and Potrac (2000) who found that expert coaches acknowledged the need for sincerity, understanding and sensitivity in their practice if they were to get the best out of their athletes.

A further characteristic of orchestration as manifest in the practice of expert coaches is that of coaching unobtrusively, where no apparent coaching takes place (Potrac 2000, Cushion and Jones 2001, Miller 1992). Far from being a case of passive practice, this relates to allowing players to focus on the exercise and its objectives. In essence, coaches intend the game or the experience to be the teacher. The trick is to structure the exercise clearly in terms of its organisation and objectives, and to know when to halt proceedings to correct and re-focus the players and when to let experiential learning take its course. Through adopting such unobtrusive practices, players are forced to consider their decisions and their consequences at a deeper level than if the coach was stopping the practice to correct every error made. The coaching role here is one of detailed observation and analysis, with little direct leadership demonstrated.

At another level, further work by Potrac et al. (2002) and Jones et al. (2004) confirms that much of the work of expert coaches takes place unobtrusively. Here, such practitioners shape the experiences for their athletes both through setting frameworks for goals and largely deciding on the exercises through which they can be realised. Consequently, when athlete consultation is requested, the already set agenda confines any input to the asking of 'safe' questions, a strategy that enables coaches to determine outcomes from behind the scenes (Jones et al. 2002). This ensures that the team has a definitive focus and direction.

Conclusion

This chapter has been concerned with enhancing our understanding of the complex coaching context that we believe cannot be a wholly managed concern. It has attempted to highlight the effects of misguided rationalistic thinking on the work of coaches. Such an ideology, which seeks solutions without taking into account the endemic nature of the coaching context and its inherent dilemmas has, we contend, resulted in the irony of creating more problems for coaches than it has solved.

Alternatively, we believe that the coaching context is one characterised by ambiguity, which cannot be simply managed away. Coach education, therefore, needs to reflect how such complexity and ambiguity can be handled, not eliminated. The goal should be to help coaches cope with the relatively unmanageable character of coaching situations by learning to live with ambiguity, and so rendering them relatively manageable. Additionally, being realistic about the complex coaching environment implies accepting that it is beyond the agency of coaches (and coach educators) to eliminate uncertainty and unpredictability from the coaching process. Although the adoption of strategies such as orchestration may help to reduce ambiguity, this can only be achieved up to a point. Alternatively, if we would only get real about the futility of trying overly hard to reduce or even eliminate ambiguity by simply easing back on rationalistic models of coaching, the agency of coaches could be more profitably channelled towards more risk taking and experimentation. Coaches need to be able to accept the risk of some loss of control for the sake of innovation; so being able to think the unthinkable and make the undoable more doable (Wallace 2003).

In turn, we believe that a promising direction for improvement lies in the realm of coping strategies, headed by orchestration, rather than more grandiose notions such as visionary leadership, which treat coaches' agency as potentially unlimited. Effective coping implies ameliorating ambiguity, where both feasible and desirable. It also implies accepting a significant degree of ambiguity as a fact of coaching life, not an aberration. While we are tentative in transferring the notion of orchestration from one context to another, we believe that it has enough face validity to form a basis for further research.

Chapter 6

First among equals

Shared leadership in the coaching context

Robyn L. Jones and Martyn Standage

Introduction

Few would argue that success in coaching depends in large part on the capacities of people to work together productively in teams. Indeed, the principle that coaches should involve athletes in differing facets of the latter's development appears to be finding increasing credence both among coaching scholars and some coaches themselves (e.g. Thorpe 1997, Kidman 2001). It could even be said that the role of the coach is on the cusp of a fundamental re-think, as the belief in the need to empower athletes by transferring decision-making to them gathers momentum.

Although many generalist statements about the benefits of a more athlete-centred approach have been made, an in-depth examination of its implementation and numerous implications has not yet taken place (Jones 2001). This is particularly so in terms of its effect on the power dynamic inherent in the coach–athlete relationship. Many questions then continue to exist surrounding not only if coaches can realistically fully share their leadership function with athletes, but if so which aspects should be shared, how equally and under what circumstances? Consequently, we believe that many of the seemingly unproblematic claims made on behalf of adopting a shared leadership approach to coaching should be treated with a little caution. Applying such changes in a dynamic and complex human context can never be so straightforward.

The purpose of this chapter is to argue that although leadership in the athletic domain should ideally be shared, as coaches live in the real world, which is characterised by much uncertainty and tension (and where results often matter), the extent of sharing that is justifiable in practice depends on a variety of contextual factors. The intention is to progress our understanding of the phenomenon of coaching leadership and how it can be carried out. This is particularly so in relation to sharing power with athletes, as we believe that many still labour under serious apprehensions about the nature of such an arrangement which prohibits its practical exploration and application. Following a critique of the deficiencies in previous arguments in relation to shared coaching leadership and athlete autonomy, the aim then is to sketch a framework of what we believe holds greater promise to achieve such goals. It is a framework, drawn predominantly from the work of Gronn (2000) and Wallace (2001) in education, based on the need to draw on principles which, as opposed to being absolute, are contingent on the situation.

The significance of the chapter lies in building on earlier work (e.g. Kidman 2001, Jones 2001) in further problematising the writings on empowerment and athlete autonomy within the coaching process. We believe that, although the groundwork has been laid, a more critical investigation is warranted to highlight the realities of implementing such an approach so that coaches and sport pedagogists are better equipped to do so successfully. Accordingly, this chapter seeks to better define the nature of possibility in relation to shared leadership within sport, in terms of if, when and how it can be viewed as a viable option.

Democratic leadership in coaching: current thoughts

Despite the widespread romance of leadership as portrayed by the charismatic director who possesses unlimited agency, anti-leadership proponents have periodically emerged (Gronn 2000). The recent tide of such and related positions have been termed new leadership theories (Bryman 1996). Although most obvious in managerial fields, the notion of athlete empowerment and shared or distributed leadership in sport can also been seen to fall under such an umbrella. It is based on the principle that coaches should empower their athletes through transferring control to them, thus making themselves increasingly redundant. Hence, it concerns moving the athlete beyond being supported by a coach to performing an activity unaided. Many sport-related pedagogists base their support for the approach on their desire to improve decision making among athletes in game situations (Rink et al. 1996, Jones 2001). Its link to the Teaching Games for Understanding (TGfU) movement developed earlier by Bunker and Thorpe (1982, Thorpe 1997), which provided greater opportunities for game-related decision making, further increased its appeal to scholars and coaches alike.

According to Wallace (2001) and his work in education, the justifications for adopting shared leadership are numerous. First, it can be seen as ethically appropriate in a democratic society where individual rights are given high priority (Blase and Anderson 1995, Sergiovanni 1996). Second is the belief that everyone is entitled to gain the experience offered through such involvement to further their professional development and career aspirations, i.e. it provides an opportunity for informal and incidental learning. Similarly, everyone can be considered morally entitled to contribute to decisions about their development and that of the organisation or club in which they work. Third is the belief that participating in shared leadership has intrinsic value, potentially providing a fulfilling experience for all (Wallace and Hall 1994). The fourth justification stems from a view of leaders as people developers who are obliged to provide opportunities and encourage the latter's holistic progress. In this regard, they should demonstrate the kind of cooperative behaviour they wish their followers to emulate. Finally, a reason often put forward in support of shared leadership focuses on outcomes rather than the process. Here, the strategy is viewed as potentially more effective in securing results than if leaders only acted alone, by securing follower investment and 'buy in' to the programme.

Many of these justifications were taken up by Kidman (2001) in her informative stance on the merits of adopting an empowerment approach to coaching. She listed that through greater involvement in their development, athletes would be more motivated to learn and improve. They would also have greater retention and understanding of tactics and skills. Additionally, their decision making and option taking would develop, while they would also become more self-sufficient and self-aware both as athletes and people. Finally, teamwork would be enhanced, resulting in greater on-field success. Undoubtedly, the notion of sharing leadership and power is attractive, particularly to more humanistic thinkers and practitioners. Indeed, it expresses an idea that few would quarrel with; that is, that all concerned can get a collective grip allowing athletes greater equity after years of being dominated and silenced in hierarchical coaching relationships. Hence, as rhetoric, it promises groups and/or individuals access to a higher degree of power than they previously had through the delegation of authority to influence policies, plans and processes. Little wonder, then, that its popularity has expanded.

In beginning to problematise the power-sharing concept, however, according to Wallace (2001) it is ironic that such an idea, which espouses a democratic, sharing ethos, is embedded in normative theories of leadership originating in the world of business (e.g. Senge 1990: 154). Here, leaders are urged

> to promote (and implement) a cultural transformation for their followers through articulating a vision of a desirable future state for the organization . . . garnering everyone's support for it and empowering them to realize (it) through . . . emphasizing dialogue, team work and mutual support.

Although not claiming that this perspective on leadership is devoid of merit, it is a position that clearly accords 'generous dollops of voluntarism to key individuals' (Gronn 2000: 318). In essence, it is an individualistic outlook on leadership; a belief in the power of one to change things. It could also be considered to reflect an 'under theorized view of task accomplishment and the division of labour to make that (i.e. those tasks) happen' (Gronn 2000: 319). Advocates assume that leaders, in this context coaches, possess unfettered freedom to determine their visions and the means to implement them, while assuming that followers (athletes) will adhere to these principles if given the chance. They also assume that it is possible to engineer change in a (coaching) culture with predictable results, that individual interests are mutually compatible and reconcilable, and that the empowerment of athletes leads to their actions which realise the vision proffered by the coaches (Jones and Wallace 2005, Wallace 2001). But precisely how realistic are such assumptions in practice?

Problematising shared leadership in coaching

Although obviously attractive at first glance, athlete empowerment within the coaching context is a notion that needs further analysis to reveal the ambiguities inherent in it if we are to better understand it and increase its accessibility. For example, and following from the concerns expressed in the above section, empowerment can immediately be seen as ambiguous in that the one with power is taken to empower those without. In this sense, power is given, never taken, which means that those in authority possess the ability to create the condition whereby the delegated power can be exercised. The immediate question that springs to mind then, is 'how really empowered are the newly empowered?' Indeed, recent research (which is discussed later in the chapter) suggests that despite involving athletes in aspects of decision making, many top-level coaches confess to only giving them an illusion of empowerment, just enough to ensure their 'buy in' to the coach's pre-set agenda (Jones *et al.* 2004).

Similarly, in the field of education, the complexity of the concept of hand-over from teacher to learner is being increasingly realised. Here, the activity of working alone is considered only a small part in a sequence of activities where the responsibility for the learning process moves back and forth from teacher to learner (Tharp and Gallimore 1991). Within this process, the teacher remains ultimately responsible for the learning, with the dependency of the child increasing or decreasing as the teacher intervenes or steps away. The teacher's action here is context dependent; for example, the introduction of a new activity could signal a high level of teacher intervention.

In further deconstructing empowerment per se, some authors (e.g. Hoyle 1986) believe that the social world is not as the concept would suggest but, rather, is shot through with a variety of unintended and sometimes intended ambiguity. Indeed, its terminology alone (and how it is interpreted) can be problematic. For example, collaboration is often considered and used as a crucial notion within it; a term that is suggestive of a collective, supportive activity. However, empowerment also implies autonomy, independence and self-sufficiency. Undoubtedly, both notions are usually considered 'positives' and are subsequently universally welcomed, but they are hardly consistent. Clearly, then, a tension exists as to precise meanings when concepts of shared leadership are discussed.

Ambiguity also surrounds the notion of participation. For example, much conventional wisdom in education continually promotes the argument for greater teacher participation, particularly at the levels of policy and planning. This is because it is believed that (1) teachers' motivation to implement decisions is higher if they have participated in making those decisions, (2) knowledge gained by participating about how goals can be achieved will enhance individual effectiveness, and (3) practitioner input into the decision-making process augments the effectiveness of a particular policy – on the grounds that only the wearer knows where the shoe pinches (Hoyle 1986).

The findings from more recent empirical work, however, don't always match this rhetoric. Results from such work indicate that, on balance, teachers would rather teach than participate in decision making, that they are most keen to be involved in decision making in order to develop personal as opposed to collective interests and, finally, that although teachers desire a degree of consultation, they welcome the clear location of authority. The ambiguity inherent here is that while being dissatisfied with the high degree of authority vested in head teachers, there exists an expectation by class teachers that heads should have, and should use, that authority. Additionally, teachers have been found to neither want nor expect to have any authority, while particularly disliking pseudo-participation, which was generally viewed as contrived collegiality (Hargreaves 1994).

As opposed to considering such and similar social ambiguities, empowerment theories to date, and particularly so in coaching, have been a little prescriptive. Leadership appears to have been reduced to merely giving power away, abandoned for a doctrine of self-sufficiency (Gronn 2000). It is a philosophy that considerably oversimplifies the endeavour, because it ignores the fundamental political economy of interest within it (i.e. the motivations, inducements and incentives for cooperation). There has been no room for representing horizontal and vertical interactions between actors (Gronn 2000), which has left substantial dimensions of the coach's work implicit, tacit, unsaid or invisible.

Wallace (2001) further developed this critique of the unproblematic implementation of shared leadership by pointing out a number of contextual considerations that appear to have been overlooked. For example, that there may well be avenues of resistance against it from those being empowered. Additionally, an institution's culture, though open to change, is not directly manipulable through leadership activity (Nias et al. 1989). Leaders just don't hold such unfettered freedom as to implement a policy so cleanly. Similarly, a culture often contains incompatible elements as manifest in contradictory beliefs and values co-existing in a tension while any attempt to alter an existing culture may lead to change in unforeseen and undesired directions (Jones and Wallace 2005, Wallace 1996). In this respect, empowerment does not mean that those being empowered will take up this entitlement in a manner acceptable to leaders. For example, research in education has found that a significant minority of staff, despite being subject to inclusive management policies, 'remain uncommitted to teamwork and may even work to undermine their colleagues' efforts' (Wallace 2001: 155). Furthermore, even when commitment is uniform, followers may act or exercise their power in ways that are outside the range of those considered acceptable or desirable by leaders. Finally, in addition to the potential for limited followership (Wallace 2001), there exists the possibility of leaders not agreeing with the consensus if and when one is reached.

A further stumbling block to the unproblematic acceptance of shared leadership in the coaching context relates to overcoming the current authoritarian culture within the profession. This has been manifest in coaches' desire to take charge of each and every situation. Not only has this resulted in coaches being caught in a particular philosophy of leadership that few are willing to forgo, but the perceived risky nature of sharing power precludes engagement with it at anything more than the most superficial of levels (Jones et al. 2004). It is a culture that also casts athletes firmly in the role of followers who, in turn, are often reluctant to accept such responsibility while believing the coach not to be doing his/her job properly if more inclusive strategies are followed as they have stepped outside the athletes' perception of the coaching role (Jones et al. 2004). Here, there appears to be an uneasy coexistence between actors believing they want more power or not, and actors wanting to devolve powers or not. It reflects part of the complex social and political conflict between change and tradition. Hence, in addition to the usual difficulties inherent in sharing power, the coaching context and culture appear to have added inbuilt deterrents against the smooth implementation of such sharing.

Taking account of the above complexity, some (e.g. Hoyle 1986, Wallace 2001) consider it ironic that a shared culture is often constraining rather than empowering. This is because it holds the potential to easily descend into conflicting micropolitics, thus encouraging people to follow individual agendas and to pull in differing directions. For them (and an increasing band of others, e.g. Jones and Wallace 2005), the problem with the concept of empowerment is that those who advocate it have usually paid too little attention to the contextual nature of power within it. This is particularly so in terms of the reciprocal relationship between culture and power, i.e. the way that culture informs the deployment of power which, in turn, contributes to the evolution and maintenance of the culture (Wallace 2001). In this respect, the current call towards empowerment clearly lacks both a critical and political dimension, and needs to take a much greater account of reality-based workplace ecology for it to be successfully implemented (Jones 2001, Wallace 2001).

How could shared leadership be effectively viewed within the coaching realm? Possible lessons from empirical research

Coaches, therefore, appear caught in a dilemma. They are faced with greater calls from athletes and many scholars to share their leadership, yet in a context of accountability they are often inhibited from doing so because empowered autonomous athletes could act in ways that generate poor standards of achievement. Indeed, the question of whether it is realistic to expect coaches to share their leadership at all exists, since it could negatively affect their reputation and job prospects.

In dealing with this issue at a philosophical level, Gronn (2000) believes that those who differentiate and privilege one distinct form of leadership over another are perpetuating a false dualism as the relationship between such differing forms is always one of interplay, with each being inherently intertwined with the other. Consequently, unlike some critics who have called for the abandonment of leadership altogether, he believes that some form of central leadership should be maintained. This could, however, incorporate a greater degree of follower power, enough to generate its associate benefits. As there are a number of possibilities and differences in the degree or focus of distribution of power, the critical issue then 'comes to do with causality and timing' (Gronn 2000: 323).

In addressing this issue, Gronn (2000) claims that we should view leadership on a distributed-focused continuum, which is constantly in a state of evolution. Any autonomy attached to it is therefore dependent on situations and contexts that both structure and mediate thinking. Hence, it is considered part of an overall system of collective relations between activities, agents and their objectives. In this respect, it echoes the foundational work of Gibb (1954) who highlighted the fluidity of circumstances as the driver behind the changing nature of leadership. Indeed, as opposed to a fixed role differentiation between leaders and followers, he believed that they were not mutually exclusive categories. Instead, each status was viewed as being potentially transient. The important idea was that leaders and followers were to be thought of as collaborators in accomplishing group tasks, with leadership being considered a fluid rather than a fixed phenomenon.

Taken within a coaching context, such a stance postulates that even though coach and athlete perform different operations, they depend on, rely on and influence one another for the successful accomplishment of the task. The interdependence and mutual influence of the two parties is sufficient to render meaningless any assumptions about leadership being embodied in just one individual (Gronn 2000). Such a position effectively re-defines empowerment to be both more sensitive to external constraints and to encompass the plurality of agents (Gronn 2000). Additionally, the actions of any individual only make sense from the perspective of contextual labour relations and their purpose. It could be argued that this altered form of shared leadership is needed if the concept is to retain the required credibility, utility and relevance. To move a little from the abstract to the practical, the question remains of how can shared leadership be realistically viewed and implemented within the coaching realm? Examining evidence from education, sport psychology and coaching research, the remainder of the chapter seeks a tentative answer.

In a review of distributed leadership in education, Wallace (2001) discovered many differing degrees of shared power apparent through the practice of head teachers. These varied from open consultation (all members encouraged to contribute) to bounded consultation (discussion within a starting framework). In the former, the flow of information was multidirectional, while in the latter it was channelled more (although not exclusively) unidirectionally. There was also variation in appreciating that team members potentially possessed knowledge and skills that could augment their own knowledge (and their closest colleagues'). Despite differences, many commonalities were also seen to emerge. These included a belief by head teachers that a working consensus with others (teachers) had to be reached, almost necessitating a degree of compromise on their part. There was also a recognition by teachers that the head teacher had authority as a formal leader, and that the management hierarchy had the right to pull rank, but only for contingent situations where equal contributions did not result in consensus. Consequently, the commitment to combining individual energies in pursuit of a shared goal was not jeopardised when the norm of inclusiveness was temporarily replaced by reversion to hierarchical operation.

The teachers' willingness to accept this way of working reduced the risk of the head teacher losing the control that relatively equal sharing can bring. Heads thus retained sufficient agency to employ their authority in orchestrating alternative approaches to shared leadership as they considered necessary. The key to making the system work was ensuring that both leader and led were aware, accepting and flexible enough to switch together temporarily to deal with such contingencies as demanded (Wallace 2001). Consequently, although much in terms of leadership was shared, the head teacher assumed the role of a more influential actor who, more-than-often, initiated and took the first steps towards change (Gronn 2000). Hence, even where there is the appearance of distributed power, Gronn reminds us that it should not be blindly interpreted as the absence of leadership. His (2000: 331) analogy of the accumulation of water stains on hard surfaces 'in which a gradual build up is not necessarily evident to the naked eye', neatly illustrates the point. It appears, therefore, that even when not plainly obvious, group leaders continue to serve 'as the primary mechanism by which the group mind revolves' (Neck and Manz 1994: 942).

In addition to such insights from education, work from the field of psychology, in particular that of self-determination theory (SDT) (Deci and Ryan 1985, 1991) can also assist in the quest to develop a greater understanding of shared leadership application.

Within sport settings, athlete autonomy has been shown to positively correspond to a number of desirable responses including task perseverance, well-being and intrinsic motivation (Gagné et al. 2003, Hollembeak and Amorose 2005, Krane et al. 1997). Consequently, autonomy-supportive environments (i.e. social contexts that support choice, initiation, and understanding) as opposed to controlling ones (i.e. contexts that are authoritarian, pressuring and dictating) have been generally found to facilitate self-determined motivation, performance, healthy development and optimal psychological functioning (Deci and Ryan 2002). Unlike many conceptualisations of personal autonomy, however, SDT considers the notion of being autonomous not to reflect *independence*, but to refer to feelings of *volitional control* toward activities. This is an important point, because, as opposed to athlete autonomy being reflected in total independence, it embraces the continuing necessary essence of support (Ryan 1993). According to such thinking, if a coach was to reinforce a coaching context conveying total freedom, he/she would be neglecting both his/her professional support for the athlete's autonomy and undermining the athlete's progression. Consequently, while the engendering of athlete contributions to elements of their training and aspects of team/squad decision making is likely to promote collaborative goals, it is perhaps undesirable to expect a coach to share *all* aspects of the leadership process.

According to SDT, then, autonomy-supportive contexts are not coaching situations that require the coach to relinquish his or her stature. Rather, the contrary holds. That is, while autonomy-supportive environments are important in interpersonal situations, SDT considers that the saliency of the interpersonal context is accentuated when there is an unequal power situation (e.g. coach and athlete) (Sheldon et al. 2003). To facilitate autonomy-support in such settings, the framework encompasses the concept of *structure* (degree of feedback, clear expectations, and understandable behaviour-outcome contingencies) that holds that coach authority can be maintained via promoting athlete choice within specific rules and limits (Mageau and Vallerand 2003). The notion that a coach's leadership behaviour would operate outside of an element of structure would seem counteractive for performance progression (i.e. too much unstructured choice would prohibit the coaching process and learning). Accordingly, in such situations, athletes can be considered relatively autonomous, but still influenced by the coach.

Within the sporting context, coaches are often required to promote the ownership of activities that are desirable, but that are not always interesting to the athlete (e.g. fitness training, drills, etc.). To help the coach gain athlete 'buy in' to 'do it for themselves', the process of internalisation as embraced by SDT offers some promise. Internalisation reflects a progressive process by which individuals become more autonomous in their motivation towards an activity and accept its value as being personally important. To facilitate the internalisation process, Deci and colleagues (e.g. Deci et al. 1994, Deci and Ryan 1991, Ryan and Deci 2002) identified various social preconditions. First, that the coach should provide a meaningful rationale to the athlete(s) expressing the future benefits of partaking in the task (e.g. espousing the payback to performance of undertaking certain training drills). Second, that there should be some expression of empathy or acknowledge-ment of the concerns that the athlete faces with regard to the requested behaviour. This would legitimise the athlete's perception of the activity, thus allowing him or her to feel understood, accepted, and believe that his or her perceptions are not incongruent with the requested behaviour (e.g. 'I know that doing fitness training is not always fun'). Third, that care should be taken in relation to how the rationale and acknowledgement of empathy are verbally conveyed by the coach to the athlete. For example, the coach should try to avoid using controlling expressions (e.g. 'you must', 'you have to', 'you should') and alternatively verbalise choice and support (e.g. 'you may want to', 'you can try to').

In exploring the theme of shared leadership further, Bergmann Drewe (2000b) placed her findings in relation to coaches' perceptions of how much autonomy an athlete should have on a continuum. At one end were coaches who wanted to 'run the ship', while at the other were coaches who felt ath-letes should predominantly do so. Unsurprisingly, there were many degrees of difference between these positions which led to the conclusion (echoing that from SDT research above) that it may well be possible for a coach to be in a position of power but still allow athletes a certain degree of autonomy (Bergmann Drewe 2000b). For her, however, arriving at a workable version of this notion required a detailed examination of differing conceptions of autonomy. According to Bergmann Drewe (2000b), many philosophers make a distinction between two fundamental notions of autonomy. First, is that of autonomy as self-sufficiency. As defined by Wolff (1970: 14), this relates to 'the autonomous man (sic), insofar as he is autonomous, [is] not subject to the will of another'. This goes further than simply being free from others' interference 'as autonomy requires awareness of control over one's relation to others' (Kupfer 1987: 82). Second, there is the notion of autonomy as self-rule. In contrast to the view of autonomy as self-sufficiency, this allows for consideration of external influences into a person's determination of action. In the words of May (1994: 141), such an interpretation believes that 'autonomy does not require detachment from external influences.

Rather, it requires that an agent actively assess these influences' before deciding, as a 'helmsman', the appropriate course to steer. An individual's direction, then, although set by him/herself, is done so as a consequence of evaluating a variety of considerations, many of which are beyond his/her control (Bergmann Drewe 2000b).

Such a conception has significant implications for the coach–athlete relationship, as how a coach conceives of autonomy will affect how much of it he or she is willing to relinquish to the athlete (Bergmann Drewe 2000b). For example, if coaches think of autonomy as self-sufficiency they may deny athletes any degree of it as they don't believe the latter can handle such unfettered decision making, or, simply, such coaches fear making themselves redundant. Alternatively, if coaches can conceive of autonomy as being more akin to self-rule, concepts such as improved decision making on behalf of athletes have the potential to occur. This is because the athlete increasingly adopts the function of helmsperson, with the coach's advice becoming one of the external considerations that athletes need to heed. Bergmann Drewe (2000b) describes such an arrangement as the coach being *an* authority as opposed to being *in* authority.

This would be quite a tidy place to leave the discussion were it not for recent empirical evidence which suggests that elite coaches believe they have, and should have, a little more control than suggested above (Jones *et al.* 2004). Although they concurred that the coach should assume the role of information giver, such practitioners also believed that the advice given ought to be viewed as coming from a 'more capable other' (Vygotsky 1978). Hence, it should be considered as coming from someone in authority and someone considered an authority; a role that assumes considerably more significance than simply just another external consideration for athletes to accept and/or reject at will. This, of course, presupposes that the coach will have the requisite knowledge to engender the influence and respect necessary. The coaches in Jones *et al.*'s (2004) study framed it in terms of setting the boundaries within which athletes were allowed to partake in the decision-making process. Thus, the athletes were permitted to be 'helmspeople' of crafts sailing on waters bounded by the coach. It is a situation that allows for considerable input from the coach while satisfying many athlete demands for greater autonomy. Control for such coaches, then, appeared to be more a matter of delimitation, that is, of allowing for different behaviours within established zonal boundaries, than of establishing directive domination over athletes.

Conclusion

Coaching exists in the uneasy interplay between uses of power, according to coaches' beliefs in a management hierarchy and in the entitlement of all athletes to have input over their preparation and destination. While the traditional arguments presented for the principle of shared leadership in coaching are persuasive as far as they go, they fail to take into account many features of the real world. For example, the possibility of such a structure resulting in an ineffective and deficient learning environment, leading to poor results. Similarly, the approach hasn't addressed the unique coaching context in terms of coaches' hierarchy of accountability when they often have to answer for everything that goes wrong.

Alternatively, we believe that any prescriptions for shared leadership should, wherever possible, be informed by evidence and rest on principles that are context sensitive. Borrowing from the work of Wallace (2001), such principles could relate to coaches having the responsibility for promoting shared leadership for the benefit of all, but retaining the right, because of their unique accountability in doing so, to delimit the boundaries of sharing and to have the final say where there is disagreement over leadership decisions. These principles justify coaches proceeding with caution towards the most extensive, equal sharing of leadership possible to maximise synergy, while allowing the contingent reversal to hierarchical operation to minimise the risk of disaster as the situation demands. It is a less romantic and more realistic conceptualisation of shared leadership, which better places it within the everyday complexity of coaching.

Chapter 7

Athlete learning in a community of practice

Is there a role for the coach?

James Galipeau and Pierre Trudel

Introduction

Authors (e.g. Cassidy *et al.* 2004, Lyle 2002) have recently suggested that coaching should not only be defined through a list of instructional methods to use and/or a specific sport knowledge content to deliver, but rather that it is a much more complex activity. According to Jones *et al.* (2004: 106), 'coaching is essentially a social practice created in the interaction of coaches, athletes and the club environment' and therefore coaching should be seen 'as a complex social encounter' (Preface). They also suggest that this special encounter takes place in a 'pedagogic setting', referring to the term defined by Leach and Moon (1999: 268):

> The term pedagogic setting encompasses a setting as a whole: the inter-actions between all its participants as well as individual actions within it as one process. It is the interdependence of all its parts over time that make a pedagogic setting a single entity. Participants create, enact and experience – together and separately – purposes, values and expectations; knowledge and ways of knowing; rules of discourse; roles and relationships; resources, artifacts; and the physical arrangement and boundaries of the setting. All of these together and none of these alone.

From this perspective, athlete learning should not be perceived as an exclusively individual process resulting from teaching or coaching, but also as an active participation in everyday activities. Using a social theory of learning, Wenger (1998) has presented the concept of 'communities of practice' (CoPs) 'for thinking about learning as a process of social participation' (Preface).

A few authors (e.g. Eckert and McConnell-Ginet 1999, Henning 1998, Wenger 1998) have suggested the possibility of considering sport teams as CoPs. Recently, Jones *et al.* (2004: 107), in their book examining top-level coaches, referred to the utility of the concept of CoPs as a framework for understanding the connection between coaching and athlete learning on a team:

Perhaps one of the most obvious ways in which this theory [CoPs] links to coaching is the recognition that the community of practice central to any sport has an important role in assuring that apprentices learn the 'culture of practice' appropriate to that sport. In these terms, the top-level coaches who appear in this book can be recognised as 'masters' in the sense that they create learning, together with the learners, in the appropriate sport-related community of practice.

Although Jones et al.'s reflection has merits, some nuances need to be provided. One of the issues is that, while most coaches certainly can be seen as 'masters', they are masters at coaching and not necessarily performing in the sport – unless of course they were or are also a successful athlete (e.g. Sage 1989). It is important to note that athletes are not apprentices of coaching (i.e. they are not all aspiring to be coaches), they are apprentices of performing the sport. In other words, the 'culture of practice' may be different between these two groups; therefore, the 'appropriate' sport-related CoP may not be the same community for coaches and athletes.

Based on Wenger's work (1998, 2000) as well as recent studies on coaching communities of practice (CCoP) (e.g. Culver 2004, Culver and Trudel 2005, Lemyre and Trudel 2004, Trudel and Gilbert 2004) and athlete communities of practice (ACoP) (e.g. Galipeau and Trudel 2004, 2005, Miller and Kerr 2002), we propose that in order to better understand the learning relationship between coaches and athletes (i.e. the pedagogic setting), it is more appropriate to view a team not as a single CoP made up of coaches and athletes but, rather, as two distinct CoPs. Viewing the team as being made up of two CoPs that are constantly in a negotiation process in relation to what is going on within it, provides new ways of understanding how learning takes place within and between these two groups.

In this chapter, we first briefly outline the characteristics and roles of coaches and athletes that make it difficult to imagine them having the same career and life expectations; differences that lead to a power differential between the two groups. Second, we present Wenger's (2000) definition of social learning systems, and expand on the three modes of belonging through which people participate in them. We focus specifically on the mode of engagement within which the concept of communities of practice fits into these social learning systems. Third, based on a study with varsity teams, an example of an ACoP and a CCoP encounter is provided. Fourth, ways of developing harmony between an ACoP and a CCoP are discussed. Finally, we address the implications of the content of this paper for the coaching process.

Characteristics and roles of coaches and athletes

In examining the different characteristics and roles of coaches and athletes in a team sport, there are many elements which, taken together, make it difficult to consider these two groups as a single homogeneous entity sharing the same outlook and responsibilities in their journey to reach the team's goal(s). While the ultimate goal(s) of both athletes and coaches on a team may be the same or very similar, the characteristics and roles of each group in achieving them can vary considerably. For example, for coaches:

1   in many countries, there is a move toward professionalizing coaching in order to display coaching expertise (e.g. National Coaching Certification Program [NCCP] in Canada). This can be seen as an attempt to distinguish coaches from athletes, thus promoting differences between the two groups;
2   when a coach starts with a new team, he/she is normally imposed on the athletes without consultation or discussion;
3   coaches select players at the beginning of the year and control their playing time;
4   many team coaching staffs meet regularly without the players;
5   coaches are often fired or released if they do not produce a winning team.

Whereas, for athletes:

•   despite coaches' attempts to be 'athlete centred', athletes must still follow and execute the game plan and tactics designed by the coach;
•   players (with the possible exception of teams of younger athletes) quite often organize events and get-togethers to which the coaching staff are not invited and are of sometimes not even aware;
•   players are often forced to compete with each other for a starting position on the team because coaches support intra-team rivalry as a means to improve performance;
•   even if they do not agree with coaching decisions, athletes must follow them or be faced with the possibility of not playing.

The literature in sport contains an abundance of studies on team cohesion (e.g. Carron et al. 1985, Paskevich et al. 2000) and leadership (e.g. Chelladurai 1984, 1993, Dwyer and Fisher 1990). Cohesion and leadership on a team can occur between players themselves and/or between players and the coaching staff. The concept of 'team' normally stirs up ideas of cohesion and leadership across both groups, whereby coaches and athletes are viewed more in terms of their similarities, as opposed to their inherent differences. Often the fundamental differences between the two groups are either minimized or ignored in an attempt to foster a better relationship between them.

Intertwined with the many differences between athletes and coaches on a team is a significant power differential between the two groups. The concept of power in the coach–athlete relationship is an issue that has not been addressed by many authors – with Jones *et al.* (2004) being a notable exception. As Jones *et al.* (2004: 150) explain: 'An understanding of the dynamic power relationship that exists between coach and athlete is necessary for effective coach education and effective coaching practice to occur.' Two types of power in particular help in understanding the dynamics of the coach–athlete(s) relationship – expert power and legitimate or positional power.

The notion of expert power (French and Raven 1959) in coaching implies that power in a relationship is based on the expertise as related to knowledge or skill possessed by the coach. This is in contrast to the concept of 'legitimate' or positional power (Erchul and Raven 1997), which empowers coaches based solely on their position within the social structure of the team. Jones *et al.* (2004: 154) argue that 'coaches are continually involved in trying to maintain or enhance their legitimate power through the use and further development of expert power'. While this argument is plausible, some questions arise. One major question that surfaces concerns the legitimacy of expert power of coaches in the lives of athletes, a topic that will be discussed later in this chapter.

One way that coaches have tried to overcome the power differential on a team is to adopt a more 'athlete-centred' approach (e.g. Kidman 2001, 2005) or to act as a guide or facilitator. However, the nature of the coaching role naturally demands that coaches exercise control over the athletes (e.g. player selection, starting line-ups, technical and tactical decisions, etc.). Thus, regardless of how 'athlete-centred' many coaches claim to be, it is nearly always he/she who makes the final decisions. As Freire and Macedo (1999: 47) explain in the context of education:

> In de-emphasizing the teacher's power by claiming to be a facilitator, one is being less than truthful to the extent that the teacher turned facilitator maintains the power institutionally created in the position. That is, while facilitators may veil their power, at any moment they can exercise power as they wish. The facilitator still grades, still has certain control over the curriculum, and to deny these facts is to be disingenuous.

We would argue that in the context of sport this situation is actually amplified, since sport takes place in a performance-oriented environment where coaches are often replaced if they do not produce a successful team. Thus coaches might occasionally make decisions that are in their own best interests, as opposed to those of their athletes.

Considering the different statuses that coaches and athletes have on a team, it makes more sense to consider them as two distinct groups. However, for a team to exist and perform, these two groups have to work together.

This ongoing interaction – the pedagogic setting – can be understood using Wenger's (2000) concept of social learning systems.

Social learning systems and communities of practice

Wenger's work is useful in the sport setting in helping us to understand the dynamics of the relationship between coaches and athletes within a team. Here he argued that 'the success of organizations depends on their ability to design themselves as local learning systems and also to participate in broader learning systems such as industry, a region, or a consortium' (2000: 225). Figure 7.1 is an application of this definition of social learning systems to the sports field.

An important point that Figure 7.1 highlights is the fact that a team does not exist on its own in isolation. In terms of structure, teams make up the smallest unit (i.e. the local learning system) of the social learning system of any particular sport. Each of these teams is part of a league, which is part of a larger regional and/or national sport structure, which, in turn, is part of an international sport structure (i.e. a global learning system). At the local level, athletes can be directly engaged with their team mates, or connect with the team via their imagination and/or alignment (described below). As they move toward the more global sport structure, athletes have less direct engagement with either the members of the sport structure itself or the athletes and teams within it, thus they most often connect with these groups via imagination and/or alignment. However, the global sport

		Athlete perspective	Coach perspective
Social learning system (SLS)		Modes of belonging	Modes of belonging
Local	A team	• Imagination • Alignment • Engagement (ACoP)	• Imagination • Alignment • Engagement (CCoP)
	A league	• Imagination • Alignment	• Imagination • Alignment
	A national sport structure	• Imagination • Alignment	• Imagination • Alignment
Global	An international sport structure	• Imagination • Alignment	• Imagination • Alignment

Figure 7.1 Social learning systems in team sports

structure can often have a strong influence right down to the local or team level through the imposition of rules, regulations and standards, etc.

Imagination, alignment and engagement, make up the three ways in which individuals can belong to a social learning system (Wenger 1998, 2000). Each mode allows for a different type of belonging based on a person's proximity and connection to others within the social learning system.

Imagination

The first mode of belonging – imagination – enables local members to stay connected to those on their team as well as those at more global levels by using their imagination as a tool to connect themselves to the broader community. Wenger explains that imagination is necessary 'in order to orient ourselves, to reflect on our situation, and to explore possibilities' (2000: 228). Imagination allows local community members to connect themselves to the local and/or global community without directly engaging with them. For example, university-level soccer players may feel a sense of belonging to the international soccer community by imagining themselves executing certain moves that are performed by players at the international level.

Alignment

The second mode of belonging – alignment – ensures that one's activities are in line with the practices of the team, other groups in the social learning system (e.g. CCoP) and/or broader social learning systems (e.g. league, governing sport body, etc.). Athletes feel a sense of belonging to the community as a consequence of such alignments. For example, university-level soccer players may feel a sense of belonging to the broader social learning system through their league's adoption of FIFA rules and regulations. Or players may feel more connected by adopting the same training or nutritional regimens as their favourite players at the international level (this is why some companies use sports heroes to advertise their products).

Engagement

The final mode of belonging – engagement – places the emphasis squarely on participation at the local level, within a CoP (Wenger 1998). A CoP is defined as a group of 'people who share a concern, a set of problems, or a passion . . . and who deepen their knowledge and expertise in this area by interacting on an ongoing basis' (Wenger et al. 2002: 4). Said another way, members of a CoP (e.g. a group of athletes) are interested in achieving a certain task (e.g. winning a championship), thus they will engage in actions and will interact with each other to negotiate the meaning of their participation in this enterprise. Over time, this negotiation process creates routines, words, tools, stories and ways of doing things, which are essential in order to know how to be a fully involved member of this particular CoP.

Engagement is the actual doing part of the practice in a CoP (i.e. athletes engage in performing the sport, coaches engage in coaching, etc.). It is the mode through which the community develops and sustains its practice. Only by engaging in the community's practice can members fully develop the mutual engagement, joint enterprise, and shared repertoire that are neces-sary for full membership in the CoP. Such terms are defined as follows:

Mutual engagement   The first essential element of membership in the CoP – mutual engagement – is the requirement that each member must actively engage (with the other members of the community) in the community's practice. This is the element that defines belonging within a CoP: 'Practice does not exist in the abstract. It exists because people are engaged in actions whose meanings they negotiate with one another' (Wenger 1998: 73).

Joint enterprise   The second essential element of community membership – joint enterprise – is the requirement that all members of the community must share a common enterprise (or 'goal'). This does not mean that everyone's goals will all be exactly the same, merely that they share a common purpose or reason for participation in the community. Building from the common enterprise that they share, community members will engage with each other and negotiate the meaning of their participation in the community and what they hope to get out of it.

Shared repertoire   The third essential element of membership in the CoP – a shared repertoire – 'includes routines, words, tools, ways of doing things, stories, gestures, symbols, genres, actions, or concepts that the community has produced or adopted in the course of its existence, and which have become part of its practice' (Wenger 1998: 83). This is important to the CoP because it enables members to speak about and understand issues rele-vant to the community using a common language and similar ways of doing things. It is also what distinguishes one CoP from another and contributes to forming the identity of people as members of a particular community.

For most athletes, participating in a CoP will consist of being engaged at the local (team) level with other athletes, as well as using their imagination and aligning their practices. One of the main tasks of each of the members of the ACoP will be to negotiate the meaning of their involvement in the community and the manner in which they engage in the community's practice. As Wenger (2000: 228) explains:

Each mode contributes a different aspect to the formation of social learning systems and personal identities. Engagement, imagination, and alignment usually coexist and every social learning system involves each to some degree and in some combination ... Each mode requires a different kind of work ... The demands and effects of these three modes of belonging can be conflicting ... The modes can also be complementary, however.

A CCoP follows a similar make-up to the ACoP in terms of the modes of belonging and levels of engagement. At the local level, head coaches often form a CoP with other members of their coaching staff to make decisions regarding the team, and then proceed to 'negotiate' these decisions with the ACoP. (For more information on CCoP, see Chapter 8 by Culver and Trudel in this book.)

The athlete community of practice (ACoP): an example from varsity sports

Research (Adler and Adler 1985, Galipeau and Trudel 2004, 2005, Meyer 1990, Miller and Kerr 2002) has shown that participation (i.e. engagement) in collegiate/university sport involves not only athletic participation, but also athletes' academic and social lives. As Miller and Kerr explain: 'The relationships between these three spheres were described as competitive and student-athletes unable to completely fulfill any of them, were forced to make a number of compromises and negotiations between the three' (2002: 352). Galipeau and Trudel (2004, 2005) expanded on this negotiation process using a CoP approach to understand how athletes navigate the athletic, academic and social demands of their student-athlete life. The results of this work help to illustrate an 'encounter' between an ACoP and a CCoP, in this instance in the context of varsity sport.

An encounter between an ACoP and a CCoP: intersecting at the boundaries

As Wenger (2000: 232) explains: 'The very notion of CoP implies the existence of boundary.' In a sport team, the major boundary that separates the ACoP from the CCoP is the nature of each community's practice. The practice of the ACoP is the actual performance of the sport, while the practice of the CCoP is the coaching/teaching/leading of the ACoP. The fact that 'boundaries are often unspoken does not make them less significant' (Wenger 2000: 232).

In examining the criteria mentioned above for designation of a group as a CoP, divisions between the ACoP and the CCoP emerge. While both groups generally share some degree of a joint enterprise (e.g. being successful as a team, becoming more skilled, having fun, etc.) and a shared repertoire (sport specific terminology, unique team words or language), the two groups do not engage in the same practice. Figure 7.2 illustrates how these two communities intersect.

Keeping in mind the suggestion that participation in university/college sport consists of participation in an athletic, academic and social sphere, the diagram in Figure 7.2 could be replicated – and be slightly different – for each of the three spheres (with more or less overlap between circles) and for every team. Exploring the interplay of these three spheres at the boundaries between the ACoP and CCoP reveals how each one intersects in terms of mutual engagement, joint enterprise and shared repertoire.

Athletic sphere

The athletic sphere is where the ACoP and the CCoP overlap boundaries the most. While the differing nature of the practice of each community creates a separate engagement or practice within the respective CoPs, the joint enterprise and the shared repertoire of each community can overlap significantly. The shared joint enterprise of the two communities is akin to the concept of team goal setting, in that it pertains to a shared view between players and coaches on what the team hopes to accomplish and how it plans on doing it. Here, the coaches' degree of authoritativeness and the degree of commitment and effort made by athletes can influence how shared the enterprise truly is. The repertoire of athletic words, tools and ways of doing

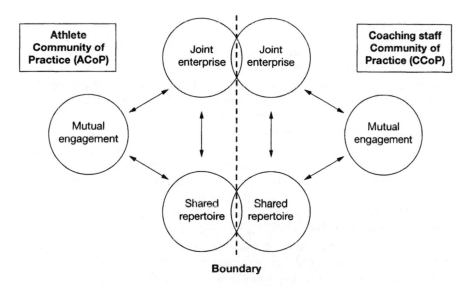

Figure 7.2 Intersection of the Athlete and Coach Communities of Practice

things will often be quite similar between CoPs and will often include a sport-specific as well as team-specific repertoire. However, the CCoP will have a unique portion of its repertoire related to coaching, while the ACoP will likely have some words, routines and stories that are unique to their community and the practice of the sport.

Expert power in the athletic sphere

On almost all sport teams, there is no question that coaches do possess expert power in the athletic sphere. Coaching courses such as the NCCP in Canada (National Coaching Certification Program, n.d.) and other coach education programmes ensure that coaches obtain minimal training/certification in the physical, technical, tactical and psychological elements of their sport. Coaches may also have gained experience from being coached as athletes, by observing other successful coaches, or by reading books and articles about effective coaching (Irwin *et al.* 2004, Lemyre and Trudel 2004). It can also be argued that most often athletes willingly attribute expert power to their coaches in the athletic domain, fully expecting and trusting that their coaches have the knowledge and abilities to help them improve and become more successful. For this reason, athletes will often adhere to the practices and advice of their coaches and participate fully in the training and athletic recommendations made by the coaching staff. In some instances, however, it is possible that athletes may not respect the knowledge and/or skills of the coach and may not attribute him or her expert power in the athletic domain.

Academic sphere

As is the case with the athletic sphere, the ACoP and the CCoP differ on the practice in which they engage. Coaches are generally not university students, and even if they are, their authorization to coach or be a member of the team is not contingent on their grades. Thus the coaches' role in the academic sphere becomes one of supporting students in maintaining academic eligibility to continue playing varsity sport. This would appear to create a significant overlap in the joint enterprise of the two CoPs, however oftentimes this overlap is not as simple as it may first appear.

The main reason for this is that while some athletes place a high priority on their education, others do not (Galipeau and Trudel 2004, Miller and Kerr 2002). In the broader social learning system, the governing body for university sport – in this case Canadian Interuniversity Sport (CIS) – has general regulations on academic eligibility (e.g. Canadian Interuniversity Sport 2005), however students participating in university sports will still individually negotiate the importance of grades within the regulations set forth by the governing body. In terms of identity, this can be understood as the difference between being a student-athlete and being an athlete-student. A student-athlete may strive for high academic marks, even at the expense of his/her sport, while the athlete-student may attempt to do the bare minimum academically in order to be able to play sports in university. Depending on the policy of the coach (or the university) regarding academics, this can create a very large or very small overlap between the academic joint enterprises of each CoP.

In terms of shared repertoire, the educational experiences of the CCoP can play a large role in the amount of overlap between communities. All athletes must be university students, but the same cannot be said of all CCoP members. Thus, in some instances the head coach (or other CCoP members) may be a current or former university student (or varsity athlete) and will have an overlapping repertoire of words, tools and stories with the ACoP. In other instances, the overlap will be small if members of the CCoP can't relate to the academic demands faced by the ACoP.

Expert power in the academic sphere

Here, we propose the idea that most coaches do not have expert power in the academic sphere. We suggest that, while coaches do have a responsibility to ensure that their players remain in good academic standing in order to maintain academic eligibility, they (for the most part) do not possess the academic expertise necessary to have expert power in this area. As Potrac et al. (2002) suggest, expert power is essential to obtain and maintain the respect of athletes. Thus, it can be argued that the lack of expert power in the academic sphere could result in the loss of respect for the power of coaches regarding academics. As Tauber (1985: 7) explains: 'people must consent to power being used on them before such power can be effective.' Coaches, then, are left with only legitimate or positional power when it comes to the academic sphere, and athletes are forced to comply with this legitimate power or face the possibility of not playing or even being expelled from the team.

Social sphere

The social sphere is somewhat more variable than the athletic or academic ones because there are no universal guidelines regarding the social development of varsity athletes. Instead, the coaching staff is mostly left to decide how the social development of the team will unfold. In general the mutual engagement (or practices) of the ACoP and the CCoP will not overlap in the social sphere, since this creates the potential of dual-role relationships (e.g. coach and friend) between the coaching staff and athletes.

The overlapping of the joint enterprise of the two CoPs can vary quite dramatically, depending on the mandate of the coach. If a coach places a high value on the social development of athletes, he or she will likely schedule opportunities for them to engage socially with each other (e.g. have a movie night, or do an activity together) or occasionally give them time off from training to spend time with family and/or friends (e.g. during holidays, non-competition weekends, etc.). However, if a coach places less emphasis on the social aspect, he or she may feel it is more important to spend the time training (or studying) and will provide few opportunities for athletes to socialize. The shared repertoire of the CoPs may also overlap more or less depending on such factors as the age, gender, history and sociability of the CCoP compared to that of the ACoP.

Expert power in the social sphere

Similar to the argument in the academic sphere, we propose the notion that coaches do not possess expert power in the social sphere either. While in most instances there is no official responsibility for the social development of athletes on a team, many coaches do place limits on the social lives of players, mainly for concerns over limited training time and performance issues. For example, coaches may opt for practices during religious or academic holidays, forcing some players to remain at the university to practise instead of returning home to visit family or friends. Coaches can also impose rules, such as curfews and sleeping arrangements when the team travels, in an attempt to improve the team's performance. As with the academic sphere, if the coach is not seen by the athletes as possessing expert power, the coach will not have the respect of players on his/her authority to make decisions regarding their social lives. Once again the athletes will be forced to adhere to the legitimate power of the coach or face possible discipline.

Creating a harmonious pedagogic setting: boundary dimensions

While some of the propositions made above appear to cast coaches in an unfavourable light, their intention is simply to highlight the limits to the power of coaches and emphasize the notion that the ACoP maintains some authority and responsibility for its own learning and development. If we are proposing that coaches do not have expert power in some areas, then how can coaches have a positive impact on the academic and social development of their athletes? Wenger (2000) suggests that there are three dimensions that can help CoPs connect and harmonize their practices in deep ways: coordination, transparency and negotiability.

Coordination

Coordinating actions between CoPs entails making processes and actions workable for both CoPs. Wenger (2000: 234) explains that: 'Across boundaries, effective actions ... require new levels of coordination. They must accommodate the practices involved without burdening others with the details of one practice and provide enough standardization for people to know how to deal with them locally.' In other words, processes and actions must be clear enough to enable the two CoPs to work together, but not so thorough that they burden the other CoP with the intricate details of one community's practice. For example, coaches may demand that the athletes on a team develop better cohesion with each other. While this can be a very important aspect of performing well as a team, in and of itself, the coaches' demand gives no instruction on how to make the team more cohesive. Coordination in this instance would involve coaches and players engaging with each other to develop some problem-solving strategies instead of the coaches imposing ways to develop cohesion or for players to be left on their own to develop strategies. Players would not need to know all of the coaching and mental training science that goes into developing cohesion on a team, while coaches would not need to know every detail of how the team develops a more cohesive group.

Transparency

Transparency here refers to sharing access to the meanings behind particular processes or actions. While coordination creates a method for joint problem-solving, transparency allows for an understanding of why particular processes, actions, objects, stories, etc. are important to each of the CoPs. Continuing from the example above, we can argue that while developing strategies for enhancing cohesion on the team is important, it does not reveal anything about the meaning behind such decisions. Said another way, coaches and athletes may be able to coordinate their activities to develop some cohesion-building ideas and exercises, but athletes may not understand the reasons why it is important to the coaching staff to develop cohesion on the team. Coaches adopting a more transparent approach might take the time to explain to the ACoP the importance of team cohesion and the links between cohesion and performance.

Negotiability

The ability of both CoPs to negotiate meanings and processes with each other is paramount to maintaining a healthy boundary relationship. As Wenger (2000: 234) explains: 'Boundary processes can merely reflect relations of power among practices, in which case they are likely to reinforce the boundary rather than bridge it. They will bridge practices to the extent that they make room for multiple voices.' Coordinating actions between CoPs and remaining transparent about intentions, reasons and meanings will be ineffective in connecting the boundaries of the CoPs if there is no room to have a two-way negotiation process between communities. Again, following the example above, a CCoP may work with the ACoP to develop strategies to increase cohesion and may even provide reasons to the ACoP why doing so is important to performance. However, if the CCoP then imposes a plan of action to increase cohesion and offers the ACoP no possibility for negotiation, the CCoP has served to reinforce the divisions or boundaries between the respective CoPs. Adopting a policy of negotiability in this case would entail the development of a flexible plan that could be adjusted to accommodate the changing needs of both CoPs. This action would serve to bridge the gap between communities and strengthen the development of the team.

Table 7.1 uses the modes of belonging (imagination, alignment, engagement) from Figure 7.1 and combines them with the three dimensions (coordination, transparency, negotiability) for developing deep, harmonized

	Coordination	Transparency	Negotiability
Imagination (on the team)	Good enough understanding of the others' perspective: ensuring understanding of each others' (coaches' and athletes') perspectives.	Building a picture of the others' practice: stories, experiences, etc., which allow coaches and players to gain an appreciation of the others' perspective.	Overarching social learning system can be seen: can players and coaches see themselves as one 'team' (i.e. 'being on the same side')?
Alignment (with the team)	Instructions, goals, etc. interpretable across boundaries: are coaching and players' demands of each other realistic?	Traditions, norms, etc. clear enough to reveal common ground and differences: clarity in intentions and actions which demonstrate player and coach expectations of each other.	Who has a say in devising compromises?: determining leadership on the team and how decisions/ compromises between coaches and players will be made.
Engagement (in the team)	Joint activities, problem solving, etc.: opportunities for players and coaches to problem-solve together and discuss differences.	Explanations, demonstrations, etc.: explaining coach and player decisions, sharing thoughts and reasoning behind decisions.	Joint activities structured for multiple perspectives: being flexible in organizing and conducting activities in order to accommodate others' perspectives.

Table 7.1 Boundary dimensions (adapted from Wenger 2000: 235)

connections between the practices of the ACoP and the CCoP. We propose that this deep connection between the practices of the ACoP and the CCoP is what brings these two groups together to form a single sport 'team'. Given the earlier propositions made about the independent learning potential of the ACoP, the limits to coaches' expert power, and the criteria for developing a deep connection between the practices of the ACoP and the CCoP, what can coaches do?

Implications for coaching

Adopting the view of coaches and athletes forming two distinct CoPs opens up the possibility of understanding new ways in which the two groups can interact with each other. Building on the advances in understanding from the coaching literature, further suggestions are now made on ways to enhance the relationship between the ACoP and the CCoP in an effort to further the development of both communities' practices. In particular, we explore the view of coaching as pedagogy, re-conceptualize the make-up of power dynamics on a team, and introduce the notion of cultivating or nurturing the ACoP.

Coaching as pedagogy

In examining the working lives of elite coaches, Jones et al. (2004: 1) suggest that they are complex and involve more than simply instructing players on technical and tactical aspects of their sport: 'coaches' stories are complex, messy, fragmented, and endlessly fascinating and . . . they demonstrate a need to understand the interconnections between coaches' lives and their professional practice'. The authors thus make the proposition that

> future inquiry into expert coaching practice [should] expand upon the traditional focuses of 'what to coach' and 'how to coach' to more adequately examine the complex question of 'who is coaching' . . . We need to view each coach as a whole, as a unique being.
>
> (Jones et al. 2004: 2)

Taking this idea one step further, we propose that it is equally important to view the athletes in the same way. Understanding who is being coached as well as who is coaching could help lead to better coaching practices, better athlete–coach relationships, increased satisfaction and, ultimately, better athletic performance.

One way for coaches to better understand the complexities of athletes' lives is to adopt a coaching style based on the concept of pedagogy instead of assuming a constrained role of 'teacher'. Referring to the work of Savater (1997) on the historical use of the word 'pedagogy', Jones et al. (2004)

explain that the scope of the work of a pedagogue was once much more comprehensive than simply being a teacher: 'In contrast with the teacher . . . who was merely responsible for delivering specific instrumental knowledge, the pedagogue had a broad-ranging and holistic role in the moral development of a young person' (Jones *et al*. 2004: 96). This description of pedagogy fits our views on the multiple roles that coaches play on a team as opposed to simply being the person who teaches skills and drills. Support for this argument comes from Jones *et al*. (1999: 12) who state: 'Seeing as the objectives inherent within both the teaching and coaching domains are different, one would therefore expect the behaviours to be similarly different.' Thus, to assume that coaching is merely a varied, narrowly defined form of teaching would be to miss the complexity of the coaching process. Viewing athletes only as learners (of coach delivered knowledge) perpetuates the power imbalance between coaches and athletes and denies the competence of the ACoP in certain areas (e.g. academics and social).

Coaching and power

The traditional notions of power in team sports place the control of the team directly in the hands of the coach through the designation of legitimate power. One of the recent trends in sport has been for coaches to empower athletes, giving them some degree of control over certain aspects of their participation on the team (e.g. Blinde *et al*. 1993, 1994, Lindgren *et al*. 2002). While this is generally seen as a step in the right direction, adopting a CoP approach reveals a somewhat different view.

Empowering athletes assumes that the ACoP is inherently powerless, a position that we have argued against in this chapter. While it is certain that most coaches possess expert power in the athletic domain, oftentimes athletes do not accord coaches expert power in other domains, such as academics or their social lives. Thus, it can be argued that coaches, by definition, cannot empower athletes on these latter matters, since they are not the ones who hold the (expert) power in these areas. Therefore, coaches – in an attempt to improve their relationship with players – will often try to delegate power that they do not, in fact, have. This then becomes an issue of legitimate power and serves only to perpetuate the imbalance that exists between the ACoP and the CCoP. Given all of this, again, what can coaches do?

Cultivating the ACoP

Given the view that the ACoP and the CCoP have expertise in different areas (i.e. CCoP are experts in the athletic sphere, ACoP – veterans in particular – are experts on other aspects of the ACoP), the emphasis shifts from issues of power and control, to the process of negotiation between

CoPs. Since part of the CCoP mandate is normally to assist in the development of players, one potential option is to adopt a nurturing (Galipeau and Trudel 2004, 2005; McDermott, 1999) or cultivating (Wenger *et al.* 2002) role in relation to the ACoP. Wenger and colleagues (p. 13) liken the concept of cultivating a CoP to the manner in which a gardener cultivates his or her plants:

> You cannot pull the stem, leaves, or petals to make a plant grow faster or taller. However, you can do much to encourage healthy plants: Till the soil, ensure they have enough nutrients, supply water, secure the right amount of sun exposure, and protect them from pests and weeds.

To expand this analogy, we would suggest that while a gardener can do many things to help a plant grow, they do not actually control the growth of the plant. The proof is that many plants will continue to grow in a natural environment even if they are not tended to by the gardener. The same can be said about athletes in the sense that although coaches can certainly do much to help them grow (learn), growth or learning also takes place without the coach (Galipeau and Trudel 2004, 2005).

Cultivating the ACoP requires coaches to re-conceptualize their role based on who is being coached, that is, who the athletes are, not only what they are doing or how they are doing it. To do so requires an understanding that, while coaches certainly possess the expert knowledge and power to educate athletes on the physical, technical, tactical and mental aspects of their sport, their expertise in terms of knowledge and/or power in other areas of athletes' lives (e.g. academics, social, etc.) may be limited. Respecting such limitations and focusing on ways to cultivate athlete learning in these other areas without exercising legitimate power can lead to new shared understandings between the ACoP and the CCoP on what it means to be a 'team'.

Conclusion

Coaches play many roles on sport teams, including being teachers and leaders devoted to the growth of their players. However, re-casting the coach–athlete relationship in terms of a social learning system invites coaches to ponder a new role vis-à-vis their athletes – the role of cultivating the ACoP. Cultivating this CoP entails an understanding that while coaches possess knowledge and expert power in certain areas of the life of the team, athletes also possess knowledge and expert power in other areas, or are able to access expert knowledge/power from people (inside and outside the CoP) other than the coach.

Understanding the team as being made up of two distinct CoPs that share a number of boundaries can be helpful in developing ways of negotiating understanding of the intricacies of each community's practice and finding ways of working together. Developing a relationship based on coordination, transparency and negotiability will ensure that the needs of both CoPs are met and that each group can serve to support and enhance the practice of the other. This view of the coaching process is not meant in any way to take power or credibility away from coaches, rather it is designed to challenge coaches to understand and respect the notion that the ACoP can and does learn apart from them. The hope is that this understanding will release coaches from feeling totally responsible for athletes' development, thus freeing them to share knowledge in their areas of expertise and focus on helping to cultivate or nurture the growth of athletes in all areas of their lives.

Part III

Re-conceptualising coach education

Chapter 8

Cultivating coaches' communities of practice

Developing the potential for learning through interactions

Diane M. Culver and Pierre Trudel

Introduction

Recent works on coaching have highlighted the nature of its complexity and the accompanying failure of formal coach education to fulfil its mandate by overly focusing on sport-specific knowledge (Cushion *et al.* 2003, Lyle 2002, Saury and Durand 1998). It would make sense that, if coaching is complex and dependent on many factors, the training of coaches should not be limited to a list of courses 'based on the assumption that learning is an individual process, that it has a beginning and an end, that it is best separated from the rest of our activities, and that it is the result of teaching' (Wenger 1998: 3). However, in many of our current coach education programmes, coaches register as individuals to participate in a few courses that will correspond to a specific number of credits or hours provided in the classroom or on a practice field by a designated course conductor, with the evaluation being a solitary test where collaborating is considered cheating.

When coaches are asked about the usefulness of such forms of coach education programmes, whether they be elite coaches (e.g. Fleurance and Cotteaux 1999, Jones *et al.* 2003, Salmela 1995) or amateur coaches (e.g. Gilbert and Trudel 1999b, Wright *et al.* in press), their opinions are mixed. While such programmes have contributed to the dissemination of the scientific principles of coaching, coaches feel that skills relating more to the art of coaching, such as communication and pedagogy, are not well served within them (Dickson 2001). However, there is agreement among coaches that learning from experience plays an important role in their development. If coaching is to be seen as a complex social encounter (Jones *et al.* 2004), it makes sense that learning from experience is significantly influenced by the types of interactions that coaches have.

Among the conceptual frameworks that could be used to study learning as it occurs in day-to-day activities, Wenger's (1998) notion of communities of practice (CoP) is of interest. Using a social theory of learning, not to be confused with Bandura's (1977) social learning theory, Wenger begins with the assumption that 'engagement in social practice is the fundamental process by which we learn and so become who we are' (Preface).

In the first part of this chapter we will define, using Wenger's (1998) framework, a coaches' community of practice (CCoP). This will be accomplished by first describing what is not a CCoP, before defining what it is and situating it within the sport social learning system. The second part of the chapter describes the results of two studies, which will provide concrete examples of attempts to facilitate coaches' learning through their interactions with others.

A coaches' community of practice: what is it?

In defining a concept it is often constructive to say what it is not. From the start, we wish to say that it is of use to avoid considering that coaches at large form a CoP. Wenger (1998: 73–74) helps us with this when he states:

> A community is not just an aggregate of people defined by some characteristic. The term is not synonymous for group, team, or network ... Membership is not just a matter of social category, declaring allegiance, belonging to an organization, having a title, or having personal relations with some people ... A community of practice is not defined merely by who knows whom or who talks with whom in a network of interpersonal relations through which information flows ... Neither is geographical proximity sufficient to develop a practice. Of course mutual engagement requires interactions, and geographical proximity can help.

Considering the above, a CCoP has alternatively been defined as 'a group of people [coaches] who share a common concern, set of problems, or a passion about a topic, and who deepen their knowledge and expertise in this area by interacting on an ongoing basis' (Wenger et al. 2002: 4). It has been recognized that coaches will inevitably engage in interactions with others (Cassidy et al. 2004, Gilbert and Trudel 2001, Jones et al. 2002, Lemyre and Trudel 2004). However, the fact that coaches interact with others does not necessarily mean the existence of a CoP. Therefore, it is important to differentiate learning within CoPs, from two other ways to interact and learn from others; informal knowledge networks (IKNs) and networks of practice (NoPs). To show the differences and complementarities of these three ways of interacting, we will adapt Galipeau and Trudel's figure (see Chapter 7) regarding the social learning system in sport.

Using Wenger's (2000: 225) suggestion 'that the success of organizations depends on their ability to design themselves as social learning systems and also to participate in broader learning systems', Galipeau and Trudel suggest that a team, being amateur, elite or even professional, is the local unit of a more global system. A team is part of a league, which can be affiliated with a national federation/association, and representatives of many nations

Social learning system (SLS)		Modes of belonging	Modes of interacting
Local ↑	**A team**	• Imagination • Alignment • Engagement	• CCop (through mutual engagement)
	A league	• Imagination • Alignment	• (Few interactions)
	A national sport structure	• Imagination • Alignment	• IKN • NoP
↓ **Global**	**An international sport structure**	• Imagination • Alignment	• IKN • NoP

CCoP = Coaches Community of Practice
IKN   = Informal Knowledge Network
NoP   = Network of Practice

Figure 8.1 Coaches' modes of belonging and interacting in a sport social learning system

will regroup to form an international federation. Wenger (2000: 227) suggests that 'our belonging to social learning systems can take various forms at various levels between local interactions and global participation', and he also presents three modes of belonging: engagement, imagination and alignment. It is important to note that although each of these modes of belonging will co-exist in a social learning system, their respective import-ance will vary from the local to the global. Engagement will often dominate at the local level (team). But as we move to the global level, coaches will use their imagination to orient themselves, to reflect on their situation, and to explore possibilities, and will use their alignment to 'make sure that [their] local activities are sufficiently aligned with other processes so that they can be effective beyond [their] own engagement' (Wenger 2000: 228). Thus, any coach will, up to a certain point, influence and be influenced by the interactions he/she has with the others who participate in the social learning system of a particular sport.

As indicated earlier, members in a CoP work together closely with a 'sense of mission – there is something people want to accomplish or do together that arises from their shared understanding' (Allee 2000, Communities of practice section, para. 8). Therefore, we suppose that the coaching staff of a team or a club have the possibility of forming a CCoP. The nature of their interactions will be influenced by three elements: mutual engagement, joint enterprise and a shared repertoire (Wenger 1998). In a CCoP, coaches will be mutually engaged in negotiating the meanings of their actions. This does not mean that coaches who participate in a CCoP do so identically.

Engagement in practice is individual, and tensions and challenges are accepted as common elements of participation. Coaches' meetings to discuss how to prepare for the season, which exercises to include in training sessions and which strategies to use during competitions, are examples of contexts where coaches negotiate their practice. The second element, joint enterprise, implies that the enterprise is cooperative not because all the coaching staff agree on all things but because it is collectively negotiated, allowing it to always be uniquely indigenous, thus 'never [being] fully determined by an outside mandate, by prescription, or by any individual participant' (Wenger 1998: 80). For example, a national federation can suggest that having fun should be pursued over winning at the amateur level, but a coaching staff that realizes the potential of their team might come up with the enterprise of winning the championship of their league. Finally, the development of a shared repertoire is the third element of practice that acts as a source of community coherence. The repertoire of a community allows for the negotiation of meaning because it reflects the community's history of mutual engagement, while remaining ambiguous. Here, we can think of specific ways to do things (routines) and all the materials developed by the coaching staff over the years. When coaches sustain mutual engagement in their enterprise long enough to share significant learning, a CCoP is the result.

In sum, coaches of the same team or club have the potential to form a CCoP, but only if they decide to learn through their interactions with each other. They must take the time to meet not only to discuss schedules and other organizational issues but also to deepen their knowledge and expertise. At the amateur level, a team's coaching staff is often limited to a coach with one assistant (Gilbert and Trudel 2001) and the potential to learn through a CCoP is therefore limited. At the elite level, the coaching staff is bigger and the possibility to learn from others is greater, but not necessarily automatic.

Some people might suggest that coaches of teams in a specific league form a CCoP. Based on certain researchers' analyses of the coaching field and on some of our studies on coaches' learning through interactions, we will argue that in the actual sport culture it is almost impossible to find a CCoP outside of a team or a club. The sport culture does not facilitate collegiality between coaches of the same league (Lemyre and Trudel 2004, Wright et al. in press) because 'in a sporting context it may be difficult for coaches who wish to be reflective practitioners to be part of a like-minded group, given the varied aspects of the sport culture that act as constraints in this regard' (Cassidy et al. 2004: 23). Trudel and Gilbert (2004: 169–170) in their analysis of the sharing of knowledge among coaches in the ice hockey structure similarly concluded that:

> Results of studies on ice hockey coaches at the youth level suggest that [they] do not participate in a community of practice, or that their

community of practice is very limited. Coaches do share a repertoire in the sense that they know the rules of the game, they are aware of good and bad penalties, they usually are familiar with events in the shared ice hockey model (i.e. the National Hockey League), and so on. In a sense, they have a communal view of ice hockey. Unfortunately in hockey, like in most sports, the dominant goal often seems to be winning. In itself, winning is not bad and in fact it is an important component of a competitive sport. The problems emerge when winning overshadows other goals such as providing children with a safe and fair-play environment. When winning at all costs drives coaches, isolationism takes root and coaches see other coaches as enemies – not partners. This individualistic approach refrains coaches from engaging with other coaches in their league while searching for solutions to common problems. This context is best described in terms of an individual, instead of a joint, enterprise.

In fact, it seems that coaches are more open to sharing knowledge with coaches outside of their leagues (Wright et al. in press). Two other modes of interacting that a coach might use beyond sustained mutual engagement with his/her team's coaching staff are an IKN or a NoP. In IKNs, people know one another and exchange information but these discussions are loose and informal because there is no joint enterprise that holds them together, such as the development of shared tools. They are just 'a set of relationships' (Allee 2000, Communities of practice section, para. 8). Despite this, many studies (e.g. Durand-Bush 1996, Gilbert and Trudel 2001, Jones et al. 2003, Lyle 2002) have indicated that coaches will often call an ex-coach, a colleague, and/or sport specialists (e.g. nutritionists, sport psychologists, athletic trainers) when looking for information to solve coaching problems.

In NoPs on the other hand 'most members are unknown to one another . . . The members hardly meet face-to-face, yet they contribute and help each other out regularly. This type of community readily adapts to the Internet and other communication technologies' (Nichani and Hung 2002: 50). While these NoPs have a large reach there is 'relatively little reciprocity across such networks' (Brown and Duguid 2000: 142). More apt for sharing information, NoPs are not usually known for producing action and knowledge although they are well developed in certain areas such as commerce (Brown and Duguid 2000). All the websites where coaches can, through chat rooms, discuss coaching issues, are possibilities of NoPs.

To summarize, an important part of learning how to coach is through coaches' interactions within a sport social learning system. Nowadays, coaches can chat with people that they do not personally know through their NoP, they also can keep in touch with a certain number of respected and knowledgeable colleagues or friends, that is, their IKN. Finally, they can work closely with a restricted group of people and develop a CCoP. The question then is: can we help coaches increase their knowledge by influencing any of these three modes of interaction? In an attempt to answer this question, two studies have been conducted.

Coaches learning through interactions: two clubs, two stories

The remainder of the chapter will describe how one of us (Culver) acted as the initiating researcher, seeking to collaborate with coaches from two different clubs to promote learning through their everyday work experiences.

An athletics club: adding to the coaches' IKN

This study was conducted over a six-month period in an athletics club operating in a major city in eastern Canada (Culver 2004). The staff at the club included 17 coaches from all levels of competition and nearly every track and field discipline; a rarity, as most athletics clubs focus on only one such discipline, e.g. distance running, sprints or jumps. The aim of the project, which focused on six of the club coaches, was to observe their interactions and also to be available as a sport psychology/pedagogy consultant, that is, to be another potential member of their IKN. For the purposes of this study the consultant was non-prescriptive, unlike more traditional approaches in which a consultant may act as a supervisor who is a content expert and/or who would analyse the coaching situation, define a number of problems, and then recommend solutions. She did not convey new concepts to the coaches. Instead, when requested by coaches, she helped them define their own practice-related problems and discuss possible actions in relation to solutions. Data were collected using interviews, field notes, e-mail and the researcher's journal.

Findings

A close examination of the types of interactions that occurred between the coaches showed that there was not really a CCoP in operation. There were very few instances where coaches interacted to exchange their coaching knowledge. Instead, their interchanges were usually one-on-one and related largely to three types of issues: (1) asking about a specific athlete's progress, usually because this athlete would eventually be moving into the asker's training group, (2) organizational issues and (3) requesting that another coach work with one of his or her athletes such as when a distance coach sent an athlete to a speed and power coach to improve strength. The structure of the club, the precariousness of the head coach's position at that time, and the absence of a clubhouse to serve as a meeting room could be factors contributing to the absence of a true CCoP. This, however, did not preclude coaches developing their own IKN. When asked about sharing information with other coaches, the international-level coaches in the club said they did so, for instance, at competitions. Interestingly, when asked if It was always that way for them, the story was different:

> You could say there is the inner circle and an outer circle, and you have to penetrate the inner circle. I am sure it is like that in any sport. And once you are in the inner circle, everybody talks to you, and if you are not in the inner circle then you sort of poke at it. Then, like at any sport, in track and field if you start producing athletes that get on the national team, well, obviously that kind of wakes people up. And that took me a long time. I was essentially like an outsider, but that's fine. I understood that.
>
> (Ron, interview 1) (Pseudonyms are used)

Another coach echoed similar thoughts:

> Usually the [more senior] coaches are not going to talk to the young coaches, and pass that stuff on. But you find that as soon as you put that first person on a national or international team, then they start watching, then all of a sudden you have got two and three, in different disciplines ... There is a level of respect I guess that they see what is going on. And yeah, we get into conversation and start passing ideas.
>
> (Colin, interview 1)

These quotes suggest that developing an IKN is not so easy; it's often a 'breaking through' adventure.

In relation to the question of whether the presence of a sport psychology/pedagogy consultant could be seen as an addition to the coaches' IKNs, the findings were positive. By being there on a consistent basis over a six-month period, the researcher/consultant became more than a familiar face. She served as a partner in the coaches' reflections and a sounding board. Four of the six coaches verified this. In the case of the head coach, the consultant's role went beyond that of a sounding board to therapeutic listening. For example, he said that, other than his girlfriend, the consultant was the only person with whom he could really let off steam and talk about his job. Having a consultant available for them to talk to about their work was new to the coaches, the impact of which was evaluated nonetheless by their subsequent actions and reactions. For instance, many of the coaches used face-to-face conversations, and three also used e-mail to seek advice from the consultant. Furthermore, the three coaches who were shown a knowledge sharing network 'map' of the club, produced as part of the study, confirmed the presence of the consultant/researcher in this network.

A ski club: cultivating CCoPs

The following description of a collaborative inquiry will show how this particular research approach was used to promote coaches' learning through their interactions, the ultimate goal of which was the negotiation of a coaching practice that puts a priority on athlete development. The defining characteristics of collaborative inquiry are 'a group of peers, engaging in repeated cycles of action, and reflecting on a question of importance to all of them' (Bray *et al.* 2000: 12).

This study had three phases: Part One in the winter, Part Two in the summer and Part Three during the following winter. The context of this study was a large alpine ski club at a major resort in the east of Canada. The club employs about 20 coaches for the winter season to look after athletes ranging in age from 11 to 19 years. One of us (Culver), acting as the initiating researcher/facilitator, approached the head coach about the study. He was instantly interested and suggested the group of six coaches who coached the K1s (11 and 12 year olds) in the club. Part Two was a summer ski camp organized by the same club. The participants in this second part were the same head coach, three different club coaches, and two coaches from other clubs. In Part Three, the initiating researcher stepped back as facilitator and observed how three coaches from Part One and three from Part Two, now coaching two different age groups, managed their interactions.

Findings Part One: the first winter

The seven practitioners in Part One were a mixture of very experienced, novice and intermediate coaches. This blend turned out to be an ideal starting point from which to launch a CCoP. Based on interviews conducted early in the season, the coaches appeared to believe they had a strong support network. The following quotations, one by first-year coach, Ben, and the other by experienced Gord sum up the opinions of the coaches regarding coaching support:

> We have so many good coaches here, in my opinion . . . even some not in the club that I can talk to. Everywhere here there are incredible resources.
>
> (Ben, interview 1)

> We're surrounded by amazing coaches, just in the room downstairs there is a wealth of experience. There is no shortage of talent around and I'm not afraid to ask, big-time.
>
> (Gord, interview 1)

With the endorsement of the head coach, the researcher set out to facilitate the learning of the coaches in the group from their everyday working experiences. Using a non-prescriptive approach, she sought to move the group forward by creating an open, participative environment, and by paying attention to the purpose and culture of the group. In this case, being an experienced skier (ex-racer and coach), and having a long acquaintance with several of the coaches helped the early establishment of a trusting, respectful atmosphere. The coaches were very receptive to the idea of meeting to further their learning, which was initiated by the facilitator's request to arrive at the first few discussion groups, labelled Round Tables (RTs) by the coaches, ready to share three lessons learned from their daily coaching. It was explained that these lessons could be things that worked well or the opposite, or ideas to be tested through discussion and then experimented with in practice.

Like other vibrant organisms, CoPs have a rhythm: 'At the heart of a community is a web of enduring relationships among members, but the tempo of their interactions is greatly influenced by the rhythm of community events' (Wenger et al. 2002: 62). A crucial role of the facilitator was to monitor this rhythm and organize activities that afforded members the opportunity to interact in such a way that the community developed the quality of 'aliveness', that there was a sense of moving forward in a productive manner. Every community evolves in different ways, therefore the ideal rhythm changes with this evolution. Being familiar with the rhythm of the ski season, the facilitator knew that it was essential to establish a good beat to the CCoP's activities early on so that the members would experience the satisfaction of learning, which would sustain the community when the season became hectic. Thus, the early objective was to establish value based on the aliveness of the interactions related to everyday coaching issues, and to create a rhythm that was sustainable.

Initially the coaches felt unsure about their 'lessons'. At the first RT there were very few interactions; the coaches presented lessons ranging from peda-gogical (related to the delivery or application of coaching knowledge), to technical (to do with ski technique), to the psychological (involving mental preparation). It was not so much the nature of the lessons that was important at that time but the fact that they resulted from the coaches' reflections about their day-to-day, recently experienced, coaching practice.

At the second RT, the coaches immediately interacted to a greater extent with each other and by the third one they began to take responsibility for the process. They came ready to share their lessons without being asked. The role of the facilitator was becoming less directive, involving mostly managing who spoke when and making links. By the time RT 5 took place, the process was well established and different types of learning were occur-ring, including novice coaches learning from experienced ones and vice versa. For example, when one coach, Gord, told the others how he used time in the chalet to warm up (it was very cold outside) and to teach the children about skiing the correct line in turns, Chris, a novice, said that this reminded him 'of something that he learned from John who used his hand to explain the radius of a turn to a skier' (Chris, RT 4, notes). This is a type of modelling in which a coach observes another's strategy and then tests it, modifying it to suit his or her context. A total of eight RTs were conducted and at the end of the winter, the coaches' evaluation of the process was very positive, as indicated by the following comment:

> Number one, the programme that we set up with you, and with the group, the coaches and the kids, it just became tighter and tighter all winter. And it was really ... the exchange of ideas and information and the camaraderie, was amazing! Like really amazing ... And one thing is we had a lot of amazing results. After the first race we just about owned the podium for the rest of the year. And what was really cool in the last couple of races is that it wasn't the same people.
>
> (Gord, interview 2)

Another of the coaches said:

> I think we have been an example in the club, and outside of the club. I have seen coaches from other mountains, like MB, come and see us, and say, 'How do you work it? What do you do to have those kinds of results? How do you make your groups, and how. . .?'
>
> (Sebastian, RT 8, transcription)

Similarly, Chelsea said, 'In the four seasons that I have coached, this has been my best season. Yeah, I am going to remember it forever' (Chelsea, RT 8, transcription). The head coach validated the process when, at an RT, he told the group about a meeting he had recently held with another group of his coaches with a view to establishing a similar structure:

> You know what? I had a meeting with my K2 coaches the other day after talking to Diane about this; this ... what you did and, the results we are having now in the K1 with the coaching. The bonding together, it's fun, we are performing, everybody seems to do a good job, and the K2's ... I talked maybe for two minutes, and then they were all like ... 'Okay you don't talk to me, I do my own stuff' ... so that is what came out of it. I said, 'You see guys, a lack of communication. It [communication] does not exist at all and that is why you are all working differently here. And what we did with the K1's, it is unbelievable; I mean the harmony is this! I'd rather spend more time with them because I am having more fun. You guys are boring! (*Laughs*). Everybody here is like a guru' ... I said, 'Come on you guys, open your wings . . . .'
>
> (Jean, RT 6, transcription)

Toward the end of the winter the facilitator was asked by the club president if she would work with the coaches who were going to the summer ski camp. In a peer debriefing session, we decided that it would be good to ask the leader of the K1 coaches, who would not be coaching at the summer camp, if he would like to write a letter to the summer coaches about participating in a similar process to the one we had engaged in throughout the winter. The main paragraph of this letter is presented here and is a reification of the evolving practice:

> In a nutshell, it [the CCoP] promotes a method of working together as coaches and helps create an environment that is proactive, positive, and sharing of ideas and methods. It is more than enhancing communication. It is creating work habits and procedures that truly enhance our coaching ability. It brings a group of coaches together making them a team, which is much more effective and focused than the 'vacuum of coaches' approach. What I mean by this is that too often as coaches we work alone or even if we do work alongside other coaches; we tend to guard our problems and knowledge, keeping them to ourselves, instead of sharing them with others.
>
> (John, letter to summer coaches, 5 June 2002)

Findings Part Two: the summer camp

The second part of this study was located in a resort in the French Alps with a glacier ski area. The ski club organized a three-week summer ski camp with six coaches and about 30 athletes (11–15 years old). All except one coach stayed in the hotel, providing ample opportunity for the coaches to spend time together as compared to Part One where the coaches went home at the end of the day. Another difference between the winter and the summer programmes was in the orientation of the coaching work. A summer ski camp is a training camp, a time to work on technique rather than trying to train and prepare for competitions, as is the norm in the winter. During the camp several other coaches dropped in to the RT meetings. In this part of the study, the coaches participated in 16 RTs, 11 of which were held in the first two weeks, and five more after the facilitator had left. Every CoP is unique; this small group of elite coaches, which was gathered together in an isolated setting by a ski club for a summer camp that aspired to develop not only the athletes but also the coaches, showed its uniqueness from the very start. Even though the facilitator asked the coaches to come to the first few RTs with 'lessons learned' from their daily coaching practice, as in Part One, this approach didn't appear to be as productive with this group.

Influenced by the nature of the CCoP, the types of issues raised in this part of the study were of a more general, philosophical nature. For example, at the first RT, only one or two issues were discussed. The second RT began with Bjorn, the oldest and most experienced coach, asking the question, 'Have you thought of the price of being a coach? The cost to your family life?' (Bjorn, RT 2). This question, he declared, was related to the fact that he had sacrificed his family life for coaching. There followed an animated dialogue relating to the costs of leading the life of a coach, who is trying to balance surviving financially, which means doing other work, and keeping a family together. Skiing, unlike some sports that can be practised almost anywhere, requires coaches to spend large amounts of time away from home. Due to the less defined joint enterprise, stories, which tend to have broad applications, were one element of the shared repertoire that was frequently used in this context. Storytelling has recently received quite a lot of attention in the field of organizational change and knowledge management. Authors such as John Seely Brown and Steve Denning (Brown *et al.* 2004, Denning 2001) have investigated how stories work to ignite change. According to Brown (cited in Kahan 2003: 1), 'stories talk to the gut, while information talks to the mind . . . [storytellers] can get to [people] emotionally . . . [creating] some scaffolding that effectively allows them to construct a new model'.

The CCoP continued to meet throughout the camp, including during the last week after the head coach and the researcher/facilitator had left. During this latter week, Bjorn, the most experienced coach, fell naturally into the role of leader for the RTs. The nature of the discussions remained broader than in Part One, reflecting the local enterprise. There were also examples of individuals who straddle the boundaries of different communities brokering interactions between the two (Wenger 1998). This was the case in RT 11, when Nick, a former club coach, acted as a broker, asking Connor, another former club coach, to share with the CCoP some of the ways in which he prepared for and worked for a camp such as this one.

Follow-up interviews with the coaches revealed three important elements about their participation in the CCoP; the pleasure of being involved in the process, the necessity of having this type of interaction, and, perhaps most interesting, the coaches' apparent understanding of the process and their ability to explain what it did for them. For example, Bjorn talked about listening to advice from another coach, thinking about it, and then trying it out. He said:

> When you talk . . . whatever the information, you are going to take what you think is good . . . adjust it, and try it out. All of a sudden it clicks, for four students; the others might not change but at least it worked for four.
>
> (Bjorn, interview 2)

Another explained the process as being like scientists in a laboratory:

> The approach is like an experiment; it is a laboratory. You arrive with this and that, then you question your approach, you put the timer back to zero, then you restart and you search for the solutions.
>
> (Florian, interview 2)

Paul, the coach who was the most forthcoming about his limitations when working too closely with others said:

> I guess in the end it was to discover what and how the others were thinking . . . I know who I want to work with and when, and when it's good and when it's not good compared to what I want to do with the athletes that are assigned to me . . . so it's good to know when you need something, who to go to right away, versus, sometimes losing an entire day or two trying to figure out who am I going to get . . . so right now it's very easy . . . but it was really impressive. The others got to know the way I work, and vice versa.
>
> (Paul, interview 2)

Paul had experienced the sense that 'it is more important to know how to give and receive than to try to know everything' (Wenger 1998: 76).

Findings Part Three: the following winter

The co-participants in this third part of the study came from two groups of coaches, a K1 (11–12 years) and a K2 (13–14 years) group. Two of the five K1 coaches and four of the six K2 coaches had been exposed to learning within a CCoP, either the previous winter or during the summer camp. As these six coaches had expressed their desire to continue to work within a CCoP in the future, they were interviewed to see how well they could manage the process of doing so without the help of the facilitator.

The K1 group faired better than the K2 group. The K1 coaches asked the facilitator to attend their first coaches' meeting, during which they explained the process to the other K1 coaches who had not previously been exposed to a CCoP. This was the only K1 meeting attended by the facilitator. Then the group carried on with some of the learning activities as in Parts One and Two; in particular, four meetings, all in the first half of the season. However, without a facilitator and the structure of a meeting schedule, their interactions were less based on everyday learning through negotiating, and were more organizational in nature.

The K2 coaches, who were equally exposed to the facilitator, had their only meeting just two weeks before mid-season. Indeed, this group never operated as a CCoP as it lacked a strong leader interested in promoting learning through social co-participation. The head coach was interested but too busy with other administrative tasks to take on this role and the two coaches who might otherwise have taken it on were, instead, concerned about stepping on each other's toes. In other words, there were ego problems, which led to a lack of leadership. One of the other coaches, who had also participated in Part One, but who would not be considered a leader for this group, said that she did learn a lot during the season but that it was through asking other individual coaches for advice. Thus, without the CCoP, learning from experience was very much left up to the individual.

This third part demonstrates that even with coaches who have previously benefited from a CCoP and who have said they want to continue to work within one, it is not sufficient to leave them on their own. We need to provide them with a facilitator who understands the principles of cultivating CoPs (Trudel and Gilbert 2004, Wenger *et al.* 2002).

Conclusion

We started this chapter by saying that coaching is a complex process and therefore it is illusionary to think that any formal coach education programme will, by itself, prepare coaches to solve all the potential problems they could face. It might be for this reason that many coaches are saying that much of what they know is a result of their experience. But what does 'learning from experience' really mean? To investigate this way of learning, Wenger (1998: 3) suggested the adoption of a perspective 'that placed learning in the context of our lived experience of participation in the world [and] assumed that learning is, in its essence, a fundamentally social phenomenon, reflecting our own deeply social nature as human beings capable of knowing'. The question to answer then becomes: 'What kind of understanding would such a perspective yield on how learning takes place and what is required to support it?' (Wenger 1998: 3).

Using Wenger's (1998, 2000) work, we suggested in answer that coaches belong to a social learning system that goes from a local unit (the team) to a more global structure using three modes of belonging: engagement, imagination and alignment. For example, a coach belongs to a team by doing things together with the other members of the coaching staff (engagement). At the other levels of the social learning system, the coach will generally have to use two other modes of belonging: imagination and alignment. Based on the results of studies we have conducted on coaches' learning paths (Culver 2004, Lemyre and Trudel 2004, Trudel and Gilbert 2004, Wright *et al.* in press) we propose that the sharing of coaching knowledge, the interactions through which a coach will learn how to coach from/with others, can take at least three modes. Through a CCoP, a coach will negotiate ways of coaching through his/her direct and sustained engagement with other coaches. Unfortunately, because of the competition sub-culture so present in sport's social learning system, the sharing of knowledge between coaches is most likely to be restricted to a team/club and will not appear between rival coaches. This situation is particularly unfortunate at the amateur level where all coaches within a league should be working together to create an environment where safety and fair-play are valued (Trudel and Gilbert 2004). The second mode of interacting through which coaches learn is with respected and knowledgeable colleagues and friends, the coaches' IKN. A coach's IKN is generally composed of a restricted number of people coming from any level of the sport learning system. Finally, advances in technology allow coaches to develop an NoP, that is, to interact as often as they want with people they have never met and will probably never meet in person. What is of interest here, in relation to use of the internet, is that it is very easy to interact with coaches from all over the world at any time. Similar to the two other forms of learning through interactions, NoPs have advantages and limitations (Wright *et al.* in press). Nevertheless, undoubtedly coaches would certainly maximize their learning if they could use to the full potential each of these three modes of interacting.

Once we have acknowledged the potential of learning by interacting from/with others, what is the next step? Can we teach coaches how to make better use of their interactions? For Wenger (1998: 225), learning cannot be designed but 'those who can understand the informal yet structured, experiential yet social, character of learning – and can translate their insight into designs in the service of learning – will be architects of our tomorrow'. In a modest effort to be among the coach development architects of tomorrow, we have conducted two studies in an attempt to facilitate the learning from experience of the coaches from two sport clubs.

From the study with the athletics club we learned that even when coaches are part of the same organization and share the same sport stadium they do not necessarily form a CCoP, or, said another way, their CCoP might not be very healthy. The coaches in this club seemed to get along pretty well on an informal basis but their discussions, although important, were restricted to organizational aspects of the club. Rarely were these interactions an occasion to exchange their coaching knowledge, limiting the development of the club. Organizations will often request the services of specialists to improve the performance of the team/club but such personnel generally focus on the athletes instead of the coaches. In this study, one of us acted as a consultant to work with the coaches using a non-prescriptive approach. Such an approach leaves the responsibility for initiating interactions largely to the coaches. Therefore, we saw some coaches behave in a way that seemed to indicate, 'Don't call me. I'll call you whenever I need your help.' This left us wondering if changing the role of the consultant, still without being prescriptive, might lead to greater enrichment of the coaches' learning. The challenge was to convince the coaches of the power of interacting on a regular basis in an attempt to 'negotiate' their practice.

In the study with the ski club, we decided to be more pro-active and to address the classic problem of 'we do not have time to meet'. With the collaboration and support of the club's head coach a strategy to bring coaches together was proposed. The intent was not to regroup the coaches to lecture them but to have them discuss their coaching knowledge. This study has shown that coaches will benefit from such round table discussions and the approach can contribute to the nourishment of a CCoP. However, the study has also demonstrated that a facilitator/coordinator is necessary because 'the most important factor in a community's success is the vitality of its leadership' (Wenger *et al.* 2002: 80).

The two studies presented demonstrate how learning can be enriched through social co-participation, as theorized by Lave and Wenger (1991). However, to talk about improving learning through a CoP or a network does not mean that we reject the individual side of learning. The concept of identity is very present in Wenger's work; 'issues of identity are an integral aspect of a social theory of learning and are thus inseparable from issues of practice, community, and meaning' (p. 145). Furthermore, for Wenger, learning 'is an experience of identity. It is not just an accumulation of skills and information, but a process of becoming – to become a certain person or, conversely, to avoid becoming a certain person' (p. 215). We did not address the concept of identity in this chapter, but we strongly recognize the importance of conducting studies on the possible tensions or conflicts between the demands of groups and the needs of individuals.

Chapter 9

The coach as a reflective practitioner

Wade Gilbert and Pierre Trudel

Introduction: the coach as a reflective practitioner

To accomplish their various roles, coaches at all levels (recreational, developmental and elite) are expected to understand and use an increasingly complex and specialized body of knowledge. Therefore, comprehensive large-scale programmes to assist them in this task are now available in many countries around the world (Campbell 1993, Mills and Dunlevy 1997, The International Council for Coach Education, n.d.). Coach education has grown to the point where there is now an International Council for Coach Education (www.icce.ws). When coaches are asked to comment on the role of this type of formal education on their professional development, they do not value it nearly as much as the learning that occurs through actual coaching (Fleurance and Cotteaux 1999, Jones *et al.* 2004, Wright *et al.* in press). The importance attributed to learning to coach through experience compared to large-scale coach education programmes is not a surprise. If required at all, the number of hours mandated for coaching certification is minimal compared to the formal educational requirements of similar professions such as teaching or allied health positions. Recent studies show that successful high school and college coaches in the US spend an average of 25 hours per year in coach education clinics (Gilbert *et al.* 2006). This is minimal when compared to the thousands of hours required to obtain a college degree and professional certificates mandated for teaching. Furthermore, at the elite level coaches are often hired based on their playing and/or coaching experience instead of their educational certification (Lyle 2002). Finally, an analysis of coaching science shows a lack of systematically collected data on many related topics (Gilbert and Trudel 2004a), leaving coaches to generate solutions to many of their coaching problems without the benefit of any related scientific coaching literature.

What is troublesome with learning to coach through experience is that we do not know what it really means. Is learning through experience as simple as only spending time in the field? For Bell (1997: 35) this 'is not the case. To become better skilled at one's professional practice, a novice teacher or coach needs to do more than simply spend time on the job'. It has been repeatedly suggested that the key to experiential learning is reflection (Cassidy *et al.* 2004, Cushion *et al.* 2003, Gilbert and Trudel 2001). That is, ten years of coaching without reflection is simply one year of coaching repeated ten times. Integrating reflection into coaching practice is the key to what Cassidy *et al.* (2004) termed a holistic approach to the activity. It is suggested that holistic coaching allows for risk-taking and promotes intrinsic motivation in coaches.

Moon (1999, 2004) provides a comprehensive overview of the different ways to conceptualize reflection. For example, she differentiates reflective learning that 'simply emphasizes the intention to learn as a result of reflection' (2004: 80) from Schön's concept of reflective practice that 'emphasizes the use of reflection in professional or other complex activities as a means of coping with the situations that are ill-structured and/or unpredictable' (p. 80). As coaching has often been conceptualized as a decision-making or problem-solving process in a complex environment (Lyle 2002), Schön's conceptual framework is particularly relevant to analyse the informal way through which coaches learn to coach.

This chapter is divided into three sections. We start by outlining the terminology used by Schön. A model of coach reflection based on an empirical study is then presented. Finally, we discuss potential strategies through which coaches could be introduced to reflective practice, thus preparing them to become better reflective practitioners.

The reflective practitioner

Schön's literature on reflection has made a significant contribution to the discourse on learning and education, across a wide array of professions. In addition to Schön's own texts (1983, 1987, 1991), many overviews of his work are available for those interested in learning more about his approach (e.g. Cassidy *et al.* 2004, Farrell 2004, Moon 1999). We use this opportunity simply to provide a primer to those who may not be intimately familiar with Schön's contributions and how they can provide a framework for the role of reflection in coach development.

To understand Schön's work, it is important to become familiar with a few key terms. For Schön, the importance attributed to basic and applied science in formal education is referred to as *technical rationality*. In this view, practice 'is instrumental, consisting [of] adjusting technical means to ends that are clear, fixed and internally consistent, [with] instrumental practice becoming professional when it is based on the science or systematic knowledge produced by the schools of higher learning' (Schön 1995: 29). From the perspective of technical rationality, the professionals' behaviours should be based on science and not on intuition. Schön suggests the term *knowing-in-action* to define what 'makes up the great bulk of what we know how to do in everyday and in professional life' (1995: 30). This type of knowledge is tacit, meaning that it is often difficult to explain. Our knowing-in-action allows us to execute our daily activities without having to make a special effort to think about them. However, an unexpected result or an unfamiliar situation might create an element of surprise and these 'situations of practice are not problems to be solved but *problematic situations* characterized by uncertainty, disorder, and indeterminacy' (Schön 1983: 16). In order to convert a problematic situation into a problem, a process of *problem setting* must be completed. When we set a problem 'we set the boundaries of our attention to it, and we impose upon it a coherence which allows us to say what is wrong and in what directions the situation needs to be changed' (1983: 40).

Practitioners will experience very few problematic situations if they prefer to follow a well-established routine that prevents them from falling outside the boundaries of their comfort zone. Others might like to push the boundaries and see how they can do things differently. For Schön: 'There are those who choose the swampy lowlands. They deliberately involve themselves in messy but crucially important problems' (1983: 43). In those circumstances, competent practitioners will not limit their effort to a trial and error approach but will enter into a reflective process. When the reflection is done after the fact, it is called *reflection-on-action*: 'thinking back on what we have done in order to discover how our knowing-in-action may have contributed to an unexpected outcome' (1983: 26). Schön suggests that a person can also engage in *reflection-in-action* in a sense 'that his thinking occurs in an action-present – a stretch of time within which it is still possible to make a difference to the outcomes of action' (Schön 1995: 30). A repeated spiral of appreciation (problem setting), action (strategy generation, experimentation, evaluation) and reappreciation (problem setting) is referred to as a *reflective conversation*.

The knowing-in-action, the reflection-in-action, the reflection-on-action and the reflective conversation, are what make a practitioner different to another practitioner. However, no person is an island and as Schön (1987) states, 'A professional's knowing-in-action is embedded in the socially and institutionally structured context shared by a community of practitioners. *Knowing-in-practice* is exercised in the institutional setting particular to the profession' (1987: 33).

If we regroup all the terms we have just defined and apply them to coaching we can construct the following story. Paul, an elite soccer coach, has recently completed a 50-hour coach education programme. The content delivered was based on applied science (sport psychology, sport physiology, sport pedagogy, etc.) and his 89 per cent obtained on the final test confirms that Paul is worthy of certification and should be able to use this scientific knowledge in his coaching (technical rationality). If Paul is questioned about the usefulness of this formal training his answer might look like this:

> The way I coach hasn't changed that much because of the training. I have my bag of tricks and I know from experience what works and what does not. It is difficult to explain like this, but put me in a situation and I will show you (knowing-in-action). What I do is not that much different from what other coaches do in the sense that there is a common body of knowledge that all coaches know (knowing-in-practice). I do recognize though that some of the course documents like the season planning matrix and the tournament checklist will be very useful. However, when I face a new dilemma (problematic situation) the theoretical content presented during the training often seems irrelevant. The dilemmas are often so complex that before applying the techniques they taught us I need to define what the problem is (problem setting). Once I have set the problem then I can start to work on it (reflective conversation). If the problem does not need to be solved on the spot I will reflect on what happens after the fact (reflection-on-action) but sometimes I have to find a solution very quickly (reflection-in-action).

Schön's work has been influential in the literature on reflection (Farrell 2004, Moon 1999) but his conceptual framework has sometimes been criticized (Moon 1999). For example, Ixer (1999: 513) questions its applicability in a profession such as social work: 'Not only do Schön's own ideas tend to lack practical application to social work and to have been superseded by later theorists, but the entire oeuvre to date leaves more questions than answers.' In the teaching profession authors such as Johansson and Kroksmark (2004) conclude that reflection-in-action 'needs and requires either a 'freezing' of the ongoing situation or the possibility to make it the subject of reflection afterwards. Our study clearly shows that teachers have no other possibility than the latter, and therefore teachers' reflection-in-action seems impossible' (Johansson and Kroksmark 2004: 377). One reason for the reflection-in-action controversy is Schön's definition of the *action-present*:

> There are indeed times when it is dangerous to stop and think. On the firing line, in the midst of traffic, even on the playing field, there is a need for immediate, on-line response and the failure to deliver it can have serious consequences. But not all practice situations are of this sort. The action-present (the period of time in which we remain in the 'same situation') varies greatly from case to case, and in many cases there is time to think what we are doing. Consider, for example, a physician's management of a patient's disease, a lawyer's preparation of a brief, a teacher's handling of a difficult student. In processes such as

these, which may extend over weeks, months or years, fast-moving episodes are punctuated by intervals which provide opportunity for reflection.

(Schön 1983: 278)

As one can see from this quotation, the difference between reflection-in-action and reflection-on-action is not obvious, but a strategy might be to define, for a particular practice (example coaching), what is the most appropriate time period to consider for reflection-in and on-action. In the next section, we present the results of an extensive study that examined how model youth sport coaches learn to coach through experience and how we have defined three types of reflection.

Reflective coaches

While investigating youth sport coaches' behaviours, beliefs and decision making (Gilbert *et al.* 1999, Trudel *et al.* 1996, Trudel and Gilbert 1995, Wilcox and Trudel 1998), we started to wonder how coaches learned to coach the way they did. Considering that their formal training was limited and suspect on at least some accounts we searched for a conceptual framework that would help understand their learning from experience. After reviewing the work of Schön (1983, 1987) we concluded that his conceptual framework could 'be used as a [guide] to examine how coaches transform coaching experience into coaching knowledge. His emphasis on the development of domain-specific knowledge in the context of professional practice differentiates his work from other experiential learning theories' (Gilbert and Trudel 1999a: para. 18). We then completed an exhaustive study to determine how model youth sport coaches learn to coach through experience. The research questions were:

1 What are the types of coaching issues (dilemmas) experienced by youth sport coaches?
2 What are the components in the process of learning through experience?
3 To what extent do youth sport coaches engage in reflection?
4 Do youth sport coaches proceed through reflection alone or do they consult other sources?
5 What are the components of a model youth sport coach's role frame?

Only a brief overview of the methodology is presented as it has been discussed elsewhere in detail (Gilbert and Trudel 2001, 2004b). Three ice hockey coaches and three soccer coaches were selected as model youth sport coaches. For each coach, data were collected over an entire sport season using semi-structured interviews, observations and documents. The reflective

model presented in Figure 9.1 is based on the analysis of 6 background interviews, 93 pages of documents, 59 videotaped games and practices, 118 on-site
interviews, 18 interval summary interviews, 6 member check interviews, and
discussion on 90 coaching issues.

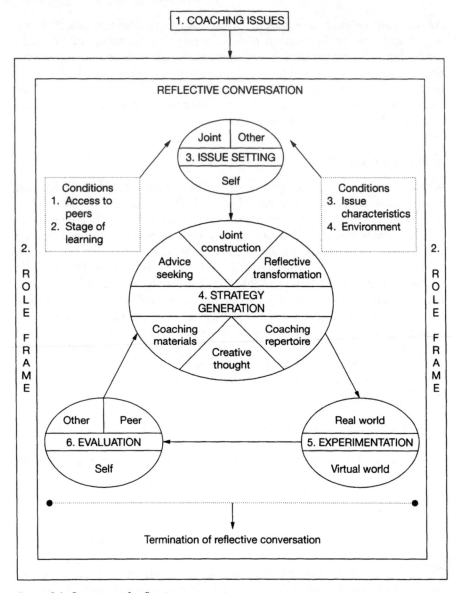

Figure 9.1 Overview of reflection

From W. D. Gilbert and P. Trudel, 'Learning to coach through experience: Reflection in model
youth sport coaches', *Journal of Teaching in Physical Education*, 21(1): 23, Figure 1. © 2001 by Human
Kinetics. Reprinted with permission from Human Kinetics (Champaign, IL)

The model starts with *coaching issues* which are the surprises, the problematic coaching situations. The issues reported by the coaches were regrouped into five types: (1) athlete behaviour (attendance, discipline, focus and team morale), (2) athlete performance (consistency, individual techniques and team tactics), (3) coach and athlete personal characteristics that influence communication and parent–coach interactions, (4) parental influence and (5) team organization (coaching staff, fundraising, line-up and practice planning) (Gilbert *et al.* 2001a, 2001b). For the coaching issues to be considered worthy of reflection, they had to be filtered by the coach's *role frame* (i.e. the coach's personal approach to coaching). On average, the coaches' role frames comprised two boundary components (age group and competitive level) that were considered objective conditions of the environment that influence an individual's coaching approach (Gilbert and Trudel 2005). There were also nine common internal components (discipline, emphasis on team, equity, fun, personal growth and development, positive team environment, safety, sport-specific development, and winning) which were personal views regarding youth sport coaching framed by boundary components. Two internal components (personal growth and development, and winning) often caused an internal conflict for the coaches resulting in a psychological struggle to find a balance between them. It was also interesting to note that none of the coaches were fully aware of their role frame. When, at the end of the study, we presented individually the results to the coaches, some were surprised and thought about reviewing the way they conducted themselves as youth sport coaches.

When a problematic situation is considered important enough, the coach initiates a *reflective conversation* composed of four components. The first component, *issue setting*, can be done by the coach alone or through informal discussion with someone else. Once the issue is set, the coach then proceeds to *generate a strategy* through one or more options. Coaching repertoire, creative thought and coaching materials are independent of coaching peers, while advice seeking, joint construction (often with the assistant coach) and reflective transformation (i.e. observing and adapting what other coaches are doing) are dependent on coaching peers. Coaches will often use more than one option to generate a strategy. Before *experimenting* with the strategy in the real world, coaches will often conduct a virtual experimentation by testing it on a person referred to as a peer sounding board. Finally, the strategy is *evaluated* for its effectiveness. The sub-loop (strategy generation, experimentation and evaluation) can be processed many times.

A reflective conversation is influenced by four *conditions*: (1) access to respected and trusted peers, (2) a coach's stage of learning (coaches with more experience are less likely to consult coaching material, instead relying on creative thought and joint construction), (3) issue characteristics (for challenging dilemmas it is more likely that coaches will consult during strategy generation, experimentation and evaluation) and (e) environment, for example, the support provided by the community (Gilbert and Trudel 2005).

Due to the research design used in the study, the model of coach reflection refers largely to the coaches' reflection-on-action, although examples of coaches' reflection-in-action were also evident. We concluded that in coaching, reflection-in-action and reflection-on-action must be clearly differentiated by making a distinction between the 'midst of activity' and the 'action-present'. Reflection-in-action is interpreted to apply only to the reflection that occurs in the midst of activity (during a game or a practice). But 'reflection that still occurs within the action-present, but not in the midst of activity, is defined as reflection-on-action (e.g. the coach who reflects about an issue in-between games or practices)' (Gilbert and Trudel 2001: 30). A third type of reflection, retrospective reflection-on-action, was 'defined as reflection that occurs outside of the action-present (e.g. after the season or after a coach's reflection can no longer affect the situation)' (p. 30). Retrospective reflection-on-action is consistent with what Van Manen (1991) labels recollective reflection.

In brief, we found that model youth sport coaches were, to some extent, reflective practitioners. Other recent coaching literature has begun to unpack the reflective process in coaching (Cassidy et al. 2004, Jones et al. 2004). Given the importance of reflection in coaching, and the importance of reflection to experiential learning, how can we facilitate the development of reflective practice in coaches?

Reflective practicum in coaching

In the education literature there are numerous books and articles on how to nurture reflection in teachers. Books such as *Reflective practice in action: 80 reflection breaks for busy teachers* (Farrell 2004) and *A handbook of reflective and experiential learning: Theory and practice* (Moon 2004) are two such examples. Hinett (n. d.-a, n. d.-b) is also a good source of information about websites that present ways of supporting reflection and experiential learning. Much of the material available to enhance learning through reflection helps participants reflect on their practice and not necessarily on an ongoing problem. In such cases, 'reflection is the means by which awareness of experience is recognized as knowledge and is made explicit and generalizable to other situations' (Moon 2004: 158). Individuals can be required to reflect on an artificial experience (the experience to reflect on is suggested) or on a recalled experience, but in both cases it is a simulated experience and not an actual experience, i.e. 'an experience that occurs at the present time' (Jarvis et al. 1998: 56). In our study with model youth sport coaches we became particularly sensitive to this important distinction:

In terms of how the different types of reflection influence experiential learning, the first two types [reflection-in-action and reflection-on-action] can be considered modes of learning *through* experience, while the third type [retrospective reflection-on-action] can be considered a method of learning *from* experience.

(Gilbert and Trudel 2001: 31)

Training coaches to become reflective practitioners within the episte-mology of practice as defined by Schön (1987) will have to be different from traditional professional development models:

In the normative curriculum, a practicum comes last, almost as an after-thought. Its espoused function is to provide an opportunity for practice in applying the theories and techniques taught in the courses that make up the core of the curriculum. But a reflective practicum would bring learning by doing into the core.

(310–311)

This quote from Schön suggests that the training should be done in the field outside of a controlled environment. However, how can coaches start using reflection in their practice if they are not aware of its existence? Based on the literature on reflection in education and sport, as well as the needs, expectations and preferences of coaches regarding their education, we discuss six different ways to introduce coaches to reflective practice and prepare them to become reflective practitioners.

Description of reflective practice

If we expect coaches to become reflective practitioners, we must first share with them our definitions of reflection and reflective practice. The model presented in Figure 9.1 can be described to coaches to show them a visual representation of this abstract concept of reflection. Examples of the three types of reflection (in-action, on-action and retrospective reflection-on-action) could complement this introduction. Other examples of how reflection is conceptualized in teaching could be included, such as Van Manen's (1991) types of reflection (anticipatory, interactive, recollective) or Zeichner and Liston's (1996) dimensions of reflection (rapid reaction, repair, review, research, retheorize and research). Stories of coaches addressing common coaching dilemmas through a reflective conversation could also be included as a reading in a coach education course.

If the presentation is well received, we can presume that coaches will have learned *about* reflective practice. However, this is still far from being able to conclude that the coaches will become reflective practitioners. Learning about is very common and 'most of anyone's knowledge might best be described as knowledge *about*. Many people learn *about* a lot of things', while 'learning to be requires more than just information. It requires the ability to engage in the practice in question' (Brown and Duguid 2000: 128). Therefore, describing a reflective practitioner might be a first step but it certainly is not enough to expect coaches to become reflective as a consequence of it.

Reflection on typical coaching problems

Coaches can be asked by a course instructor to discuss typical coaching issues. Several ways to use this strategy in a coach education course have been described in the coaching literature. According to Cassidy and colleagues (2004) both a critical task-based approach and problem-based learning can be used to teach coaches how to reflect. In a critical task-based approach coaches view coaching scenarios that serve as 'primers' for critical group discussion on coaching topics (i.e. coach power, communication, leadership). In a sense, this is a form of reflection-on-action, but it is still limited in that it is someone else's action. Consequently, as the relevancy of the scenario may be partial, coaches' reflection on it may be superficial. Furthermore, particularly for novice coaches, the scenario may be completely foreign because they have no personal experience upon which to draw for reflection. With problem-based learning, the coach education curriculum is designed around common coaching issues. Coaches are given a set of 'real-life' problems and asked to collectively generate solutions. To increase the ecological validity of this approach, Cassidy and colleagues suggest adding interruptions to the exercises, which would more closely simulate the unpredictable and multiple-problem reality of coaching.

These exercises will be, in a sense, a reflection on the knowing-in-practice and if coaches have to explain their personal position regarding these issues they will also start to define their role frame. Knowledge-in-practice is tacit knowledge and coaches are generally not aware of their role frame. Therefore, it may take a few attempts before coaches can go deep enough in their reflection to consider making changes to the way they coach. Moon (1999) presents factors that should be considered when using writing or discussion to generate reflection. People resisting to participate because they are afraid of 'being "knocked back or laughed at"' (p. 169) and the power relationships between the members of the group that inhibits reflection are two examples.

A limitation of asking coaches to reflect on typical coaching problems is that problems are given to the coaches. This violates the primary role of problem setting in the reflective process (Schön 1983): 'In real-word practice, problems do not present themselves to practitioners as givens. They must be constructed from the materials of problematic situations which are puzzling, troubling, and uncertain' (p. 40).

Reflecting on critical incidents

One way to address the limitations of reflecting on pre-set issues is to guide coaches through the process of reflecting on their own personal incidents or coaching stories. Using the example of teaching, Farrell (2004) differentiates personal critical incidents and critical teaching incidents. A personal critical incident is an event that happened at some point in an individual's tenure as a coach. The incident could be any type of issue related to coaching (dealing with parents, fundraising, recruiting, etc.). A critical coaching incident is an event that occurred in the act of coaching (i.e. on the field or in the gym). For a novice coach these incidents could extend back into their time as an athlete observing coaches. Another way to reflect on critical incidents is to write a narrative (Cassidy et al. 2004). In this approach coaches are asked to write stories related to specific coaching issues, drawing on their own coaching experience. Coaches then deconstruct, discuss and review readings related to the issue. Last, coaches are asked to rewrite the narrative to incorporate the reflection-on-action completed in the narrative exercise.

Field-based reflection interventions

Although some coaches may use reflection effectively, many others may find it difficult to adequately set a problem or to reflect-in-action without any training. That training might start with showing coaches how 'to create opportunities for reflection-in-action' (Schön 1983: 279). Based on some of our previous work, we can provide two examples of intervention strategies used to train coaches to make time for reflection-in and on-action.

In the first example (Trudel 1987), a multiple baseline design across subjects (four youth ice hockey coaches) was used to evaluate the influence of a training programme on Academic Learning Time in Physical Education (ALT-PE) variables (e.g. motor engaged, waiting, listening). The training programme was individually presented and consisted of three parts. The first consisted of a two-hour meeting (1) to introduce the coach to the concepts related to Academic Learning Time, (2) to present him (all the coaches were male) with material such as a lesson plan model that facilitates note taking during practice, (3) to show him a video of another coach conducting a session and, for each drill, completing a reflection-in-action inventory (e.g. how many players are engaged and what is the quality of this engagement). In the second part, the coach was video-taped during a training session. The third part (about two hours) consisted of a meeting with the coach to watch the video and discuss (1) how closely he respected the basic concept of ALT-PE, (2) the appropriate use of the material to collect information on the quantity and the quality of the players' motor engagement and the coach's on the spot reactions (reflection-in-action) and (3) how he would use this information to prepare the next training session (reflection-on-action). Coaches were observed and positive changes were noticed on many of the ALT-PE variables for three of the coaches.

A second study (Trudel *et al.* 2000) was conducted with 28 youth ice hockey coaches to verify the effects of an intervention strategy on aspects related to violence. Coaches met individually for about two hours and, with the aid of a specially made video, the researcher (1) made coaches aware of the problem of injuries, penalties and illegal body checking, (2) demonstrated the importance of teaching appropriate body-checking skills and (3) provided teaching materials to facilitate reflection-in and on-action. The process of reflection was based on the following scenario. Before each game, the coach would remind the players about some criteria regarding body checking. Then the coach observed and took note of the players' use of body contact. Feedback was then given to the players when they returned to the bench or between periods (reflection-in-action). At the end of the game, the coach, alone or with assistants, would reflect on how the players used body checking and who received penalties (reflection-on-action). Although the coaches expressed a high level of satisfaction with the content of this intervention strategy and stated that they would use it in the future, no significant differences were noticed in any of the dependent variables (frequency of legal body checks per game, the type and frequency of penalties, and the number of injuries).

The results of these two studies show that some coaches will respond positively to an intervention strategy that focuses on training coaches to reflect on a specific coaching issue during games or practice sessions. However, we do not know if by practising these suggested strategies coaches will transfer them to other coaching issues on their own.

Working with a mentor

For Schön, the role played by mentors (he called them coaches) is central to helping students learn to be reflective practitioners:

> In a reflective practicum, the role and status of a coach [mentor] takes precedence over those of a teacher as teaching is usually understood. The coach's [mentor's] legitimacy does not depend on his scholarly attainments or proficiency as a lecturer but on the artistry of his coaching [mentoring] practice.
>
> (Schön 1987: 311)

The mentor that Schön is referring to is different from a person in charge of coach assessment. It should be a person with experience in coaching; although by itself this will not be enough:

A facilitator is both a part of the learning environment and will influence other aspects of the learning environment. They will understand the nature of reflection, how it relates to the qualities of learning (deep and surface learning) and will be clear about what they are attempting to achieve in the learners . . . They should particularly be aware of the role of reflection as a means of upgrading learning and enable more mature learners to become aware of how they can use reflective techniques to upgrade their previous less organized but valid levels of knowledge and understanding.

(Schön 1987: 167)

Many authors have already indicated the important role that mentors play or could play in coach education (Bloom *et al.* 1998, Campbell and Crisfield 1994, Cassidy *et al.* 2004, Cushion *et al.* 2003, Lyle 2002, Saury and Durand 1998). Unfortunately, mentorship in coaching lacks clarity and hence has had only limited success (Cassidy *et al.* 2004). It has traditionally served as a way to pass along knowledge and values and as such has not provided coaches with a critical perspective on their practice. The primary objective of a coach mentorship programme should be to foster exploration and inquiry in context.

It seems that in most cases, mentors are not assigned to coaches: 'finding a mentor was often the case of being at the right place at the right time. With a bit of luck and personal persistence, novice coaches were able to find a mentor with whom they shared their passion for their sport and for coaching' (Bloom *et al.* 1998: 274). In this context, if mentors are not reflective coaches they will only transmit to the apprentice-coach the knowledge-in-practice and their own routine. A further difficulty relates to where mentors are reflective coaches, will they be willing and able to take the time to share the reflective process? Therefore, the following question to ask is: are informal mentors willing to be trained to permit apprentice-coaches to have access to their reflective process? Another option is to have mentors attend the coach's practice instead of the apprentice-coach entering the coach-mentor practice. The mentor will then be more prepared to play the mentoring role, but to what extent will a formalized and structured mentoring programme that is imposed on coaches be effective? Can sport organizations afford such initiatives in terms of the number of qualified mentors that will be required? One of the key factors to a successful reflective mentoring experience is the time allocated to this experience:

The work of a reflective practicum takes a long time. Indeed, nothing is so indicative of progress in the acquisition of artistry as the student's discovery of the time it takes – time to live through the initial shocks of confusion and mystery, unlearn initial expectations, and begin to master the practice of the practicum.

(Schön 1987: 311)

Facilitating access to peers

The idea of collective coach reflection conducted in a supportive community of practitioners has been suggested by several authors (Cassidy *et al.* 2004; Trudel and Gilbert 2004). Trudel and Gilbert (2004) provide an example of what a community of practice approach to coach development might look like in action using an ice hockey league example. The community of practice ideally would include not only coaches, but all stakeholders in the sport context (officials, administrators, etc.).

Through our study with model youth sport coaches we discovered that coaches will often consult peers across the different phases of a reflective conversation (Gilbert and Trudel 2005). The most important peers are probably the coach's assistants. At the elite level the accessibility of competent assistant coaches is less problematic than at the recreation or developmental level. Unfortunately, community sport associations will often encourage head coaches to develop their knowledge but do not invest as much in the assistant coaches. To have a competent coaching staff is a first step, but the learning will be much richer if the coaching staff has access to other peers. Unfortunately, coaches tend to limit knowledge sharing with other coaches: 'in a sporting context it may be difficult for coaches who wish to be reflective practitioners to be part of a like-minded group, given the varied aspects of sport culture that act as constraints in this regard' (Cassidy *et al.* 2004: 23). The isolation of many coaches, particularly at the recreation and developmental levels of sport, is detrimental to coach and athlete development. This situation may be the result of decades of an outcome (win) orientation evident with many coaches: 'When winning at all costs drives coaches, isolationism takes root and coaches see other coaches as enemies – not partners. This individualistic approach refrains coaches from engaging with other coaches in their league while searching for solutions to common problems' (Trudel and Gilbert 2004: 169–170).

Conclusion

The purpose of this chapter was threefold: (1) to review Schön's (1983) reflective practitioner conceptual framework, (2) to discuss Gilbert and Trudel's (2001) coach reflection model and (3) to present six strategies for nurturing reflective coaches. The language and value of reflective practice has infiltrated the field of coaching. It is increasingly common to find coaching science articles that address reflective practice in coaching and coach development. The impact of this literature on coach education is much less evident. Although there is a global initiative to professionalize and standardize coach education, it is not clear what role a reflective practitioner framework will play in this movement. The practical application of reflection strategies in large-scale certification-driven coach training programmes will certainly be a challenge. Efficiency of course delivery (i.e.

cost effectiveness) is a driving force behind such programmes that increasingly are offering self-study and online courses. The immediate challenge for coaching scientists and coach educators will be to work together to find creative ways to meet the needs of developing coaches. Ultimately the objective of these partnerships should be to create what Cassidy and colleagues (2004) have termed reality-based coach education programmes. Clearly much research is needed to determine what types of coach education programmes are most effective at creating long-term behavioural changes in coaches. In other words, which programmes best demonstrate the ability to create and nurture reflective practitioners? This best practices approach to research will surely drive much of the coaching science in years to come.

Chapter 10

Mentoring

Harnessing the power of experience

Chris Cushion

Introduction

Traditionally, the coaching environment has been viewed as a place where athletes learn. However, more recently, it has also begun to be thought of as a place in which coaches' professional learning and development takes place (e.g. Cushion *et al.* 2003, Gould *et al.* 1990, Gilbert and Trudel 2001). Despite the individual nature of each coaching position, coaches form a sub-society of interlocking groups, 'a community rooted in sport and what it symbolises, and [a means of identifying] themselves collectively as a meaningful social segment' (Sage 1989: 88). This makes a social network or structure that enables the expression of similar attitudes and value orientations, and through which cultural traditions flow (Coakley 1986, Sage 1989). Through this network coaches develop a personal set of views on coaching, issues in sport and how things should be done (Lyle 1999). These views evolve over time, flow through practice and are a result of education (formal and informal) and experience. In exploring this further, Cervero (1992: 91) contends that the 'popular wisdom among coaches is that the knowledge they acquire from practice is far more useful than what they acquire from more formal forms of education'. In developing as practitioners, therefore, coaches are 'initiated into the traditions, habits, rules, cultures and practices of the community they join' (Merriam 1983: 37), and key to this initiation is the process of mentoring (Cushion *et al.* 2003).

According to Merriam (1983) mentoring is derived from Greek mythology, where a father trusted his son to learn from a wise old man, 'Mentor'. However, because of the diverse use and the variety of contexts in which mentoring occurs, there remains some confusion as to what a mentor is and the role that he or she should play. For example, according to Alleman *et al.* (1984: 327) mentoring is a 'relationship in which a person of greater rank, experience or expertise teaches, guides and develops a novice in a profession'. Similarly, Merriam (1983) defined a mentor as a supporter, counsel and guide to a protégé, while for Fletcher (2000) mentoring is synonymous with guiding and supporting a trainee through difficult transitions.

Developing such a definition further, Carmin (1988: 10–11) characterises mentoring as:

> a complex, interactive process, occurring between individuals of different levels of experience and expertise which incorporates interpersonal or psychosocial development, career and/or educational development, and socialisation functions . . . Further, the mentoring process occurs in a dynamic relationship within a given milieu.

Although these are selective descriptions it is important to emphasise the common 'guidance' function of a process that dovetails with the belief that real development, in terms of professional expertise, cannot come from cloning but through reflection on interaction, researched knowledge and practice (Cassidy et al. 2004, Fletcher 2000). Mentoring, then, involves doing something *with* as opposed *to* a trainee; it is seen as an investment in the total personal growth of the individual and, by its nature, is heavily contextualised (Cassidy et al. 2004).

In coaching, while many in the field agree on its value, mentoring seems to lack a clear conceptual definition (Bloom et al. 1998). Furthermore, the existing literature regarding mentoring, by and large, considers it in a very functional, positive and unproblematic way, with 'how to' guides extolling its benefits, of which there would seem to be many. The purpose of this chapter, as with all the concepts discussed in this book, is to engage with the process of mentoring in a more critical way. In doing so, a number of key issues will be considered. The chapter is divided into two halves. The first comprises two key sections; first, looking at the nature of experiential learning and mentoring as it currently exists in coaching, and why more formal mentoring could have particular relevance for it. Second, in trying to understand why mentoring works (or indeed, doesn't work) theoretical approaches to experiential learning are drawn upon to give greater conceptual depth to a largely descriptive concept. In this case, borrowing broadly from the field of education, the chapter will examine the concepts of reflection (Schön 1983), communities of practice (Lave and Wenger 1991) and zones of proximal development (ZPD) (Vygotsky 1978) as frameworks for understanding mentoring and for considering possible reasons for its success or otherwise. In doing so, the implications for mentoring relationships, the role of the mentor, and the mentoring process are discussed.

The second half of the chapter considers mentoring in action; specifically examining roles, relationships and processes. This includes the nature of the mentor–protégé relationship and how it feeds into the broader role of the mentor. Currently considered unproblematic, a more critical examination is undertaken that considers the nature of power and control in the mentoring relationship and the 'hidden curriculum' of mentors, thus questioning to what extent social and cultural norms are being reproduced and uncritically passed onto protégés. This section also proposes a shift in our thinking in relation to our current conceptualisation of mentoring. This shift involves relocating the locus of learning from the individual mind of the coach or mentor, to a broader process that unfolds within a participatory framework which, itself, resides in practice. Within this framework, the role of the mentor is considered, along with recommendations for mentoring in practice.

Learning from experience: the case for mentoring

Coaches' knowledge and action are both the product and manifestation of a personally experienced involvement with the coaching process. They are linked to the coach's own history and are attributable to how they were learned, suggesting that learning and development are inherently social, and that the construction of knowledge and meaning is situated within a socially constructed context (Doherty et al. 2002). The implications of such a stance, both in this particular case and in coach education generally, lie in understanding how knowledge and experience are passed on and become translated into coaching. Despite the implementation of coach education programmes worldwide (Campbell 1993, Gilbert and Trudel 2001) it would seem that a large part of coaching knowledge and practice is based on experiences, and personal interpretations of those experiences (Cushion et al. 2003, Gould et al. 1990, Gilbert and Trudel 2001). However, this is not to say that all experienced coaches are competent (Bell 1997, Gilbert and Trudel 2001), although to become a competent coach, it would appear that significant experience is required (Cushion et al. 2003, Lyle 2002).

Coaches learn to be coaches while competing as athletes and as 'junior' coaches or assistants working with and observing experienced coaches. As players themselves, coaches had an unusually good opportunity to learn about coaching from their own coaches. Coakley (1978: 241) notes that these experiences 'are the channels through which the traditional accepted methods of coaching become integrated into the behaviour of aspiring young coaches'. Coaches and sports leaders then serve as experts who facilitate learning by modelling problem-solving strategies and guiding learners in approximating those strategies, while also articulating their thought processes (Kerka 1998). Observing the behaviour of more experienced coaches during practice and games, and listening during informal periods, is highly influential and resonates with the career development of coaches. It is largely through these types of experiences that collective understandings begin to develop, and the shared meanings about the occupational culture of coaching start to take shape (Cushion et al. 2003). Therefore, much of what a new coach learns is through ongoing interactions in the practical coaching context, as well as a variety of informal sources. This enculturation provides continuity with lessons learned earlier as a player, no matter what the level. Crucially, in this process of learning from experience, mentoring in coaching is already 'just happening' (Kerka 1998).

Indeed, a key finding from coaching research (e.g. Cushion 2001, Gould *et al.* 1990) is its confirmation that mentoring is already very much in operation. The fact that experience and other coaches are still highlighted as the most important facet in the development of coaches bears testimony to this. Mentoring in its current form is however, unstructured, informal and uneven in terms of quality and outcome, uncritical in style and, from the evidence, serves to reproduce the existing culture and power relations found in existing coaching practice (Cushion 2001). Not surprisingly then, as Rossi and Cassidy (1999) remind us, formal coach education is a relatively low impact endeavour in terms of generating coaching knowledge compared to that gleaned from the hours spent as a player, assistant coach and coach. Indeed, coach education seems unable to compete in this respect with the coaches' integrated sporting and coaching experiences (Cushion *et al.* 2003). It would seem logical, therefore, for coach education to harness the obvious power and influence of experience and other coaches to work toward sound coach development objectives. This line of argument certainly presents a strong case for formalised mentoring programmes which is further developed later in the chapter when discussing the operation of mentoring in practice.

It would seem that the relevance of formal mentoring programmes is readily apparent, and evidence from other practice fields (e.g. health care, education) lends weight to this position. However, mentoring, whether formal or informal, must contribute to the transformation of experience into knowledge and expertise. As has been highlighted by other authors in this book, then:

> it would be a relief to believe that one need only spend a certain amount of time teaching or coaching, and the lessons learned in the experience would elevate one to the next level of expertise. Unfortunately, that is not the case. To become better skilled at one's professional practice, a novice teacher or coach needs to do more than simply spend time on the job
>
> (Bell 1997: 35)

Indeed, not all education results from experience, nor is all experience educational (Dewey 1933), as meaningful learning and development will not occur simply by being involved. Consequently, mentoring must be part of a framework through which coaches construct knowledge. Additionally, there must be conditions that make the process more or less successful. Understanding these conditions has obvious benefits to any formal mentoring programme, and it is to these that the chapter now turns.

Theories of learning, social practice and mentoring

All theories of learning are based on assumptions concerning the individual, the world and the relationship between the two. In theories of social practice (e.g. Bourdieu 1977, Giddens 1979) the emphasis is on the relational interdependency of not just the individual and social world, but also of activity, meaning, cognition, learning and knowing (Lave and Wenger 1996). It is a way of looking at learning, thinking and knowing, as relations among people arising in, with and from the socially and culturally structured world. Consequently, understanding and experience are in constant interaction and, through action, other persons and the world are inherently connected in knowing and learning (Lave and Wenger 1996).

A traditional view of the person as a primarily cognitive individual tends to promote an impersonal view of knowledge, skills, tasks and learning, with the resulting theoretical analysis and subsequent instruction driven by knowledge domains (Lave and Wenger 1996). However, by situating learning within social and cultural contexts the individual is less involved with objective de-contextualised knowledge acquisition, but is constructing knowledge through direct experience of social practice (Gilbert and Trudel 2001). This can be seen as an active process, with coaches seeking out information related to the task and the given context, and testing this within the context formed by the task and the environment.

This constructivist approach also stresses the developmental nature of learning, in that there are phases of learning skills, and the way these are learned will change over time with experience. A further feature of a social practice approach is that learning is multidimensional, in that more than one thing at a time can be learned, and that this can be both implicit and explicit. Perhaps more interestingly, when thinking about mentoring, it can be argued that learning occurs best when novices collaborate with more experienced and more knowledgeable others on a shared task (Vygotsky 1978).

Several theories of how individuals construct knowledge exist, with the common thread running through them suggesting that learning is most effective when new knowledge and skills are used and individuals construct meanings for themselves within the context of interaction with others (Kerka 1998). This approach provides a useful starting point to a theoretical consideration of mentoring and why learning may or may not occur in a mentoring relationship.

Mentoring as communities of practice and legitimate peripheral participation

Lave and Wenger (1991) were unhappy with what they perceived as overly simplistic views of learning *by doing* (Fuller *et al.* 2005), arguing instead for learning to be conceived as a complex relational, situated endeavour. This required a conceptual shift from the traditional view of 'the individual as learner to learning as participation in the social world, and from the concept of cognitive process to the more-encompassing view of social practice' (Lave and Wenger 1991: 43). They also argued that social practice is the primary generative phenomenon, with learning being one of it characteristics; hence, it should be analysed as an integral part of social practice (1991).

Lave and Wenger (1991) originated the community of practice framework as an approach to conceptualise learning and as a way to consider methods of knowledge production and dissemination in practice fields. The notion of a community of practice is particularly helpful in this case as it challenges the perception of experts as knowledge generators with novices being 'knowledge translators' (Palinscar et al. 1998). Teaching and learning can, therefore, be usefully viewed in a mentoring relationship as bi-directional, with both mentor and protégé contributing to the community's knowledge base. As a result, the community of practice framework recognises that knowledge is generated and shared within a social and cultural context. Mentors are therefore viewed as not working on the world of practice but with it (Waddock 1999), and engaged in considerably more than merely passing on survival tips or the tricks of the trade or even in simply caring about protégés' well-being.

Participation in social (communities of) practice, by definition, will involve learning. The process of becoming a member of a community allows learning to take place, thus the processes, relationships and experiences that constitute a participant's sense of belonging underpin the subsequent learning (Fuller et al. 2005). Lave and Wenger (1991: 29) characterise this notion of legitimate peripheral participation as such:

> Legitimate peripheral participation provides a way to speak about the relations between newcomers and old-timers, and about activities, identities, artefacts and communities of knowledge and practice. It concerns the process by which newcomers become part of a community of practice.

Learners progress from less important tasks toward crucial core tasks, thus moving from peripheral to full or central participation. As this occurs, understanding unfolds with the learner developing a view of what the activity entails. This process ensures that learning itself is an improvised practice where the curriculum unfolds in opportunities for engaging in practice (Fuller et al. 2005). According to Lave and Wenger (1991) learning is particularly effective under certain conditions, conditions a mentor is able to influence such as: providing access to different parts of the activity, enabling eventual full participation in core tasks, allowing horizontal interaction between participants, and ensuring that the structures and workings of the community of practice are transparent.

Importantly, a community is not simply a repository for technical knowledge and skills, so a protégé needs more than just being shown 'the answer'. The mentor, to be effective, must not only command the appropriate knowledge and skills but must be a full participant themselves in the cultural practices of the community. The mentor then locates the protégé within the community of practice and facilitates learning through mutual engagement in an activity that is defined by negotiations of meaning both inside and outside the community (Fuller *et al*. 2005). As communities are social structures they involve power relations, and the way power is exercised can make legitimate peripheral participation empowering or disempowering (Lave and Wenger 1991, Fuller *et al*. 2005). Moreover, given the nature of sport and coaching, its traditions and cultures, there remains a dynamic tension between continuity and displacement within a given community thus impacting the nature of mentoring relationships and the subsequent success or failure of the mentoring process.

In order to develop coach expertise Salmela and Moraes (2003) argue that formal coach-centred training and education should be carried out in a range of settings, including academic, technical and social. This should also be located within a context of constant interaction with peers, which has been shown to be one of the best sources of learning for expert coaches (Salmela and Moraes 2003, Cushion *et al*. 2003). Consequently, they argue that:

> Sharing of knowledge with other passionate coaches provides a rich forum for better understanding the complexities of coaching, as well as testing the effectiveness of one's particular ways of interaction and behaving in practice and games.
>
> (Salmela and Moraes 2003: 289)

From this relational perspective of persons and their actions within a socially and culturally constructed world, understanding and experiences are in a constant state of dynamic interconnection (Buysse *et al*. 2003). Thus, mentoring can be understood as a function of communities of practice and as legitimate peripheral participation. Mentor and protégé operate within an environment of shared enquiry and learning revolving around issues, ambiguities and dilemmas that emerge from situations in practice settings. The mentor is able to create meaning from activities and situations from protégés' lived experiences which become reinforced because the community of practice is *the* practice environment. Finally, learning occurs within the context of social relationships with other members of the community, who have similar, if not identical, issues and concerns from the realm of practice.

This section has considered mentoring as legitimate peripheral participation within communities of practice. These concepts provide useful insight into the nature of mentoring, mentoring relationships and experiential learning generally. Mentoring viewed as situated learning is a sociocultural phenomenon, rather than an isolated activity in which an individual acquires de-contextualised knowledge. When viewed in this way, mentoring and the conditions contributing to its success or failure can be better understood. First, learning must be grounded in daily activities and cannot be separated from the complex environments in which knowledge is applied. Second, knowledge has to be acquired through experience and transfers only to broadly similar situations. Finally, learning is the result of social processes that require negotiation and problem-solving with others (including the mentor) and results from engaging with difficult issues, ambiguities and dilemmas.

A key part of learning from communities of practice and mentoring is ongoing critical reflection. Indeed, Lave and Wenger (1991) contend that communities of practice result in an ongoing flow of reflective moments as a result of monitoring in the context of practice, which can be either tacit or explicit. Further, the flow of reflective moments is organised around the trajectory of participation (Lave and Wenger 1991). In this sense, reflection refers to the ongoing process of critically examining current and past practice as a method of improving future practice and increasing knowledge (Han 1995, Hatton and Smith 1995), and it is to reflection that this chapter now turns.

Mentoring as reflection

Ongoing reflection with others about the integration of professional knowledge and expertise is a key part of coaching practice. Indeed, the assumption that coaching knowledge is derived largely from coaches' experiences and observations as well as formal knowledge gained from theory, research and education, with each informing the other, seems well founded. It is, in fact, this interaction that predicates reflective practice (Buysse et al. 2003). Rooted in an experiential learning tradition that is 'dependent on the integration of experience with reflection and of theory with practice' (Osterman 1990: 135), the term reflective practice has been popularised by Schön (1983, 1987) and characterises a dialogue of thinking and doing to become more skilful (Giovannelli 2003). The practice of reflection is more than casual speculation on success and failure of practice but is a 'dialectic process in which thought is integrally linked with action' (Osterman 1990: 134) with the objective of improving a dilemma of practice (Kruse 1997, Gilbert and Trudel 2004b).

Hatton and Smith (1995), based on a review of literature, describe four distinct forms of reflection: (1) technical examination of immediate skills and competencies, (2) descriptive analysis of performance, skills and competencies, (3) dialogic exploration of alternative methods to solve problems and (4) critical thinking of the effects of a course of action. Usefully, these forms of reflection fit very well with concepts surrounding the role of the mentor. Indeed, mentors and protégés could be engaged in one or more of these types of reflection within a mentoring relationship. This collaborative reflection has the potential to develop individuals' professional practice and knowledge, and can also contribute to the development of the field in a meaningful way. In addition, reflection, regardless of the form it takes, is a useful concept in the discussion of mentoring as it enables an examination of practice and, in particular, the considered taken-for-granted assumptions that influence it to occur (Loughran 2002).

In a coaching environment, practice can be characterised by both technical skills (applying a set of rules to a problem), and by what is sometimes considered its 'art' (solving complex problems in unique or uncertain situations) (Schön 1983). Indeed, Schön argues that professional growth through experience is accomplished through a process of reflecting-in and on-practice dilemmas, referred to as a reflective conversation (a concept explored previously in this book) (Gilbert and Trudel 2004b). In other words, individuals may learn best through observing, doing, commenting and questioning, rather than simply listening. Schön proposes four key components in the reflective process: role frames, issue setting, strategy generation and experimentation. Recent coaching-specific work by Gilbert and Trudel (2004b, 2005) has added a further two components: coaching issues that precede issue setting, and evaluation that follows experimentation. Critically considering these components against the mentoring process has the potential to further develop our understanding of experiential learning in coaching and contribute to the development of effective mentoring practice.

First, role frames are how the coach would view his or her coaching role and the world in which they operate. Experience offers coaches opportunities to live through alternative approaches to practice, but it is the framing of these that impacts on what is 'seen' and the potential for learning. How a coach engages with practice and their own actions shape the possibilities for seeing as a result of experience. There remains an important interplay between experience and reflection, and effective reflective practice involves careful consideration of both seeing and action to enhance the possibilities of learning through experience (Loughran 2002). Mentors quite clearly influence coaches' role frames in that they will be instrumental in constructing the reality in which the protégé functions (Schön 1983) and what is seen and how it is seen.

Gilbert and Trudel (2001, 2005) identified that any reflection and engagement with experiential learning is triggered by a 'coaching issue'. The process of deciding why an issue is an issue is defined as issue setting. Mentors are significant in identifying issues and those issues that are important in a given situation. Not unlike role framing, this is not a culturally neutral process, and may be either enabling or constraining; a notion developed later when considering mentoring in action.

The mentor will influence the timing of reflection, and set out the necessary skills and framing. Professional repertoires are developed through ideas
and action strategies and form the basis of experiments that are attempts
to resolve the problem. These, in turn, are continually evaluated thus further
informing problem solving. The mentor then, through the reflective process
is effective when he or she leads the protégé to take meaning from situations that give understanding to the practice setting from a variety of
viewpoints. Thus, knowledge from the mentor through a process of reflection is 'genuine wisdom-in-practice' (Loughran 2002: 38) as the knowledge
becomes recognisable and articulated. This process is considerably more than
highlighting the problem and then providing the solution. There remains
a subtle difference between being told what to do and understanding the
practice (Loughran 2002). This means that experiencing situations in a
certain way becomes a genuine learning experience, an episode that carries
personal meaning (White 1988). This developed personal meaning through
ownership of a reflective process appears key, as coaches 'will pay more
attention to information that has immediate and personal meaning for them,
or when their "operative attention" is high' (Gilbert and Trudel 2001: 32).

The presence of a significant other, such as a mentor, however, is not
sufficient to invoke reflection. Mentors must be accessible, must be respected
and trusted for their knowledge of coaching. Indeed, Gilbert and Trudel
(2005) suggest that significant others, such as peers, or mentors, are pivotal
in the experiential learning process, as sounding boards in a range of circumstances and at different stages within the process.

Reflection and, therefore, mentoring needs both seeing and action. This
is a complex endeavour in a fast-paced decision-demanding domain such as
coaching. A common misconception of mentoring is to try to post-practice
'extract' the learning for the protégé so that it may be presented back in a
helpful way with insights previously unrecognised (Loughran 2002). The
key for successful mentoring it would seem is to assist the protégé to become
the focus, and to develop their abilities to analyse and draw meaning from
the experiences that matter most. It could be that the knowledge developed may be the same but the process is very different, as it has meaning
as a consequence of ownership for the protégé because of the link to their
own experience. The aim of this process, and a key objective of the mentor,
should be to assist the protégé to recognise, develop and articulate knowledge about practice. Loughran (2002) argues this process to be a powerful
way of informing practice as it makes the tacit explicit, meaningful and
useful.

This section has considered mentoring as reflection. Through reflection
coaches develop both knowledge and practice (Gilbert and Trudel 2001).
However, both reflection and mentoring require significance and meaning
(alongside application), so that the value of experiences is realised. In other
words, mentoring as reflection requires 'contextual anchors' (Loughran 2002:

33) to make learning episodes meaningful. For this to happen however, effective mentoring and reflection require a 'way in'; that is, a need, a context, a recognised problem and a recognised value. This ensures that the professional knowledge developed through effective mentoring and reflection has the opportunity to offer insight into the practice setting where the perhaps contradictory views of mentor and protégé create a diversity of ways of seeing actions in the coaching environment.

Mentoring as 'Zones of Proximal Development'

Vygotsky's work attempts to link the social and the individual levels of cognition (Hung 2002). A key proposition in understanding this is the ZPD (Vygotsky 1978). While developed as a theory of child-development, the ZPD has been applied to any type of learning task where individuals are developing mastery of a practice or understanding of a topic (Tharp and Gallimore 1988, Wells 1999). The underlying assumption behind ZPD is that psychological development and instruction are socially embedded (Hedegaard 1996).

The concept of a ZPD has been subject to a range of interpretations. First, as the distance between the problem-solving abilities of an individual when working alone and when assisted by or collaborating with more experienced people (e.g. a mentor). This interpretation, characterised by a 'scaffolding' analogy, has led to notions of learning that provide initial support for tasks that are later performed alone (e.g. Greenfield 1984, Wood et al. 1976). The second interpretation sees the ZPD as the distance between cultural knowledge and everyday experiences (Davydov and Markova 1983). Hedegaard (1996) describes this as the distance between understood knowledge (e.g. provided by instruction or mentor) and active knowledge owned by the individual. The third interpretation, not unlike Lave and Wenger's work, sees social practice as central, with the ZPD being the distance between the everyday actions of individuals and the collectively generated activity embedded in those actions (Engestrom 1987). These interpretations, while differing in their degree of 'socialness' share a common pre-supposition, namely an interaction between a more and a less competent person, with the less competent person becoming independently proficient in what was a jointly accomplished task (Chaiklin 2003). Once again this seems a useful concept through which to consider mentoring.

In viewing learning in these terms, it should be recognised that the learner is more than a passive recipient of information, as learning by 'doing' can often lead to the acquisition of immature or incorrect concepts and the possible neglect of key skills. This led Vygotsky to look at the concept of mediation. Here, he (1978, 1981) emphasised symbolic tools, such as artefacts, signs or language, that could be used to mediate between subjects (as part of the community) and objects, with learning being reflected in the internalisation process (i.e. from external action to internal activity). Two further types of mediation have been proposed; through another human being, and mediation as a form of organised learning (Kozulin 2003).

Of particular relevance to a discussion of mentoring and the mentor–protégé relationship, is the human form of mediation. Vygotsky (1978) considers the role of human mediator as manifest in two principal ways: that is, in the interaction between people and as a subsequent internalised form of that function. Looking at mentoring, then, what is important is the transition from the interpersonal to the intrapersonal (Kozulin 2003), rather than the properties of the mentor's mediation. Thus, the process assumes greater significance than the action.

There are many parameters for human mediation that facilitate internalisation, and these are largely context dependent. That said, Rogoff (1990, 1995) and Hung (2002) distinguish strata of mediation that are useful when considering the role of the mentor. These include apprenticeship, guided participation and appropriation. Each is now considered with mentoring in mind. First, apprenticeship provides a model of activity that mediates the sociocultural patterns of the activity to the protégé. The protégé then becomes able to undertake activity within particular contexts and under specific norms or rules of working that he or she would not have been previously able to do. Second, Rogoff (1990) stresses the importance of contextual learning, the significance of guided participation in activities and intersubjectivity, i.e. the sharing of focus and purpose between the learner (protégé) and the skilled partner (mentor). In particular, Rogoff (1990) argues that skilled partners help novices with difficult problems by structuring sub-goals or problem solving to help the novice focus on manageable aspects of the problem, and advocates the importance of routine in respect of skilled cultural activities. Finally, appropriation, which relates to the changes occurring within a protégé because of their involvement in mediated activities. This is a concept closely related to reflection.

Research on elements significant in human mediation has been inspired by Feuerstein's (1990) theory of mediated learning experiences (MLE). Feuerstein argued that the quality of MLE will only be achieved if certain criteria are met. Once again, these criteria provide useful thinking tools when considering mentoring. Among the most important criteria are intentionality and reciprocity of interaction, its transcendent character (i.e. having significance beyond the here and now situation) and the mediation of meaning. The first two of these criteria would seem relatively straightforward when thinking about mentor and protégé in action. The final criterion, that of mediation of meaning, is interesting when thinking about mentoring relationships. In structured learning environments, the meaning embedded in activities and action is sufficiently transparent. However, this is not the case necessarily in less formal learning, thus the protégé who learns most in an everyday setting has, perhaps, worked with a mentor who has mediated meaning, thus making situations and their embedded meanings clear.

This section has considered mentoring in terms of Vygotsky's ZPD and some of the supporting theory. These concepts are useful thinking tools in a discussion of mentoring, a mentoring process and why this may be more or less effective. First, the ZPD fits particularly well with mentoring as it is learning through interaction, with the interaction being from the more knowledgeable to the less knowledgeable. Second, the notion that learning is a transactional or dialectic interaction between subject, community and object is also significant. This suggests that not only are mentors and protégés constructing knowledge but that it is a negotiated or even a contested process. Third, through mediation, the mentor appears key in learning proceeding from external action to internal activity. This process and the influence of the mentor (either formally or informally) mean that the patterns of coaches' behaviour become more recognisable and hold the potential for coaches to better understand their external activity. Through this understanding of coaching comes the internalisation of action (Hung 2002). In turn, the coach becomes less dependent on the external support of people and objects in the coaching world.

Mentoring in action

Coaches' previous and ongoing experiences remain significant in the development of coaching practice. The power of these experiences should not be underestimated, therefore formalising them within coach education would seem to be a necessity. This would involve providing opportunities for developing coaches to acquire hands-on experience through structured educational programmes that include mentoring. Indeed, in an investigation of training methods of coaches where mentoring was in operation, it was found that a formalised and structured related programme was considered by the participants to be the most important factor in their development (Bloom et al. 1995). In light of this, and the evidence presented in this chapter, it could be contended that more formalised mentoring programmes would be a worthwhile addition to coach development (Bloom et al. 1998).

It would seem that the challenge for coach education and the development of mentoring is not to ignore or downplay the personal knowledge and experience of the trainee (or perceived lack of it) but to elevate and build upon it (Snow 2001). By doing this through a mentoring process, coaches could be given the opportunity to integrate information 'relevant to crystallizing their own philosophies and unique coaching styles' (Bloom et al. 1998: 278). All the concepts discussed in this chapter, while taking a slightly different perspective to learning from experience, seem to converge and present evidence supporting that such a strategy should be based on the need to situate coaches' learning in practical experience and within a supportive framework. This would also enable coach education to get its 'hands dirty' by extending its thinking into practice (Cassidy et al. 2004). Thus, coach education programmes should include mentoring in a variety of contexts, to enable coaches to consider differences, make mistakes, learn from them and try again. This would provide coaches with multiple opportunities to test and refine knowledge and skills, make coaching judgements that are meaningful within given situations, and understand the pragmatic constraints of coaching contexts (Cushion et al. 2003).

Within this mentoring process, the ability to recognise, develop and articulate knowledge about practice is crucial as it gives a real purpose for, and value in, effective practice; indeed, it is a powerful way of informing practice as it makes the tacit meaningful and helpful (Loughran 2002). With this in mind, the mentoring process has to be drawn from the ability to frame and re-frame the practice setting, and to develop and respond to this framing through action so that the practitioners' wisdom-in-action is enhanced. The various theoretical approaches to understanding mentoring taken in this chapter contribute to this process. Indeed, by considering mentoring from a more theoretical basis, it becomes increasingly clear that what is learned and how it is learned, as a result of mentoring, is as important as mentoring itself. It is through the development of knowledge and understanding of the practice setting and the ability to recognise and respond to such knowledge that the mentoring process becomes truly responsive to the needs, issues and concerns that are important in shaping coaching practice (Loughran 2002).

This chapter has provided evidence that mentoring supports much of what is known about how individuals learn, particularly the socially constructed nature of learning, and the importance of experiential, situated learning experiences (Kerka 1997). Mentors can assist with effective learning that is situated in context, where new knowledge and skills are used and where individuals construct meaning for themselves but within a context of interaction with others (Kerka 1998). This understanding leads towards the evolution of a mentoring process and the development of an understanding of the role of the mentor.

Process role and relationships

Simply copying the behaviours of experienced practitioners is limited to 'imitation or cloning, devoid of insight and initiative' (Ethell 1999: 2). By the same token, protégés have a perception of their needs and of the world around them and, as such, are not simply empty vessels waiting to be filled with professional dogma. One could reasonably ask how do protégé perceptions influence the role of the mentor, their ongoing relationship and the mentoring process? The mentoring literature, at times, can be benign, and lacks a critical depth when it characterises the mentor as simply a supporter and provider of information, and an articulator of practical knowledge. This chapter has demonstrated that the role of the mentor is clearly greater than that. Mentors model problem-solving strategies and provide guidance to approximate strategies while encouraging learners to articulate their thought processes. Indeed, mentoring involves a 'capacity to foster an inquiring stance' (Field and Field 1994: 67), which has the potential to inform insightful learning, particularly in relation to understanding the holistic and complex nature of coaching.

In some ways practice leads theory in this regard as instances of informal mentoring are occurring on a daily basis. It would seem logical, therefore, that an essential first step underpinning the role of the mentor and the development of a mentoring relationship, has to be formalising the process. As Wright and Smith (2000) argue, formalising mentoring adds to consistency, a quality in the occurring interaction and, ultimately, effectiveness. In addition, once formalised, the mentor's remit, according to Fletcher (2000), is substantial, and should extend to a number of areas. Although such a list could well appear on a mentor's job description, for a full appreciation of the depth of engagement and to understand some of the issues that arise, a more critical stance needs to be taken.

First in this respect, the mentor needs to explore the personal dimensions and related anxieties of the novice in beginning a new or different post. Mentoring is crucial at this stage as new and/or inexperienced coaches have to deal with issues of marginality, isolation, role conflict, reality shock and the washout effect (Wright 1997). Indeed, Huling-Austin (1990), while reviewing teacher induction programmes, suggested that 'the most consistent finding across studies is the importance of the support teacher (mentor)' (p. 542). Second, the mentor needs to assist with integrating the neophyte coach into the club or institution. Kerka (1998) argues that mentoring is a personalised and relatively systematic way to be socialised into a culture, and cultural competence remains important in coaching settings (Cushion et al. 2003). However, this form of socialisation can be constraining if the protégé is exposed to a 'limited repertoire of practice views, and expectations' (Cleminson and Bradford 1996: 255), hence, mentoring can be a vehicle for both assimilation and exclusion. Indeed, the power the mentor may wield over a protégé is rarely discussed and recognised (Hansman 2001). Mentors may have too much control over a protégé, thus stifling the protégé's ability to create and reflect upon knowledge gained. Indeed, professionals, either implicitly or explicitly, may be caught up in producing, reproducing and passing on the organisational and social norms by which they operate without reflecting upon the appropriateness of the process (e.g. Cushion 2001). Mentoring is instrumental in defining what is necessary knowledge for coaches to practice. Tinning (1997) contends that this implies a choice between different views of what knowledge is essential for practice. This is a form of social editing, where some themes are eliminated and others are promoted (Lawson 1993). Therefore, the mentoring process becomes a political act, intimately linked with power and control, regarding what constitutes legitimate knowledge and who holds that knowledge in the culture and profession (Cushion *et al.* 2003). It is a possibility that the mentor needs to become acutely aware of.

The third, fourth and fifth items, respectively, relate directly to practice and are: providing guidance in relation to where helpful coaching resources can be gleaned; assisting with the preparation and delivery of coaching sessions; and guiding the new coach's practical coaching and indicating alternative appropriate strategies within a supportive framework. Within these steps it is clear that a mentor should empathise with the novice as the latter experiences the various stages of professional development, namely 'early idealism', 'personal survival', 'hitting the plateau', and finally 'moving on' (Furlong and Maynard 1995). He or she should also systematically challenge novice coaches as they progress through these stages with the intention of forcing them to constantly evaluate their whole understanding of the coaching role and their performance within it (Fletcher 2000). What is key here is the posing of insightful open-ended exploratory questions by the mentor to de-mystify the coaching process, thus supplying novice coaches with the confidence that they can survive and thrive in a complex environment (Cassidy *et al.* 2004). Relating this process to the theories discussed earlier in the chapter, through these steps mentors provide learners with ZPD appropriate aids, including scaffolds (Vygotsky 1978), access to and guidance through legitimate peripheral participation (Lave and Wenger 1991) and an informed process of reflection (Schön 1983) to assist with construction of their own knowledge and understanding. Through the mentoring process then, the mentor can provide authentic, experiential learning opportunities for the protégé that can be viewed as true co-operation between the two.

The process and role of the mentor is closely linked to the nature of the mentoring relationship, and the discussion so far has suggested a relationship defined by co-operation. Indeed, within education Napper-Owen and Phillips (1995) found a strong co-operative relationship produced an increased sense of accountability to teach effectively, and seek new knowledge. Within this, the matching of mentor and protégé was key with the relationship being carefully cultivated through regular contact ensuring the success of the process. This relationship needs to be constructed within the goals and objectives of the programme. Therefore, it is imperative that potential mentors and protégés are identified and matched carefully, not simply thrown together; 'the dyad must be encouraged to foster a positive, committed relationship between them' (Wright and Smith 2000: 210). Importantly, this coming together cannot be assumed but developed for the pair, ensuring a customised interaction and strategy. It may be that mentors are persons with more experience but, regardless of who assumes the role, how this relationship is formed usually determines its nature, with trust at its core being a pre-requisite (Kaye and Jacobson 1996). This ensures that mentors provide a safe environment, where experiences are authenticated by links to real-world activities, ensuring that knowledge acquired is reinterpreted and developed through practice (Cleminson and Bradford 1996). Regardless of the nature of the mentor/protégé dyad, it would seem imperative for mentors to have established the appropriate position in the social field (Cushion 2001). They would have to have the required mix of social, cultural and symbolic capital. The mentor would also have to hold expert power (French and Raven 1959), which is based not only on the knowledge of the mentor but upon the perceptions of the novice coaches regarding it (Tauber 1985).

Some conclusions

Within coaching, as has been argued, evidence suggests that both the experience of the coach and encounters with experienced coaches are fundamental to the shaping of coaching practice; hence, mentoring is 'just happening' (e.g. Cushion et al. 2003). Clearly then, influencing such experiences would affect the acquisition and development of coaches' knowledge. Indeed, sections of the coaching literature have argued that coach education should incorporate sources of experience other than the standard coaching manuals (Gould et al. 1990, Lyle 2002).

Harnessing the power of experience, arguably, requires a shift in thinking for coach education. Taking on board the arguments presented in this chapter, this would mean that the role of coach education is to facilitate construction of knowledge through experiential, contextual and socio-cultural methods in real-world communities. The learning environment should reproduce key aspects of the practice, such as authentic activities grounded in complexity, multiple experiences, examples of knowledge application, access to experts and a social context in which learners collaborate on knowledge construction. Central to this process, as suggested in this chapter, lies mentoring.

Chapter 11

The development of expert coaching

Paul G. Schempp, Bryan McCullick and
Ilse Sannen Mason

Introduction: the development of expert coaching

One of the significant challenges facing sport organizations is finding ways to improve its coaching corps. Discovering ways to increase the expertise of current coaches and prepare better coaches for the future is a daunting task. Research has conclusively shown that expertise is neither a birthright nor an innate characteristic. Rather, excellence in coaching is gained through years of deliberate practice and study. While certain abilities may account for someone coaching better than others, or ultimately being able to perform at a higher level, one cannot reach the highest levels of instructional performance without extensive education and experience.

Borrowing from the work of David Berliner (1994) in educational psychology, the purpose of this chapter is to describe the developmental stages in becoming an expert coach. Specifically, the skills, knowledge, characteristics and perspectives common to coaches as they pass from beginner, to competent, to proficient, to expert coach will be identified (Bell 1997, Berliner 1994). While these stages seem to imply a hierarchy, everyone passes from one to the next on the journey toward improvement. One can, however, choose where one stops in developing expertise. To help meet the new challenges of sport, these stages will be presented so that sport coaches may identify their current stage and recognize the skills, perspectives and knowledge necessary to elevate to the next level and beyond. Also, suggestions for preparing and working with beginning coaches will be offered.

After an extensive review of research in expertise, Anders Ericsson (Ericsson and Charness 1994) concluded that it takes at least ten years of deliberate practice to reach the level of expert. That is, one must *consciously* perform and refine the requisite skills of a profession in order to get better. That offers good news for those who aspire to become great coaches because it means that investing in experience, intentional practice of specific coaching skills and extended learning, will pay dividends in developing coaching expertise. Simply knowing the characteristics and qualities of an expert is, however, not enough. Remember, too, that experts are individuals and their thoughts and actions often take on an idiosyncratic, at times eccentric, quality. Therefore, in considering the stages and the characteristics of each, understand that they represent commonalties among coaches rather than a prescription for being a great coach.

Everyone starts as a beginner

Those who enter coaching seldom do so as pure novices. The years spent in classrooms as students, on playing fields as athletes and in preparatory or certification programmes have familiarized neophytes with the skills, perspectives and responsibilities of the role. While the athletic setting may feel intimately familiar, beginning coaches must still prove themselves as capable contributors. By definition, beginning coaches are those with less than three years of professional experience. But it is more than the lack of experience that characterizes beginners. The following traits can be found in most early career coaches.

Learning the job means learning the rules

To learn their new role as coaches and prove themselves worthy, beginners learn the rules and norms governing life in their new workplace. Their conception of doing the job correctly includes following the organizational rules and procedures, particularly those centered on establishing order and managing the practice environment. Beginners view neat, orderly practices with compliant and happy athletes as characteristic of competent coaches. In essence, it means that coaches in this stage are more "concerned about student behavior than about transmitting a body of knowledge" (Placek 1983: 49). This seems natural because through the naive eyes of a beginning coach, it is relatively easy to notice players on-task, listening, following directions and enjoying the experience. It is more difficult to discern athletes who are actually gaining knowledge, developing skills or improving performance. Only with experience, will these coaches begin to detect these subtle, but significant changes in athletes.

Because of their dependence on rules to guide practice, for those working with beginning coaches such as player coaches or first year coaches, it is important to make sure they clearly understand the rules and procedures that guide life both in practice and during game situations. In this respect, they need assistance to establish rules they feel comfortable with and opportunities to discuss situations that fall outside given rules and procedures. Providing this information and support will help ensure a positive and productive start to a coaching career.

Routines

During their initial coaching experiences, beginners try to detect the commonplace through objective facts and features of the situation, but they seldom sense the overall task or see relationships between events. There are times when novices get lost in mundane or everyday tasks due to the lack of established routines and an inability to see the interconnection of in-practice events. A beginning coach may, for example, get caught up in taking attendance, securing equipment or managing athletes, while overlooking more important instructional tasks such as practicing skill progressions, activity pacing, or player assessment (Carter *et al.* 1988, Leinhart and Greeno 1986).

With increased experience and discussions with other coaches, novices begin developing effective routines that minimize management functions and maximize the instructional focus of the practice. Once again, providing beginners with examples and alternatives for opening and closing a practice, moving athletes from one location to the next, establishing team rules, distributing equipment and the like, will help novice coaches select and cultivate the routines that permit their practices to progress purposefully and smoothly.

Perhaps the best example of an expert coach who developed and utilized significant and effective routines is legendary US college basketball coach, John Wooden. His most famous routines were used to make sure his players did not unnecessarily miss practice time. Each year at the first team meeting, Coach Wooden personally demonstrated how to properly put on a pair of socks (remember these were college athletes). Take note of his reason for having this routine:

> This may seem like a nuisance, trivial, but I had a very practical reason for being meticulous about this. Wrinkles, folds, and creases can cause blisters. Blisters interfere with performance during practice and games. Since there was a way to reduce blisters, something the player and I could control, it was our responsibility to do it. Otherwise we would not be doing everything possible to prepare in the best way.
>
> (Wooden and Jamison 1997: 61)

Repeating this ritual each year with his players, Wooden was able to ensure that they were not battling blisters and missing valuable preparation time. This routine allowed for more learning to take place and no excuses to be made for not being better basketball players. If you were to ask him, this probably contributed greatly to his success as a coach (ten National Championships, including seven in a row).

Lack of a sense of control and responsibility

Because beginners are so focused on learning their workplace regularities and enforcing rules, they seldom feel any personal control over the conditions and events of the practice and, therefore, may lack a sense of responsibility for their own actions. One manifestation of this is the common belief among beginning coaches that athletes are solely to blame for misbehavior and lack of achievement. Rookie coaches often abdicate responsibilities for athletes' learning difficulties as well, often blaming the players' backgrounds or personal characteristics for deficiencies in learning or performance (Schempp *et al.* 1998b).

Believing that athletes bring their problems into practices or games, and that the problems reflect current social ills and a lack of parental support, coaches with low levels of expertise often don't even attempt to support or assist struggling athletes because they believe such efforts would ultimately prove futile. This feature is a watershed mark in coaching, for those with the highest levels of coaching expertise never willingly give up on a player, while coaches with low expertise levels give up on athletes all too quickly. The drive to inspire and guide all athletes to their full potential is one factor that propels great coaches to the heights they achieve. A coach who gives up on a player, is at the same time giving up on him/herself as a coach. Refusing to give up on athletes and searching for ways to help them will benefit both the coach and player – regardless of the latter's ultimate success or failure in sport.

Experience is a beginner's best coach

Perhaps reflecting their limited practical experience, novices find their "real world" practice to be their most important source of information for increasing coaching competence. Verbal or written information takes second place to trial and error in acquiring instructional skill and knowledge.

There is no substitute for experience, and it is critical to developing one's coaching skills. Novices usually develop their instructional repertoires by combining observations of more experienced coaches, personal trial and error, and recalling coaches from their days as athletes. The more experiences and the greater diversity of those experiences (i.e. different athletes, facilities, coaching strategies, etc.), the more the beginning coach learns and the faster he or she will improve.

It would be soothing to believe that one need only spend a certain amount of time coaching, and the lessons learned through experience would elevate you to the next level of expertise. Unfortunately, there is no script that reads the same for all coaches. A coach needs to do more than simply spend time on the job to become better skilled. She or he needs to learn from experiences and gain more knowledge to reduce the number of mistakes they make and increase the number of successes they gain. Combining experience with activities such as reflective practice, journal writing, professional meetings, and networking with other coaches, all help the beginner get better. A coach must, however, make purposeful and sustained efforts to improve. In the next stage, the characteristics that signal the rise from beginner to competent professional will be identified and described.

Cultivating competence

With experience and increased knowledge, coaches begin to develop skills that allow them to minimize time spent on non-coaching tasks such as management, leaving more time and attention for improving player performance. Unfortunately, a common problem among sport coaches, particularly those working in secondary schools, is to simply be satisfied with having the managerial functions under control. Despite having efficient management routines, many coaches never aspire to develop instructional prowess or help athletes learn. To these coaches, if the athletes are busy, happy and good (Placek 1983), they have achieved sufficient success as a coach.

Fortunately, there are coaches who yearn for more than simply mollifying athletes. These coaches set their sights on helping athletes learn, develop and grow. These are the coaches who seek to make the most of their time with athletes. They have an impact on the athletes' lives, and lead athletes to realize their potential as both sport participants and people. These are the coaches who transition from beginning coach to the next level of expertise: competent coaches. In the following section, the characteristics of competent coaches will be identified and suggestions for moving from a beginner to competent coach will be offered.

Seeing and connecting similarities

As beginning coaches gain experience, recurring instructional events are remembered and recognized. As their knowledge of situations, players and events expand, they see similarities across contexts. Identifying commonalties over different coaching situations allows coaches to select a current response from a variety of responses tested in prior experiences. Coaching competence begins to emerge when a coach examines a new experience and then searches for a solution or decision from previous experience rather than relying strictly on following established rules or a set game plan (Leinhardt and Greeno 1986).

Because they recognize similarities across situations, competent coaches make applications from one situation to the other. For example, if a competent coach detects a player having problems learning an underhand serve in volleyball, he or she may relate the problem to a similar player from a previous team. With the connection made, the competent coach can recall successful solutions for the previous player and offer them to the current player.

Developing strategic knowledge

Competent coaches may still be somewhat rule oriented, but are now guided by circumstances and context when applying rules. They develop a strategic knowledge that allows one to ignore or flex the rules as the situation dictates.

A coach, for example, may choose to ignore athletes whispering and sacrifice the "no talking when the coach is talking" rule in order to move ahead with a practice. As a beginner, the same coach would likely enforce a strict policy of no talking during instruction and thereby stop the learning of the athletes who were paying attention and on-task.

Another example of the strategic knowledge of competent coaches may be illustrated in their feedback. Beginning coaches are schooled in giving positive feedback to bolster an athlete's self-esteem. Following this principle, new coaches are often heard spluttering "good job," "nice try" and other well meaning but instructionally worthless responses to player efforts. Competent coaches know that praise in certain instances may communicate low expectations and that, at times, constructive criticism serves as more effective feedback (Berliner 1994). Again, strategic knowledge allows them to know what to say and when to say it.

Strategic knowledge is developed in the combination of a coach's experience and knowledge of their athletes, sport and coaching. It is in trial and error and being able to see similarities in their experiences that this knowledge is incubated and grows. Beginners looking to develop this form of knowledge need to do three things: (1) gain experience (2) use reflective coaching to learn all they can from their experiences and (3) experiment with different decisions to see their results. For example, allowing players to talk and see where it takes the team, or asking athletes to provide feedback to each other. It is only through experimenting that coaches become better at knowing what to do and when to do it – strategic knowledge.

Guided by goals and long-term plans

While novices struggle to apply the rules, competent coaches work toward the larger goal of player and team development. In other words, the practices of competent coaches are guided more by purpose, while policies and procedures tend to guide those of beginning coaches.

To move from beginner to competent coach, one must continually revisit the purposes behind the coaching practices being adopted and developed. If the purpose is simply for athletes to follow rules and maintain order, one is mired in a beginner's perspective. If the purpose of one's coaching is to nurture player learning and development, a characteristic of competent coaching is evident. Competent coaches rely on long-term goals and plans to help insure that their practices work toward the bigger picture of player progress.

Contingency planning

With experience and increased knowledge comes another characteristic of competent coaches: contingency planning. While beginning coaches rely heavily on procedures and preplanned lessons, competent coaches' planning reflects the characteristic of "if/then planning." In other words, when they devise a practice or game plan, competent coaches are able to plan for contingencies and changes by thinking "if/then." As an example, a coach might think, "*If* the players look tired in warm-ups, *then* I'll spend more time explaining the value of stretching. *If* the players look energetic, *then* I'll get them immediately into running activities." Again, experience allows the competent coach to see similarities across context (e.g. the coach realizes that athletes' energy levels impact their readiness to practice running skills), and to have the knowledge necessary to offer a variety of activities depending on the situation (i.e. strategic knowledge).

One way to develop this type of planning is simply to try it. Consequently, when planning a practice a coach could think about important characteristics that affect athletes' in-practice performance, such as motivation, energy, previous learning, equipment, weather, and the like. These characteristics should be considered with the challenge lying in finding alternatives. After some practice, this type of planning becomes almost automatic.

Practicing proficiency

If all coaches reached the proficient level on the expertise scale, the quality of coaching would be vastly improved. But gaining expertise takes copious amounts of passion, experience, knowledge and, perhaps, some talent for the coaching field. Those who aspire to be the best they can be, who actively search for opportunities to gain new knowledge and perspectives, and work to learn all they can from their experiences, can move from competent to proficient coach.

Proficient coaches represent the top 20–25 percent of sport coaches. Their proficiency was gained from a significant number of years of coaching and prolonged and sustained efforts to increase their knowledge of the sport, athletes and coaching. While proficient coaches hold many of the characteristics of competent coaches, in the following section the characteristics that set proficient coaches apart from beginners and competent coaches are identified.

Discriminating perceptual capacities

With considerable accumulated knowledge and experience, proficient coaches detect subtleties in a learning environment that have significant importance to the events taking place. Thousands of hours of experience have honed their perceptual capacities, allowing them to recognize when something isn't working in a player's performance, a practice session or a game. Possessing a keen sense of timing that comes from an intimate understanding of the present environment, they can adroitly change the course of action in a direction that leads to greater success.

Coaching is a dynamic process where many athletes are engaged in activities in a practice session or game. While keeping the whole team or other players interested and on task is important, the challenge of focusing on individual performance is critical. Proficient coaches have the perceptual capacity to attend to individual player performance while monitoring the entire practice or game. Beginners and competent coaches do not seem to have developed this skill (Housner and Griffey 1985). Because they can observe the athletes individually, proficient coaches try to meet the needs of every player and realize that athletes will be at differing skill levels. Classroom teachers have a term for this – "withitness" (Doyle 1986).

The acute perception of proficient coaches also allows them to sort the important from the unimportant. For example, a beginning coach may notice a player's dress, choice of equipment, or friends, while a proficient coach will overlook any extraneous factors that don't directly bear on athletes' performances. They thus devote more attention to player performances and lock tightly on the key components that most affect those performances. By identifying the critical components in a player's performance they can supply the information and activities that will promote the biggest improvement in the player in the shortest amount of time (Woorons 2001). Consequently, although what is deemed important by individual coaches may vary, what does not change is their ability to separate the "wheat from the chaff" when it comes to the coaching environment.

A proficient coach's perceptual capacities are not necessarily restricted to performance characteristics. Proficient coaches are also quick to recognize the degree to which such factors as player motivation, physical fitness and the like influence a player's development. Again, with an inability to discern the important from the unimportant, beginners and competent coaches are less able to do this.

While beginning and competent coaches often see the symptom, it is the proficient coach who can see past it and identify the cause. Once the cause has been identified, it is far easier to supply the appropriate cure. While a beginner flounders in futile attempts to cure all the symptoms she or he sees, the proficient coach easily cures the multitude of symptoms by eliminating the cause. In a study of the professional orientations of the top 100 golf instructors in America, many of them viewed themselves as "repair people" (McCullick et al. 1999: 18). One of the experts in the study expressed this important teaching skill as:

> If someone is slicing the ball because they are swinging over the top, I try to figure out why they are over the top versus just telling them to swing more inside ... every mistake or swing fault has a reason, when you fix a problem at its cause you can really help someone progress.

Developing the discriminating perceptual capacities of proficient coaches takes both extended knowledge and experience. Beginning and competent coaches can speed the development of this process by attempting to iden- tify the environment cues that are most pertinent to a player's performance and the lesson goals – the fundamentals as they are often called. Like any coaching skill, it can be developed with practice.

Strong sense of personal responsibility

Proficient coaches are in command of the curricular and instructional activity in their domain. Since they are not as rule focused as beginning or competent coaches, proficient coaches feel more personal control over their domain and harbor a strong personal responsibility for the successes and failures of their athletes. They hold themselves accountable for athlete learning problems and believe the solutions to these problems reside within both their capabilities and responsibilities (Tan 1997). When learning prob- lems arise, proficient coaches analyze the practice or performance, seeking alternative activities and resources that might help athletes train more effi- ciently. It is at this level of expertise that coaches begin to believe that they can teach anyone their sport or activity as long as the player wants to learn (Schempp et al. 1998b).

Respond instinctively and intuition begins developing

As they increase their proficiency, instructional routines become so familiar that coaches respond instinctively to a situation rather than having to give it careful and rational analysis before coming to a decision. At this point, intuition is developing and is gaining prominence in the coaches' decision- making. The coach no longer has to consciously consider every action he or she takes and, therefore, their coaching activities take on a natural fluidity and timing.

At this level of expertise, coaches continually analyze the flow of events in a practice or game attempting to select from a large repertoire of possible activities or information that is going to make the biggest impact on player performance. Their extensive experience and knowledge allow them to respond with less rational thought and with more instinct and intuition. It is much like driving a car. After a significant number of hours behind the wheel of a car, one does not consciously have to consider which foot to use to depress the brake pedal or even give thought to the location of the brake pedal. The response is instinctive and when certain environmental cues arise, such as a pedestrian stepping into the path of the car, the braking process begins without conscious thought. Similarly, proficient coaches anticipate likely events and respond to shifting conditions in players' performances.

Predict outcomes

We often don't credit proficient or expert coaches with having a crystal ball, but it appears they do. Because proficient coaches have become extraordinarily good at recognizing similarities across situations, they can predict potential outcomes of unfolding events with a high degree of accuracy and precision. This was demonstrated in a research study of teachers with advanced teaching skills. They were asked to look at a series of slides of classroom events and comment about what they were thinking (Carter *et al.* 1988). The teachers provided rich commentaries about their observations, and drew upon their own experiences to make judgments about what they viewed. The teachers "made many assumptions about what they saw, appeared to be looking for the meaning of events portrayed in slides in [the] task, [and] inferred relationships between actions and situations in the slides" (p. 28). Like teachers, proficient and expert coaches possess this quality, as can be seen in findings from studies of coaches in tennis (Woorons 2001), swimming (Leas and Chi 1993) and volleyball (Bian 2003).

The ability to predict potential outcomes proves useful in selecting activities because only those practice activities and game strategies with the greatest chance of success are selected. As you might imagine, having a crystal ball in coaching, while extraordinarily useful, is not easy to gain. For a player, having a coach who can predict which practice activities will help them improve in the most economical and efficient manner is a major benefit. For a coach, being able to reasonably predict the success of an activity saves time and makes for quality practice sessions.

Proficient coaches make these predictions based on years of experience. They have seen similar situations time and again and have become skilled at analyzing the outcomes of their decisions. Reflective coaching, experimenting with new ideas, conversations with other coaches and a strong desire to always find the solution that is in the best interest of the player, are all needed for proficient coaches to earn their powers of prediction.

Learn more from outside sources

Having learned the lessons of experience, proficient coaches look to sources outside their own coaching for fresh information. Other coaches and resources such as conferences, books, videotapes and the like are important sources of information for these coaches. Famed expert wrestling coach, Dan Gable, is a prime example of a coach who knows that reading is one sure way to keep informed, therefore making him a better coach. Gable contends that compiling and continually updating a library is essential to improving his coaching skills. In Gable's words:

> The library is not limited to skills alone, but includes motivational books and information on psychological preparations, nutrition, strength, and

flexibility. Besides books, several worthwhile video and audio tapes are available to help with the growing process. While the Soviet Union and several other countries were having tremendous success in wrestling, I would search out periodicals and books from these countries hoping they were translated into English. Many were not, but the photos or drawings helped to expand my knowledge anyway. I highlighted many of the pages and important points in these books for quick reference when needed.

(Gable 1999: 146)

While proficient coaches assume significant responsibility for player pro-gress, see similarities across different situations, use well-established coach-ing routines, have heightened perceptual capacities and show a greater sophistication in deriving solutions to coaching problems by developing intuitive responses, they still remain largely analytic and deliberative in their decision-making. That is, they still demonstrate a logical progression in their instructional decision-making. Most decisions are reached following a process of consciously analyzing the situation and deliberately selecting from a range of potential solutions to detected problems. As we shall see, the expert begins to make decisions that, at times, appear to defy convention, logic or even explanation, and yet still represent a superior solution to a given coaching problem.

Excelling to expert

Experts are distinguished from those with less expertise by their consistently outstanding performance. For expert coaches, this means that they are able to coach more athletes to higher levels of success in a greater variety of environments in a shorter amount of time than less expert coaches. This does not mean that an expert can necessarily coach every player to master every skill under any circumstances, but rather on an overall basis, the athletes of expert coaches learn more and perform better than athletes of less expert coaches.

We like to think that anyone can be an expert, but that is not the case. It takes years of experience and extensive knowledge, but sometimes that is not enough. Dodds (1994: 162) reminds us that, "expertise demands both experience and effectiveness, but neither alone is sufficient." Research has shown, however, that experts are made and not born (Ericsson and Charness 1994). Therefore, while not everyone may become the top coach in their sport, everyone can increase their expertise and thus become a better coach. In this section, we will analyze the characteristics of expert coaches. Suggestions will also be offered on climbing to the highest level of profes-sional practice in coaching. And while not everyone who aspires to be an expert will make it, there is plenty of room for everyone who wants to try.

Extensive knowledge

While it perhaps seems obvious that an expert coach has an extensive base of knowledge, the importance of this characteristic demands that it be examined thoroughly. There are many lessons for coaches in understanding "what an expert knows." Experts make a significant investment in learning all they can about their subject, their athletes and their coaching. Attend coaching workshops, clinics or conferences and you will surely see expert coaches there. While the experts are the ones least likely to benefit from the information in a workshop, they became experts because they attended such conferences and meetings in order to develop their expertise. It is one reason they are now considered such.

One finds that experts enjoy talking almost endlessly about their subject, gather others' views on pertinent topics and have extensive libraries devoted to their subject (Ericsson and Charness 1994). Coaches use extensive resources to build a large store of knowledge. Experience and other coaches have been most often identified as important sources of knowledge, but books, workshops, certification programs, journals and magazines, athletic experiences and even athletes have been identified as important sources for coaches' knowledge (Fincher and Schempp 1994, Schempp et al. 1999). Walk into a coach's office and look at his or her library. If there are no or few books to be found, it isn't likely that the person who works there is an expert. They may be good at what they do, but they are not at the top of their profession. As Dan Gable can testify, a well stocked library will tell you that there is a knowledgeable coach in the area.

Experts are sponges when it comes to absorbing new knowledge. Less expert coaches are satisfied with what they know. To stop learning is to stop getting better. Experts know that. For those wishing to elevate their expertise, they need to learn-read, talk with others and attend relevant workshops, clinics and conferences.

Expert coaches have a thorough knowledge of the sport they coach, team and player management, coaching principles and planning skills (DeMarco and McCullick 1997). Experts also synthesize their knowledge about a skill or activity into meaningful information for athletes to understand and apply (Siedentop and Eldar 1989). This extensive knowledge base provides them with an array of possibilities for presenting information in order to help athletes understand and develop skills (Bian 2003). If a player doesn't understand the coach's explanation of a particular skill or strategy, the expert can offer a different explanation, use a demonstration, an audiovisual, or any number of other techniques. Coaches without a large knowledge base are generally restricted to only a few instructional options.

The expert coach's superior knowledge permits him or her to use their coaching environment (i.e. equipment, facilities and supplies) to greater effect than less expert coaches. For example, they demonstrate greater flexibility in using equipment to facilitate athletes' learning. They know different ways of using the same equipment for multiple purposes. A hula-hoop may, for example, be a target, a boundary area, a throwing object or anything else the fertile mind of an expert coach might concoct (Housner and Griffey 1985). Beginners on the other hand see a hula-hoop as simply that.

Interestingly, when expert coaches are faced with a relevant topic in which they are not familiar, they take measures to gain an understanding of it and how it may benefit them or their athletes (Schempp et al. 1998a). In fact, they take pains to talk with people who are experts on the topic, read pertinent material and even work on developing their own mastery of the skills. Experts know the importance of their own personal understanding of the topics that can be brought to bear on their success.

Intuition

A major divide separating expert from less expert coaches is the use of intuition in decision-making. Experts use an intuition sharpened by years of experience and bolstered by extensive knowledge to make many of their decisions. They get "gut feelings" and have the confidence to go with them – even if those feelings run counter to accepted logic or convention. This would be a dangerous practice for beginning or perhaps even competent coaches, but it is the *modus operandi* of the expert. It takes years of reflective coaching, experimentation, trying, failing and succeeding to gain an expert's intuitive ability. The criterion that separates the expert from the less expert is not the amount of intuition used, but rather the superior performances and solutions that the process yields for the expert. In other words, quality *not* quantity counts.

Planning

Expert coaches have a high regard for planning and being prepared. Despite years of experience, successful coaches still feel the need to devise detailed practice plans to ensure they meet their desired objectives. One example is former University of North Carolina coach Dean Smith who is the "winningest" coach in NCAA (US collegiate) basketball history. In his 1999 memoir, Smith explains his view:

> Practice was the foundation of everything we did. Our practices were tough, carefully planned, and meticulously organized ... Each day, players received a typed copy of our practice plan. They would come into the locker room, and while dressing they would leaf through the plan, which would give them a precise schedule of what we would be working on that day.
>
> (Smith 1999: 127)

Experts see planning as an integral and necessary part of their duties. Basketball coach John Wooden dedicated two hours every morning to planning the afternoon's practice (Wooden 2004). Notes were made on index cards that were carried to practice. As adjustments were made to the plan, they were noted on the cards. Later, the schedule and notes were transferred to a notebook for future reference. A beginning coach who believes they can coach well without planning is much like the person who enters an unfamiliar city without a map and sees no need to ask directions to his or her destination. At best, they waste a great deal of time in reaching their destination and, at worst, they never get where they intended to go.

Automaticity of behavior

Because experts are intuitive and don't often use linear, step-by-step approaches to decision-making, their responses and performances appear fast, fluid and natural. Characteristic of the expert performance is a high degree of automaticity, which Bloom (1986) described as experts' "knowing-in-action." The extensive hours of practice are an important prerequisite in developing the automatic aspect of expert performance. Automaticity in experts' coaching practice is found in their daily routines. These routines are the repetitive activities that seemingly occur with little planning, practice or forethought. Siedentop and Eldar (1989) attribute an expert's automaticity to an ability to discriminate information early and respond quickly.

This is a characteristic that is noticeable in proficient coaches, but even more pronounced among experts. Practice openings, closings, demonstrations, explanations, activities, player movement, equipment distribution and even interactions with athletes are performed with seemingly little effort, but result in remarkable outcomes. Any coach looking to raise their level of expertise should look to the routines they currently use, or consider developing routines that will allow them more time to coach and less time managing or organizing during practice or a game. As has been mentioned previously, the routines used in opening and closing a practice seem particularly key to instructional effectiveness, so it would be wise to begin there.

Attends to the atypical

When discriminating information (i.e. sorting the important from the unimportant cues and events in the coaching environment), experts attend to the atypical in a situation. Carter and colleagues (1988) found that expert teachers assessed events as either typical or atypical, and that the assessment of typicality affected the way experts processed information. If a situation was assessed as typical, the experts let the event unfold. If a situation appeared to be unusual or atypical, experts attempted to make sense of the anomalies. While observing a swim practice, for example, a coach may notice an arm swing rising from the water in an unusual pattern. Once the atypical action is spotted, the expert coach then seeks to discover its cause and take appropriate action.

When tending to the atypical, experts draw upon their extensive and highly organized knowledge to efficiently and economically sift the information to determine their next set of actions. When things are working in a normal pattern, however, they tend not to reflect on what is occurring, but rather simply monitor the process until something seems out of the ordinary.

Problem solving

Experts invest time identifying, defining and analyzing a problem before searching for a solution. They realize that if they don't get the problem right, they have no hope of getting the solution right. Even though experts are sometimes slower than novices in the early stages of problem solving (i.e. absolute time spent on initial problem representation is longer for experts), it seems time well spent as experts still solve problems faster than novices. A study of physics professors and novices expressed this ability clearly when the professors were more accurate in their solving of the problems presented to both groups, although the novices completed the problems first (Chi et al. 1981).

Coaches face similar problems (e.g. player behavior or motivation, effective communication, planning, acquiring equipment, etc.). It is in how they analyze those problems and devise solutions that separate the experts from the less expert. Beginners often guess at a solution, try it, declare "It doesn't work" and move on to another ill-founded solution. Experts take more care in solving problems.

In the beginning of a problem-solving process, experts try to thoroughly understand the nature of the problem by analyzing it qualitatively. During this analysis, experts rely on their extensive knowledge base to construct a mental representation of the problem from which they can infer relations to help define the situation, identify constraints, isolate factors causing the problem, and evaluate and justify possible solutions. In analyzing and representing problems, experts rely more on underlying principles and metaphors rather than using literal and practical categorizations.

Experts spend time gathering all the facts before making decisions. For example, expert coaches will spend significant time considering the problem, attempting to analyze all facets and components of the situation in an effort to link specific occurrences in coaching to the purpose or goals of the player or team. In solving routine problems, experts tend to work "forward" from known facts to the unknown. "Forward" reasoning usually is contrasted with backward reasoning, in which the problem-solver works from a hypothesis regarding the unknown backward to the given facts (Patel and Groen 1991).

An example of backward and forward reasoning might be seen in a coach observing that players are not paying attention to an explanation of a football play. To a beginner, the problem is of not paying attention. He or she sees two possible solutions to this: (1) to punish those athletes not paying attention, or (2) to find a way to make the instruction more interesting (e.g. more enthusiasm, shorter explanations, rewards for paying attention). In contrast, the expert coach would take time to find out why the athletes were not paying attention before attempting a solution. Perhaps talking with the athletes would be the first step, or recalling what outside activities may be interfering with the players' ability to concentrate. It would only be after the exact nature of the problem was fully and thoroughly understood by analyzing all the available information that a solution would be attempted. With the real reason at hand, the expert coach is prepared to solve the problem efficiently and effectively.

Self-monitoring

More than one expert coach has told us, "Just because I know more than most people about coaching this subject, doesn't mean I know everything there is to know." An interesting phenomenon occurs in coaching. Beginners appear to have a great deal more confidence in their knowledge and practices than do experienced coaches. In reality, expert coaches are far better at understanding the limits of their knowledge and skills, are more critical of their work and love what they do to such a degree that they strive to be even better than they are now – regardless of any success or awards they may have received (Schempp et al. 1998b).

A recent study revealed that expert golf coaches closely and extensively monitor the things they do well and the things that they believe they can do better (Schempp et al. in press). The experts identified both goals and actions in their self-monitoring strategies. Specifically, self-monitoring goals included improving communication, adjustments to personal lifestyle, examining perspectives and increasing learning. Self-monitoring actions incorporated seeking help from others, reading, using technology, developing business strategies and adapting teaching practices. Through self-monitoring, these experts were able to identify specific areas for improvement, as well as particular strategies that would lead to achieving their goals of improving their coaching performance.

While beginning coaches may simply be unaware of how little they know, expert coaches are keenly aware of errors they make and can predict which coaching problems will prove most challenging for them. They also insightfully understand why they fail to comprehend certain elements of a problem if something doesn't work as intended. Further, they are acutely aware of the appropriateness or adequacy of the solutions they attempt and the practices they employ in their coaching. By objectively and honestly assessing their shortcomings and knowledge deficiencies, they are better able to analyze the cause of their failures and take corrective action. It is one reason why they are experts. For example, while a beginning coach may give up on a struggling player as a hopeless cause and a competent coach may be satisfied that they tried their best and made at least some progress, regardless of any initial success – or failure – an expert coach will reflect upon the athlete, until he or she discovers ways they might have taught the skill better, and then make a mental note of the discovery for the next time a similar situation arises.

Conclusion

In this chapter, four stages in coaching expertise based on Berliner's (1994) theory were identified: beginner, competent, proficient and expert. The characteristics in each of these stages were also identified. Hopefully, some of the suggestions offered will help those to become the best coach they can possibly be. Not everyone has the ability, desire or opportunity to reach the highest levels of professional practice. But by identifying, formulating and developing the elements of expertise in one's own professional practice, anyone can become more expert. In our opinion, the job of a coach today is extremely challenging. If we can discover ways of helping coaches to become better skilled and more knowledgeable, they will be better able to meet the new challenges that face them in modern sport.

References

Adler, P. and Adler, P. (1985) 'From idealism to pragmatic detachment: The academic performance of college athletes', *Sociology of Education*, 58: 241–250.

Ainsworth, J. and Fox, C. (1989) 'Learning to learn: A cognitive process approach to movement skill acquisition', *Strategies*, 3(1): 20–22.

Alexander, P. (2003) 'The development of expertise: The journey from acclimation to proficiency', *Educational Researcher*, 32(8): 10–14.

Allee, V. (2000) 'Knowledge networks and communities of practice', *Journal of the Organization Development Network*, 32 (4). Available at www.odnetwork.org/odp online/vol32n4/knowledgenets.html. Accessed 13 June 2005.

Alleman, E., Cochran, J., Doverspike, J. and Newman, I. (1984) 'Enriching mentoring relationships', *The Personnel Guidance Journal*, February: 329–333.

Bandura, A. (1977) *Social learning theory*, Englewood Cliffs, NJ: Prentice-Hall.

Bell, M. (1997) 'The development of expertise', *Journal of Physical Education, Recreation and Dance*, 68(2): 34–38.

Beltman, S. (2003) 'Fostering the will to learn: Motivation is socially shaped'. Paper presented at the European Association for Research on Learning and Instruction 10th Biennial Conference, Padova, Italy.

Bentley, T. (1998) *Learning beyond the classroom: Education for a changing world*, London: Routledge.

Bergmann Drewe, S. (2000a) 'An examination of the relationship between coaching and teaching', *Quest*, 52: 79–88.

Bergmann Drewe, S. (2000b) 'Coaches, ethics and autonomy', *Sport, Education and Society*, 5(2): 147–162.

Berliner, D. C. (1988) 'The development of expertise in pedagogy', *Charles Hunt Memorial Lecture*. American Association of Colleges for Teacher Education. New Orleans, LA.

Berliner, D. C. (1994) 'Expertise: The wonder of exemplary performances', in J. Mangieri and C. Block (eds), *Creating powerful thinking in coaches and athletes: Diverse perspectives*, Fort Worth, TX: Harcourt Brace College.

Bian, W. (2003) 'Examination of expert and novice volleyball coaches' diagnostic abilities', unpublished doctoral dissertation, Athens, GA: University of Georgia.

Bishop, K. and Denley, P. (1997) *Effective learning in science*, Stafford: Network Educational Press.

Blase, J. and Anderson, G. (1995) *The micropolitics of educational leadership: From control to empowerment*, London: Cassell.

Blinde, E. M., Taub, D. E. and Han, L. (1993) 'Sport participation and women's personal empowerment: Experiences of the college athlete', *Journal of Sport and Social Issues*, 17: 47–60.

Blinde, E. M., Taub, D. E. and Han, L. (1994) 'Sport as a site for women's group and societal empowerment: Perspectives from the college athlete', *Sociology of Sport Journal*, 11: 51–59.

Bloom, B. (February, 1986) 'Automaticity', *Educational Leadership*, 70–77.

Bloom, G. A., Salmela, J. H. and Schinke, R. J. (1995) 'Expert coaches' views on the training of developing coaches', in R. Vanfraechem-Raway and Y. Vanden Auweels (eds), *Proceedings of the Ninth European Congress on Sport Psychology*, Brussells, Belgium: Free University Press.

Bloom, G. A., Durand-Bush, N., Schinke, R. J. and Salmela, J. H. (1998) 'The importance of mentoring in the development of coaches and athletes', *International Journal of Sport Psychology*, 29: 267–281.

Bourdieu, P. (1977) *Outline of a theory of practice*, London: Cambridge University Press.

Bourdieu, P. and Passeron, J. C. (1990) *Reproduction in education, society and culture*, London: Sage.

Boyle, B., While, D. and Boyle, T. (2004) 'A longitudinal study of teacher change: What makes professional development effective?' *The Curriculum Journal*, 15(1): 45–68.

Bray, J. N., Lee, J., Smith, L. L. and Yorks, L. (2000) *Collaborative inquiry in practice*, Thousand Oaks, CA: Sage.

Broadfoot, P. (2001) 'Liberating the learner through assessment', in J. Collins and D. Cook (eds), *Understanding learning*, London: Paul Chapman in association with the Open University.

Brown, J. S. and Duguid, P. (2000) *The social life of information*, Boston, MA: Harvard Business School Press.

Brown, J. S., Denning, S., Groh, K. and Prusak, L. (2004) *Storytelling in organizations: How narrative and storytelling are transforming 21st century management*, New York: Elsevier.

Bruner, J. (1977) *The process of education*, Cambridge, MA: Harvard University Press.

Bruner, J. (1996) *The culture of education*, Cambridge, MA: Harvard University Press.

Bruner, J. (1999) 'Folk pedagogies', in J. Leach and B. Moon (eds), *Learners and Pedagogy*, London: Paul Chapman.

Brunner, R. and Hill, D. (1992) 'Using learning styles research in coaching', *Journal of Physical Education, Recreation, and Dance*, 63(4): 26–28; 61.

Bryman, A. (1996) 'Leadership in organizations', in S. R. Clegg, C. Hardy and W. Nord (eds), *Handbook of organizational studies*, London: Sage.

Bullock, K. and Wikeley, F. (2004) *Whose learning? The role of the personal tutor*, Maidenhead: Open University Press.

Bunker, D. and Thorpe, R. (1982) 'A model for the teaching of games in secondary schools', *Bulletin of Physical Education*, 18(1): 5–8.

Butler, J. (1997) 'How would Socrates teach games? A constructivist approach', *Journal of Physical Education, Recreation, and Dance*, 68(9): 42–47.

Buysse, V., Sparkman, K. L. and Wesley, W. (2003) 'Communities of practice: Connecting what we know with what we do', *Exceptional Children*, Spring, 69(3): 263–278.

Cain, N. (2004) 'Question time for the coaches: The six men plotting their countries' fortunes on the best and worst of their jobs', *The Sunday Times*, Sport Section (2): 19.

Campbell, S. (1993) 'Coaching education around the world', *Sport Science Review*, 2(2): 62–74.

Campbell, S. and Crisfield, P. (1994) 'Developing and delivering a quality-controlled coach certification programme', in P. Duffy and L. Dugdale (eds), *HPER- Moving toward the 21st century*, Champaign, IL: Human Kinetics.

Canadian Interuniversity Sport (2005) 'Canadian Interuniversity Sport Mission Statement' Available at: www.cisport.ca/e/pol_proc/_40_ eligibility.htm. Accessed 15 June 2005.

Carmin, C. N. (1988) 'Issues on research on mentoring: Definitional and methodological', *International Journal of Mentoring*, 2(2): 9–13.

Carnell, E. (2000) 'Dialogue, discussion and feedback – views of secondary school students on how others help their learning', in S. Askew (ed.), *Feedback for Learning*, London: RoutledgeFalmer.

Carnell, E. and Lodge, C. (2002) *Supporting effective learning*, London: Paul Chapman.

Carr, M. and Claxton, G. (2004) 'Tracking the development of learning dispositions', in H. Daniels and A. Edwards (eds), *Psychology of Education*, London: RoutledgeFalmer.

Carron, A. V. and Dennis, P. (2001) 'The sport team as an effective group', in J. Williams (ed.), *Applied sport psychology: Personal growth to peak performance*, London: Mayfield.

Carron, A. V., Widmeyer, W. N. and Brawley, L. R. (1985) 'The development of an instrument to assess cohesion in sport teams: The group environment questionnaire', *Journal of Sport Psychology*, 7: 244–266.

Carter, K., Cushing, K., Sabers, D., Stein, P. and Berliner, D. (1988) 'Expert–novice differences in perceiving and processing visual classroom stimuli', *Journal of Coach Education*, 39(3): 25–31.

Cassidy, T., Jones, R. L. and Potrac, P. (2004) *Understanding sports coaching: The social, cultural and pedagogical foundations of coaching practice*, New York: Routledge.

Cervero, R. M. (1992) 'Professional practice, learning and continuing education: An integrated perspective', *International Journal of Lifelong Education*, 11(2): 91–101.

Chaiklin, S. (2003) 'The zone of proximal development in Vygotsky's analysis of learning and instruction', in A. Kozulin, B. Gindis, V. Ageyev and S. Miller (eds), *Vygotsky's educational theory in a cultural context*, Cambridge: Cambridge University Press.

Chelladurai, P. (1984) 'Leadership in sports', in J. M. Silva and R. S. Weinberg (eds), *Psychological foundations of sport*, Champaign, IL: Human Kinetics.

Chelladurai, P. (1993) 'Leadership', in R. N. Singer, M. Murphey and L. K. Tennant (eds), *Handbook of research on sport psychology*, New York: Macmillan.

Chelladurai, P. and Kuga, D. J. (1996) 'Teaching and coaching: Group and task differences', *Quest*, 48: 470–485.

Chi, M. T. H., Feltovich, P. and Glaser, R. (1981) 'Categorization and representation of physics problems by experts and novices', *Cognitive Science*, 5: 121–152.

Clark, P. (2000) *Learning schools, learning systems*, London: Continuum.

Cleminson, A. and Bradford, S. (1996) 'Professional education', *Journal of Vocational Education and Training*, 48(3): 249–259.

Clontarf Aboriginal College (2003) Learning for life: Student handbook, 2003, Perth, WA: Clontarf Aboriginal College.

Coakley, J. (1978) Sport in society, St Louis, MO: Mosby.

Coakley, J. (1986) Sport in society: Issues and controversies (3rd edn), St Louis, MO: Mosby.

Collins, D. and Cook, D. (2001) (eds), Understanding learning: Influences and outcomes, London: Paul Chapman.

Corlett, J. (1996) 'The role of sport pedagogy in the preservation of creativity, exploration of human limits and traditional virtue', Quest, 48: 442–450.

Côté, J., Salmela, J., Trudel, P., Baria, A. and Russell, S. (1995) 'The coaching model: A grounded assessment of expert gymnastic coaches' knowledge', Journal of Sport and Exercise Psychology, 17(1): 1–17.

Culver, D. (2004) 'Enriching knowledge: A collaborative approach between sport coaches and a consultant/facilitator', unpublished doctoral dissertation, Ottawa, ON: University of Ottawa.

Culver, D. and Trudel, P. (2005) 'Cultivating coaches' communities of practice: Developing the potential for learning through interactions', in R. L. Jones (ed.), The sports coach as educator, London: Routledge.

Cushion, C. (2001) 'The coaching process in professional youth football: An ethnography of practice', unpublished Ph.D. thesis, Brunel University, UK.

Cushion, C. and Jones, R. L. (2001) 'A systematic observation of professional top-level youth soccer coaches', Journal of Sport Behavior, 24(4): 354–376.

Cushion, C., Armour, K. M. and Jones, R. L. (2003) 'Coach education and continuing professional development: Experience and learning to coach', Quest, 55: 215–230.

Daniels, H. (2001) Vygotsky and pedagogy, London: RoutledgeFalmer.

Davydov, V. and Markova, A. K. (1983) 'A concept of educational activity for school children', Soviet Psychology, 11(2): 50–76.

Day, C. (1999) Developing teachers: The challenge of life long learning, London: Falmer Press.

Deakin Crick, R., Broadfoot, P. and Claxton, G. (2004) 'Developing an effective lifelong learning inventory: THE ELLI Project', Assessment in Education, 11(1): 247–272.

Deci, E. L. and Ryan, R. M. (1985) Intrinsic motivation and self-determination in human behavior, New York: Plenum.

Deci, E. L. and Ryan, R. M. (1991) 'A motivational approach to self: Integration in personality', in R. A. Diensthier (ed.), Nebraska symposium on motivation: Perspectives on motivation (Vol. 38), Lincoln, NE: University of Nebraska.

Deci, E. L. and Ryan, R. M. (eds) (2002) Handbook of self-determination research, Rochester, NY: University of Rochester Press.

Deci, E. L., Eghrari, H., Patrick, B. C. and Leone, D. (1994) 'Facilitating internalization: The self-determination theory perspective', Journal of Personality, 62: 119–142.

DeMarco, G. and McCullick, B. (1997) 'Developing coaching expertise: Learning from the legends', Journal of Physical Education, Recreation and Dance, 68(3): 37–41.

Denning, S. (2001) The springboard: How storytelling ignites action in knowledge-era organizations, Boston, MA: Butterworth-Heinemann.

Department for Culture, Media and Sport (DCMS) (2001) *A sporting future for all: The government's plan for sport*, London: DCMS.

Department for Education and Skills (DfES) (2003) *A new specialist system: Transforming secondary education*, London: DfES.

Department for Education and Skills (DfES) (2004) 'What are Specialist Schools?' Available at: www.standards.dfes.gov.uk/specialistschools/what_are/?version=1; accessed 3 February 2004.

Department for Education and Skills (DfES) (2005) *Five year strategy for children and learners*, London: DfES.

Dewey, J. (1933) *How we think: A restatement of the relation of reflective thinking to the educative process*, Chicago, IL: D. C. Heath.

Dickson, S. (2001) *A preliminary investigation into the effectiveness of the National Coaching Accreditation Scheme*, Canberra: Australian Sports Commission.

Dodds, P. (1994) 'Cognitive and behavioral components of expertise in teaching physical education', *Quest*, 46: 143–163.

Doherty, R. W., Hillberg, R. S., Epaloose, G. and Tharp, R. G. (2002) 'Standards performance continuum: Development and validation of a measure of effective pedagogy', *The Journal of Educational Research*, November–December, 96(2): 78–91.

Doyle, W. (1986) 'Classroom organization and management', in M. C.Wittrock (ed.), *Handbook of research on teaching* (3rd edn), New York: Macmillan.

Dreier, O. (1999) 'Personal trajectories of participation across contexts of social practice', *Outlines*, 1: 5–32.

Duckworth, E. (1997) *Teacher to teacher: Learning from each other*, New York: Teachers College Press.

Duffy, A. and Duffy, T. (2002) 'Psychometric properties of Honey and Mumford's Learning Styles Questionnaire (LSQ)', *Personality and Individual Differences*, 33: 147.

Dunphy, B. and Dunphy, S. (2003) 'Assisted performance and the Zone of Proximal Development: A potential framework for providing surgical education', *Australian Journal of Educational and Developmental Psychology*, 3: 48–58.

Durand-Bush, N. (1996) 'Training: Blood, sweat, and tears', in J. H. Salmela (ed.), *Great job coach! Getting the edge from proven winners*, Ottawa, ON: Potentium.

Dwyer, J. and Fisher, D. (1990) 'Wrestlers perceptions of coaches' leadership as predictors of satisfaction with leadership', *Journal of Perceptual and Motor Skills*, 71: 17–20.

Eckert, P. and McConnell-Ginet, S. (1999) 'New generalizations and explanations in language and gender research', *Language in Society*, 28: 185–201.

Edwards, R. (2001) 'Meeting individual learner needs: Power, subject, subjection', in C. Paechter, M. Preedy, D. Scott and J. Soler (eds), *Knowledge, power and learning*, London: Sage.

Engestrom, R. (2004) 'Studying learning in practice', presentation to ESRC Research Capacity Building Network/British Educational Research Association Master Class, University of Birmingham, October.

Engestrom, Y. (1987) *Learning by expanding*, Helsinki: Orienta-Konsultit Oy.

Engestrom, Y. (2005) 'Non scolae sed vitae discimus: Towards overcoming the encapsulation of school learning', in H. Daniels (ed.), *An introduction to Vygotsky* (2nd edn), Hove: Routledge.

Entwistle, N. (1981) *Styles of learning and teaching*, Chichester: Wiley.

Entwistle, N. and Smith, C. (2002) 'Personal understanding and target understanding: Mapping influences and outcomes of learning', *British Journal of Educational Psychology*, 72: 321–342.

Erchul, W. P. and Raven, B. H. (1997) 'Social power in school consultation: A contemporary view of French and Raven's bases of power model', *Journal of School Psychology*, 35. 137–171.

Ericsson, K. A. and Charness, N. (1994) 'Expert performance: Its structure and acquisition', *American Psychologist*, 49: 725–747.

Ethell, R. (1999, July) 'Enhancing the learning of beginning teachers: Accessing the knowledge-in-action of expert practitioners'. Paper presented at the meeting of the International Study Association on Teachers' and Teaching (ISATT). Dublin, Ireland.

Farrell, T. S. C. (2004) *Reflective practice in action: 80 reflection breaks for busy teachers*, Thousand Oaks, CA: Corwin Press.

Feuerstein, R. (1990) 'The theory of structural cognitive modifiability', in B. Presseisen (ed.), *Learning and thinking styles: Classroom applications*, Washington, DC: National Education Association.

Field, B. and Field, T. (1994) *Teachers as mentors: A practical guide*, London: Falmer Press.

Finch, L. (2002) 'Understanding individual motivation in sport', in J. Silva III and D. Stevens (eds), *Psychological foundations of sport*, Boston, MA: Allyn & Bacon.

Fincher, M. and Schempp, P. (1994) 'Teaching physical education: What do we need to know and how do we find it?' *GAHPERD Journal*, 28(3): 7–10.

Flavell, J. (1977) *Cognitive development*, New York: Prentice Hall.

Fletcher, S. (2000) *Mentoring in schools: A handbook of good practice*, London: Kogan Page.

Fleurance, P. and Cotteaux, V. (1999) 'Construction de l'expertise chez les entraîneurs sportifs d'athlètes de haut-niveau français' ['Development of expertise in elite athletics coaches in France'], *Avante*, 5(2): 54–68.

Flintoff, A. (2003) 'The school sport co-ordinator programme: Changing the role of physical education teachers?', *Sport, Education and Society*, 8(2): 231–250.

Floden, R. (1989) *What teachers need to know about learning*. Proceedings from an NCRTE Seminar for Policy Makers, 24–26 February, USA.

Flutter, J. and Rudduck, J. (2003) *Consulting pupils: What's in it for schools?*, London: Routledge.

Forman, E. A. and Cazden, C. B. (1998) 'Exploring Vygotskian perspectives in education: The cognitive value of peer interaction', in D. Faulkner, K. Littleton and M. Woodhead (eds), *Learning relationships in the classroom*, London: Routledge.

Freire, P. and Macedo, D. P. (1999) 'Pedagogy, culture, language, and race: A dialogue', in J. Leach and B. Moon (eds), *Learners and pedagogy*, London: Paul Chapman.

French Jr, R. P. and Raven, B. (1959) 'The bases of social power', in D. Cartwright (ed.), *Studies in social power*, Ann Arbor, MI: University of Michigan Press.

Fuller, A., Hodkinson, H., Hodkinson, P. and Unwin, L. (2005) 'Learning as peripheral participation in communities of practice: A reassessment of key concepts in workplace learning', *British Educational Research Journal*, 31(1): 49–68.

Furlong, J. and Maynard, T. (1995) *Mentoring student teachers: The growth of professional knowledge*, London: Routledge.

Gable, D. (1999) Coaching wrestling successfully, Champaign, IL: Human Kinetics.

Gagné, M., Ryan, R. M. and Bargmann, K. (2003) 'Autonomy support and need satisfaction in the motivation and well-being of gymnasts', Journal of Applied Sport Psychology, 15: 372–390.

Galipeau, J. and Trudel, P. (2004) 'The experiences of newcomers on a varsity sport team', Applied Research in Coaching and Athletics Annual, 19: 166–188.

Galipeau, J. and Trudel, P. (2005) 'Athlete learning in a community of practice: Is there a role for the coach?', in R. L. Jones (ed.), Sports coach as educator: Reconceptualising sports coaching, London: Routledge.

Gallimore, R. and Tharp, R. (1990) 'Teaching mind in society: Teaching, schooling, and literate discourse', in L. Moll (ed.), Vygotsky and education: Instructional implications and applications of socio-historical psychology, Cambridge: Cambridge University Press.

Galton, M., Hargreaves, L., Comber, C., Wall, D. and Pell, T. (1999) 'Changes in patterns of teacher interaction in primary classrooms: 1976–96', British Educational Research Journal, 25: 23–37.

Garforth, F. W. (1985) Aims and values in education, Hull: Christygate.

Garner, I. (2000) 'Problems and inconsistencies with Kolb's learning styles', Educational Psychology, 20: 341–348.

Gauvin, M. (1998) 'Thinking in niches: Sociocultural influences on cognitive development', in D. Faulkener, K. Littlejohn and M. Woodhead (eds), Learning relationships in the classroom, London: Routledge.

Gervis, M. and Brierly, J. (1999) Effective coaching for children: Understanding the sports process, Marlborough: The Crowood Press.

Gibb, G. A. (1954) 'Leadership', in G. Lindzey (ed.), Handbook of social psychology, vol. 2, Reading, MA: Addison-Wesley.

Giddens, A. (1979) Central problems in social theory: Action, structure and contradiction in social analysis, Berkeley, CA: University of California Press.

Giddens, A. (1986) Sociology: A brief but critical introduction (2nd edn), London: Macmillan.

Gilbert, W. and Trudel, P. (1999a) 'Framing the construction of coaching knowledge in experiential learning theory [18 paragraphs]', Sociology of Sport On-line, 2(1). Available at: http://physed.otago.ac.nz/sosol/v2i1/v2i1.htm. Accessed 10 June 2005.

Gilbert, W. and Trudel, P. (1999b) 'An evaluation strategy for coach education programs', Journal of Sport Behavior, 22(2): 234–248.

Gilbert, W. and Trudel, P. (2001) 'Learning to coach through experience: Reflection in model youth sport coaches', Journal of Teaching in Physical Education, 21: 16–34.

Gilbert, W. and Trudel, P. (2004a) 'Analysis of coaching science published from 1970–2001', Research Quarterly for Exercise and Sport, 75: 388–399.

Gilbert, W. and Trudel, P. (2004b) 'Role of the coach: How model youth team sport coaches frame their roles', The Sport Psychologist, 18: 21–43.

Gilbert, W. and Trudel, P. (2005) 'Learning to coach through experience: Conditions that influence the reflective process', The Physical Educator, 62(1): 32–43.

Gilbert, W. D., Côté, J. and Mallett, C. (2006) 'Developmental paths and activities of successful sport coaches', International Journal of Sports Sciences and Coaching, 1(1), 69–76.

Gilbert, W. D., Gilbert, J. N. and Trudel, P. (2001a) 'Coaching strategies for youth sports. Part 1: Athlete behavior and athlete performance', *Journal of Physical Education, Recreation and Dance*, 72(4): 29–33.

Gilbert, W. D., Gilbert, J. N. and Trudel, P. (2001b) 'Coaching strategies for youth sports. Part 2: Personal characteristics, parental influence, and team organization', *Journal of Physical Education, Recreation and Dance*, 72(5): 41–46.

Gilbert, W. D., Trudel, P. and Haughian, L. (1999) 'Decision making process of ice hockey coaches during games', *Journal of Teaching in Physical Education*, 18: 290–312.

Giovanelli, M. (2003) 'Relationship between reflective disposition toward teaching and effective teaching', *The Journal of Educational Research*, 96(5): 293–311.

Gipps, C. and MacGilchrist, B. (1999) 'Primary school learners', in P. Mortimore (ed.), *Understanding pedagogy and its impact on learning*, London: Paul Chapman.

Gipps, C., McCallum, B. and Brown, M. (1999) 'Primary teachers' beliefs about learning', *The Curriculum Journal*, 10: 123–134.

Gould, D., Gianinni, J., Krane, V. and Hodge, K. (1990) 'Educational needs of elite U.S. national Pan American and Olympic coaches', *Journal of Teaching in Physical Education*, 9: 322–344.

Greenfield, P. (1984) 'A theory of teacher in the learning activities of everyday life', in B. Rogoff and J. Lave (eds), *Everyday cognition: Its development in a social context*, Cambridge, MA: Harvard University Press.

Gronn, P. (2000) 'Distributed properties: A new architecture of leadership', *Educational Management and Leadership*, 28(3): 317–338.

Han, E. P. (1995) 'Reflection is essential in teacher education', *Childhood Education*, 71: 221–230.

Hansman, C. A. (2001) 'Mentoring as professional education', *Adult Learning*, 12(1): 7–9.

Hargreaves, A. (1994) *Changing teachers, changing times: Teachers' work and culture in the post-modern age*, London: Cassell.

Hargreaves, D. (2003) *Education epidemic: Transforming secondary schools through innovative networks*, London: Demos.

Hatton, N. and Smith, D. (1995) 'Reflection in teacher education: Towards definition and implementation', *Teaching and Teacher Education*, 11(1): 33–49.

Hedegaard, M. (1996) 'The zone of proximal development as basis for instruction', in H. Daniels (ed.), *An introduction to Vygotsky*, London: Routledge.

Heffler, B. (2001) 'Individual learning style and the learning style inventory', *Educational Studies*, 27: 307–316.

Henning, P. H. (1998) 'Ways of learning: An ethnographic study of the work and situated learning of a group of refrigeration service technicians', *Journal of Contemporary Ethnography*, 27: 85–136.

Henson, R. K. and Hwang, D. (2002) 'Variability and prediction of measurement error in Kolb's learning style inventory scores: A reliability generalization study', *Educational and Psychological Measurement*, 62: 712.

Heylings, D. J. A. and Tariq, V. N. (2001) 'Reflection and feedback on learning', *Assessment and Evaluation in Higher Education*, 26: 153–164.

Hinett, K. (n. d.-a) *Improving learning through reflection–part two*. Available at: www.heacademy.ac.uk/embedded_object.asp?id=21764&file. Accessed 17 June 2005.

Hinett, K. (n. d.-b) Improving learning through reflection–part one. Available at: www. heacademy.ac.uk/embedded_object.asp?id=21694&file. Accessed 17 June 2005.

Hodges, N. J. and Franks, I. M. (2002) 'Modelling coaching practice: The role of instruction and demonstration', Journal of Sport Sciences, 20: 793–811.

Hodgkinson, P. (2005) 'Learning as cultural and relational: Moving past some troubling dualisms', Cambridge Journal of Education, 35(1): 107–119.

Hollembeak, J. and Amorose, A. J. (2005) 'Perceived coaching behaviors and college athletes' intrinsic motivation: A test of self-determination theory', Journal of Applied Sport Psychology, 17: 20–36.

Horn, T., Lox, C. and Labrador, F. (2001) 'The self-fulfilling prophecy theory: When coaches' expectations become reality', in J. Williams (ed.), Applied sport psychology: Personal growth to peak performance, London: Mayfield.

Housner, L. D. and Griffey, D. (1985) 'Coach cognition: Differences in planning and interactive decision making between experienced and inexperienced coaches', Research Quarterly for Exercise & Sport, 56: 44–53.

Hoyle, E. (1986) The politics of school management, London: Hodder & Stoughton.

Huling-Austin, L. (1990) 'Teacher induction programs and internships', in W. R. Houston (ed.), Handbook on Research on Teacher Education, New York: Macmillan Publishing.

Hung, D. (2002) 'Forging links between communities of practice and schools through online learning communities: Implications for appropriating and negotiating knowledge', International Journal on E-Learning, 1(2): 23–34.

Irwin, G., Hanton, S. and Kerwin, D. (2004) 'Reflective practice and the origins of elite coaching knowledge', Reflective Practice, 5: 425–442.

Ixer, G. (1999) 'There's no such thing as reflection', British Journal of Social Workers, 29: 513–527.

Jarvis, P., Holford, J. and Griffin, C. (1998) The theory and practice of learning, London: Kogan Page.

Johansson, T. and Kroksmark, T. (2004) 'Teachers' intuition-in-action: How teachers experience action', Reflective Practice, 5: 357–381.

Johnson, R. (1997) 'Questioning techniques to use in teaching', Journal of Physical Education, Recreation and Dance, 66(6): 44–48.

Jones, R. L. (2000) 'Toward a sociology of coaching', in R. L. Jones and K. M. Armour (eds), The sociology of sport: Theory and practice, London: Addison Wesley Longman.

Jones, R. L. (2001) 'Applying empowerment in coaching: Some considerations', in L. Kidman (ed.), Developing decision makers: An empowerment approach to coaching, Christchurch, NA: Innovative.

Jones, R. L. (2004) 'An educational endeavour: Coaching redefined'. Paper presented as part of a symposium, Exploring educational relationships at the British Education Research Association (BERA) Conference, 15–17 September, Manchester, UK.

Jones, R. L. and Wallace, M. (2005) 'Another bad day at the training ground: Coping with ambiguity in the coaching context', Sport, Education and Society, 10(1): 119–134.

Jones, R. L., Armour, K. M. and Potrac, P. (2002) 'Understanding the coaching process: A framework for social analysis', Quest, 54(1): 34–48.

Jones, R. L., Armour, K. M. and Potrac, P. (2003) 'Constructing expert knowledge: A case study of a top-level professional soccer coach', Sport, Education, and Society, 8: 213–229.

Jones, R. L., Armour, K. M. and Potrac, P. (2004) *Sports coaching cultures: From practice to theory*, London: Routledge.

Jones, R. L., Potrac, P. and Ramalli, K. (1999) 'Where sport meets physical education: A systematic observation of role conflict', *International Journal of Physical Education*, 36: 7–14.

Jowett, S. and Cockerill, M. (2003) 'Olympic medallists' perspectives of the athlete–coach relationship', *Psychology of Sport and Exercise*, 4: 313–331.

Kahan, S. (2003) Interview with John Seely Brown., in S. Denning (ed.). Available at: www.sethkahan.com/Resources_0JohnSeelyBrown.html. Accessed 2 February 2003.

Kaye, B. and Jacobson, B. (1996) 'Re-framing mentoring', *Training and Development*, 51(8): 50–54.

Kerka, S. (1997) *Constructivism, workplace learning and vocational education. ERIC Digest No. 181*. Columbus: ERIC Clearing house on Adult, Career, and Vocational Education (ED-407–573).

Kerka, S. (1998) *New perspectives on mentoring. ERIC Digest No. 194*. Columbus: ERIC Clearing house on Adult, Career, and Vocational Education (ED-99-CO-0013).

Kidman, L. (2001) *Developing decision makers: An empowerment approach to coaching*, Christchurch, NZ: Innovative Print Communications.

Kidman, L. (2005) (ed.) *Athlete-centred coaching: Developing inspired and inspiring people*, Christchurch, NZ: Innovative Print Communications.

Klein, P. D. (2003) 'Rethinking the multiplicity of cognitive resources and curricular representations: Alternatives to "learning styles" and "multiple intelligences"', *Journal of Curriculum Studies*, 35: 45–81.

Kolb, D. (1984) *Experiential learning: Experience as the source of learning and development*, Englewood Cliffs, NJ: Prentice-Hall.

Kozulin, A. (2003) 'Psychological tools and mediated learning', in A. Kozulin, B. Gindis, V. S. Ageyev, S. M. Miller (eds), *Vygotsky's educational theory in cultural context*, Cambridge: Cambridge University Press.

Kozulin, A., Gindis, B., Ageyev, V. and Miller, S. (2003) *Vygotsky's educational theory in a cultural context*, Cambridge: Cambridge University Press.

Krane, V., Greenleaf, C. A. and Snow, J. (1997) 'Reaching for gold and the practice of glory: A motivational case study of an elite gymnast', *The Sport Psychologist*, 11: 53–71.

Kruse, S. D. (1997) 'Reflective activity in practice: Vignettes of teachers' deliberate work', *Journal of Research and Development in Education*, 31(1): 46–60.

Kupfer, J. (1987) 'Privacy, autonomy, and self-concept', *American Philosophical Quarterly*, 24: 81–89.

Lave, J. and Wenger, E. (1991) *Situated learning: Legitimate peripheral participation*, Cambridge: Cambridge University Press.

Lave, J. and Wenger, E. (1996) 'Practice, person, social world', in H. Daniels (ed.), *An introduction to Vygotsky*, London: Routledge.

Lave, J. and Wenger, E. (1998) 'Legitimate peripheral participation in communities of practice', in R. McCormick and C. Paechter (eds), *Learning and knowledge*, London: Paul Chapman.

Lawson, H. A. (1993) 'Dominant discourses, problem setting, and teacher education pedagogies: A critique', *Journal of Teaching in Physical Education*, 10(1): 1–20.

Leach, J. and Moon, B. (1999) 'Recreating pedagogy', in J. Leach and B. Moon (eds), *Learners and pedagogy*, London: Paul Chapman.

Leas, R. R. and Chi, T. H. M. (1993) 'Analyzing diagnostic expertise of competitive swimming coaches', in J. L. Starkes and F. Allard (ed.), *Cognitive issues in motor expertise*, New York: Elsevier Science.

Lee, M. (1988) 'Values and responsibilities in children's sport', *Physical Education Review*, 11: 19–27.

Leinhardt, G. and Greeno, J. (1986) 'The cognitive skill of coaching', *Journal of Educational Psychology*, 78: 75–95.

Lemert, C. (1997) *Social things: An introduction to the sociological life*, New York: Rowman & Littlefield.

Lemyre, F. and Trudel, P. (2004) 'Le parcours d'apprentissage au rôle d'entraîneur bénévole' ['The learning path of volunteer coaches'] *Avante*, 10: 40–55.

Light, R. (2004) 'Coaches' experiences of Game Sense: Opportunities and challenges', *Physical Education and Sport Pedagogy*, 9(2): 115–132.

Lindgren, E. C., Patriksson, G. and Fridlund, B. (2002) 'Empowering young female athletes through a self-strengthening programme: A qualitative analysis', *European Physical Education Review*, 8: 230–248.

Loughran, J. J. (2002) 'Effective reflective practice: in search of meaning in learning and teaching', *Journal of Teacher Education*, 53(1): 33–44.

Loughran, J. and Gunstone, R. (1997) 'Professional development in residence: Developing reflection on science teaching and learning', *Journal of Education for Teaching*, 23(2): 159–178.

Lyle, J. (1999) 'The coaching process: An overview', in N. Cross and J. Lyle (eds), *The coaching process: Principles and practice for sport*, Oxford: Butterworth-Heinemann.

Lyle, J. (2002) *Sports coaching concepts: A framework for coaches' behaviour*, London: Routledge.

Lyons, C. (1999) 'Emotions, cognition, and becoming a reader: A message to teachers of struggling learners', *Literacy Teaching and Learning*, 4(1): 67–87.

McConnell, R. (2000) *The successful coach: A practical guide to beginners and experts*, Auckland, NZ: HarperCollins.

McCullick, B. A., Cumings, R. L. and Schempp, P. G. (1999) 'The professional orientations of expert golf instructors', *International Journal of Physical Education*, 36: 15–24.

McDermott, R. (1999, Fall) 'Nurturing three dimensional communities of practice: How to get the most out of human networks', *Knowledge Management Review*. Available at: www.co-i-l.com/coil/knowledge-garden/cop/dimensional.shtml. Accessed 12 October 2001.

McLaughlin, M. W. and Talbert, J. E. (1993) *Contexts that matter for teaching and learning: Strategic opportunities for meeting the nation's education goals*, Stanford, CA: Center for Research on the Context of Secondary School Teaching, Stanford University.

Mageau, G. A. and Vallerand, R. J. (2003) 'The coach-athlete relationship: A motivational model', *Journal of Sports Sciences*, 21: 883–904.

Mainemelis, C., Boyatzis, R. E. and Kolb, D. A. (2002) 'Learning styles and adaptive flexibility: Testing experiential learning theory', *Management Learning*, 33: 5–33.

March, J. and Olsen, P. (1976) *Ambiguity and choice in organisations*, Bergen: Universitetsforlaget.

March, J. and Simon, H. (1958) *Organizations*, New York: Wiley.

Martens, R. (1979) 'From smocks to jocks: A new adventure for sport psychologists', in P. Klavora and J. Starkes (eds), *Coach, athlete and the sport psychologist*, Toronto: University of Toronto.

Martens, R. (1987) 'Science, knowledge and sport psychology', *The Sport Psychologist*, 1: 29–55.

Martens, R. (1997) (2nd edn) *Successful coaching*, Champaign, IL: Human Kinetics.

Marton, F. and Säljö, R. (1976) 'On qualitataive differences in learning: Outcome and process', *British Journal of Educational Psychology*, 46(1), 4–11.

Marton, F. and Säljö, R. (1984) 'Approaches to learning', in F. Marton, D. Hounsell and N. Entwistle (eds), *The experience of learning*, Edinburgh: Scottish Academic Press.

May, T. (1994) 'The concept of autonomy', *American Philosophical Quarterly*, 31: 133–144.

Mead, G. H. (1934) *Mind, self and society*, Chicago, IL: University of Chicago Press.

Mercer, N. (2000) *Words and minds: How we use language to think together*, London: Routledge.

Mercer, N., Wegerif, R. and Dawes, L. (1999) 'Children's talk and the development of reasoning in the classroom', *British Educational Research Journal*, 25: 95–111.

Merriam, S. (1983) 'Mentors and protégés: A critical review of the literature', *Adult Education Quarterly*, 33: 161–173.

Metzler, M. (2000) *Instructional methods for physical education*, Boston, MA: Allyn & Bacon.

Meyer, B. (1990) 'The academic performance of female collegiate athletes', *Sociology of Sport Journal*, 7: 44–57.

Meyer, J. H. F. and Land, R. (2003) 'Threshold concepts and troublesome knowledge (1): Linkages to ways of thinking and practicing within the disciplines', *Improving students learning: Ten years on*, Oxford: OCSLD.

Miller, A. W. (1992) 'Systematic observation behaviour similarities of various youth sport soccer coaches', *Physical Educator*, 49: 136–143.

Miller, P. S. and Kerr, G. (2002) 'The athletic, academic, and social experiences of intercollegiate student-athletes', *Journal of Sport Behavior*, 25: 346–367.

Mills, B. D. and Dunlevy, S. M. (1997) 'Coaching certification: What's out there and what needs to be done?', *International Journal of Physical Education: A Review Publication*, 34(1): 17–26.

Moll, L. (1990) *Vygotsky and education: Instructional implications and applications of socio-historical psychology*, Cambridge: Cambridge University Press.

Moon, J. A. (1999) *Reflection in learning and professional development: Theory and practice*, London: Kogan Page.

Moon, J. A. (2004) *A handbook of reflective and experiential learning: Theory and practice*, London: RoutledgeFalmer.

Murrell, P. and Claxton, C. (1987) 'Experiential learning theory as a guide for effective teaching', *Journal of the Association for Counsellor Education and Supervision*, 27: 4–14.

Napper-Owen, G. and Phillips, D. (1995) 'A quality analysis of the impact of induction assistance on first year physical educators', *Journal of Teaching in Physical Education*, 14(3): 305–327.

National Coaching Certification Program (n.d.) 'National Coaching Certification Program: Program overview'. Available at: www.coach.ca/e/nccp/. Accessed 21 March 2005.

Neck, C. P. and Manz, C. C. (1994) 'From groupthink to teamthink: Toward the creation of constructive thought patterns in self-managing teams', *Human Relations*, 47: 929–952.

Nelson, B. (2005) 'Underpinning prosperity: Our agenda in education, science and training', Speech at the *Sustaining Prosperity* Conference, University of Melbourne, 31 March 2005.

Nias, J., Southworth, G. and Yeomans, R. (1989) *Staff relationships in the primary school: A study of organizational cultures*, London: Cassell.

Nichani, M. and Hung, D. (2002) 'Can a community of practice exist online?', *Educational Technology*, July–August: 49–54.

Ogawa, R., Crowson, R. and Goldring, E. (1999) 'Enduring dilemmas of school organisation', in J. Murphy and K. S. Louis (eds), *Handbook of research on educational administration*, San Francisco, CA: Jossey-Bass.

Osterman, K. F. (1990) 'Reflective practice: A new agenda for education', *Education and Urban Society*, 22(2): 133–152.

Palinscar, A. S., Magnusson, S. J., Marano, N., Ford, D. and Brown, N. (1998) 'Designing a community of practice: Principles and practices of the GisML community', *Teaching and Teacher Education*, 14: 5–19.

Parsloe, E. and Wray, M. (2000) *Coaching and mentoring: Practical methods to improve learning*, London: Kogan Page.

Paskevich, D. M., Estabrooks, P. A., Brawley, L. R. and Carron, A. V. (2000) 'Group cohesion in sport and exercise', in R. Singer, H. Hausenblas and C. Janelle (eds), *Handbook of sport psychology*, New York: John Wiley.

Patel, V. L. and Groen, G. J. (1991) 'The general and specific nature of medical expertise: A critical look', in K. A. Ericsson and J. Smith (eds), *Toward a general theory of expertise*, Cambridge: Cambridge University Press.

Penney, D. and Clarke, G. (2005) 'Inclusion in sport education', in D. Penney, G. Clarke, M. Quill and G. Kinchin (eds), *Sport education in physical education: Research based practice*, London: Routledge.

Penney, D. and Houlihan, B. (2001) 'Specialist sports colleges: A special case for policy research'. Paper presented at the *British Educational Research Association Conference*, University of Leeds, September 2001.

Penney, D., Taggart, A. and Gorman, S. (2004) 'Extending "at risk" students' participation in school life: A case study of progress within a Specialist Sports School'. *Report of the SPINED Clontarf Aboriginal College and Clontarf Football Academy Case Study Project*, Perth, WA: SPARC, Edith Cowan University.

Perkins, D. (1999) 'The many faces of constructivism', *Educational Leadership*, 57(3): 6–11.

Pitter, R. (1990) 'Power and control in amateur organisations', *International Review for the Sociology of Sport*, 25: 309–320.

Placek, J. (1983) 'Conceptions of success in teaching: Busy, happy and good?', in T. Templin and J. Olson (eds), *Teaching in physical education*, Champaign, IL: Human Kinetics Publishers.

Poczwardowski, A., Barott, J. and Henschen, K. (2002) 'The athlete and coach: Their relationship and its meaning, results of an interpretive study', *International Journal of Sport Psychology*, 33(1): 116–140.

Potrac, P. (2000) 'A comparative study of elite football coaches in England and Norway', unpublished Ph.D. dissertation, Brunel University, UK.

Potrac, P., Jones, R. L. and Armour, K. M. (2002) '"It's all about getting respect": The coaching behaviours of an expert English soccer coach', *Sport, Education and Society*, 7(2): 183–2002.

Potrac, P., Brewer, C., Jones, R. L., Armour, K. and Hoff, J. (2000) 'Towards an holistic understanding of the coaching process', *Quest*, 52(2): 186–199.

Prain, V. and Hickey, C. (1995) 'Using discourse analysis to change physical education', *Quest*, 47: 76–90.

Qualifications and Curriculum Authority (2005) 'What do teachers and coaches need to do to achieve high quality school sport?' Available at: www.qca.org.uk/pess/468.htm. Accessed 2 November 2005.

Quicke, J. (1999) *A curriculum for life: Schools for a democratic learning society*, Buckingham: Open University Press.

Rayner, S. and Riding, R. (1996) 'Cognitive style and school refusal', *Educational Psychology*, 16: 445–451.

Reiman, A. (1999) 'The evolution of the social role-taking and guided reflection framework in teacher education: Recent theory and quantitative synthesis of research', *Teaching and Teacher Education*, 15: 597–612.

Renshaw, P. (2003) 'Community learning: Contradictions, dilemmas and prospects', *Discourse: Studies in the Cultural Politics of Education*, 24: 355–370.

Riding, R. and Rayner, S. (1998) *Cognitive styles and learning strategies: Understanding style differences in learning and behaviour*, London: Fulton Publishers.

Rink, J. E., French, K. E. and Tjeerdsma, B. L. (1996) 'Foundations for the learning of instruction of sport and games', *Journal of Teaching in Physical Education*, 15: 399–417.

Rogoff, B. (1990) *Apprenticeship in thinking*, Oxford: University Press.

Rogoff, B. (1995) 'Observing sociocultural activity on three planes', in J. Wertch, P. Del Rio and A. Alvarez (eds), *Sociocultural studies of mind*, New York: Cambridge University Press.

Rossi, T. and Cassidy, T. (1999) 'Knowledgeable teachers in physical education: A view of teachers' knowledge', in E. A. Hardy and M. Mawer (eds), *Learning and teaching in physical education*, London: Falmer Press.

Rovegno, I. and Kirk, D. (1995) 'Articulations and silences in socially critical work on physical education: Toward a broader agenda', *Quest*, 47: 447–474.

Ryan, R. M. (1993) 'Agency and organization: Intrinsic motivation, autonomy and the self in psychological development', in J. Jacobs (ed.), *Nebraska symposium on motivation: Developmental perspectives on motivation* (vol. 40), Lincoln, NE: University of Nebraska Press.

Ryan, R. M. and Deci, E. L. (2002) 'An overview of self-determination theory', in E. L. Deci and R. M. Ryan (eds), *Handbook of self-determination research*, Rochester, NY: University of Rochester Press.

Sadler-Smith, E. (2001) 'A reply to Reynold's critique of learning style', *Management Learning*, 32: 291–304.

Sage, G. H. (1989) 'Becoming a high school coach: From playing sport to coaching', *Research Quarterly for Exercise & Sport*, 60(1): 81–92.

Salmela, J. H. (1995) 'Learning from the development of expert coaches', *Coaching and Sport Science Journal*, 2(2): 3–13.

Salmela, J. H. and Moraes, L. C. (2003) 'Developing expertise, the role of coaching, families, and cultural contexts', in J. L. Starkes and K. Anders Ericsson (eds), *Expert performance in sports: Advances in research in sport expertise*, Champaign, IL: Human Kinetics.

Salmela, J. H., Draper, S. and Laplante, D. (1993) 'Development of expert coaches of team sports'. Paper presented at the 8th ISSP Congress in Sport Psychology, Lisbon, Portugal.

Sandford, D. (2002) 'Why is football management dangerous?', *BBC News*. Available at: http://news.bbc.co.uk/1/hi/health/1600557.stm.

Saury, J. and Durand, M. (1998) 'Practical knowledge in expert coaches: On-site study of coaching in sailing', *Research Quarterly for Exercise and Sport*, 69(3): 254–266.

Savater, F. (1997) *El Valor de Educar*, Barcelona: Ariel.

Schempp, P. G. (1998) 'The dynamics of human diversity in sport pedagogy scholarship', *Sociology of Sport Online*, 1(1) Available at: http://physed.otago.ac.nz/sosol/v1i1/v1i1.htm

Schempp, P. G., Templeton, C. and Clark, E. (1999) 'The knowledge acquisition of expert golf instructors', in M. R. Farrally and A. J. Cochran (eds), *Science and Golf III: Proceedings of the World Scientific Congress of Golf*, Champaign, IL: Human Kinetics.

Schempp, P. G., Manross, D., Tan, S. and Fincher, M. (1998a) 'Subject expertise and teachers' knowledge', *Journal of Teaching Physical Education*, 17(3): 342–356.

Schempp, P. G., Tan, S., Manross, D. and Fincher, M. (1998b) 'Differences in novice and competent coaches' knowledge', *Teachers and Teaching: Theory and Practice*, 4(1): 9–20.

Schempp, P. G., Webster, C., McCullick, B., Busch, C. and Mason, I. (in press) 'How the best get better: An analysis of the self-monitoring strategies used by expert golf instructors', *Sport, Education & Society*.

Schön, D. A. (1983) *The reflective practitioner: How professionals think in action*, New York: Basic Books.

Schön, D. A. (1987) *Educating the reflective practitioner: Toward a new design for teaching and learning in the professions*, San Francisco, CA: Jossey-Bass.

Schön, D. A. (ed.) (1991) *The reflective turn: Case studies in and on educational practice*, New York: Teachers College.

Schön, D. A. (1995 November/December) 'The new scholarship requires a new epistemology', *Change*, 27–34.

Seaborn, P., Trudel, P. and Gilbert, W. (1998) 'Instructional content provided to female ice hockey players during games', *Applied Research in Coaching and Athletics Annual*, 13: 119–141.

Senge, P. (1990) *The fifth discipline: The art and practice of the learning organization*, London: Century Business.

Sergiovanni, T. (1996) *Moral leadership: Getting to the heart of school improvement*, San Francisco, CA: Jossey-Bass.

Sfard, A. (1998) 'On two metaphors for learning and the dangers of choosing just one', *Educational Researcher*, 27: 4–13.

Sheldon, K. M., Williams, G. C. and Joiner, T. (2003) *Self-determination theory in the clinic: Motivating physical and mental health*, New Haven, CT: Yale University Press.

Shulman, L. S. (1999) 'Knowledge and teaching: Foundations of the new reform', in J. Leach and B. Moon (eds), *Learners and pedagogy*, London: Paul Chapman.

Siedentop, D. (1994) *Sport education: Quality PE through positive sport experiences*, Champaign, IL: Human Kinetics.

Siedentop, D. and Eldar, E. (1989) 'Expertise, experience and effectiveness', *Journal of Teaching Physical Education*, 8(3): 254–260.

Siraj-Blatchford, I. (1999) 'Early childhood pedagogy: Practice, principles and research', in P. Mortimore (ed.), *Understanding pedagogy and its implication on learning*, London: Paul Chapman Publishing.

Sloboda, J. (2001) 'What is skill and how is it acquired?', in C. Paechter, M. Preedy, D. Scott and J. Soler (eds), *Knowledge, power and learning*, London: Sage.

Smith, D. (1999) *A coach's life: My 40 years in college basketball*, New York: Random House.

Smith, S. (1991) 'Where is the child in physical education research?', *Quest*, 43: 37–54.

Snow, C. (2001) 'Knowing what we know: Children, teachers, researchers', *Educational Researcher*, 30(7): 3–9.

Sports Coach UK (2002) National standards for higher level coaches. Project Information Bulletin, 1, April.

Sports Coach UK (2004) New research reveals 1.2 million people coaching in the UK. Press release, September.

Staffo, D. (1992) 'Clarifying physical education teacher-coach responsibilities: A self-analysis guide for those in dual roles', *The Physical Educator*, 49: 52–56.

Starkes, J. L. and Ericsson, K. A. (2003) *Expert performance in sports: Advances in research on sport expertise*, Champaign, IL: Human Kinetics.

Stones, R. (1998) 'Introduction: Society as a collection of free-floating individuals', in R. Stones (ed.), *Key sociological thinkers*, London: Macmillan.

Swailes, S. and Senior, B. (1999) 'The dimensionality of honey and Mumford's Learning Styles Questionnaire', *International Journal of Selection and Assessment*, 7: 1–11.

Tan, S. (1997) 'The elements of expertise', *Journal of Physical Education, Recreation, and Dance*, 68(2): 30–33.

Tangaere, A. (1997) 'Mäori human development learning theory', in P. Te Whäiti, M. McCarthy and A. Durie (eds), *Mai I Rangiätea. Mäori Wellbeing and Development*, Auckland: Auckland University Press.

Tauber, R. T. (1985) 'French and Raven's power bases: An appropriate focus for educational researcher and practitioners'. Paper presented at the Educational Research Association Craft Knowledge seminar, 12 April, Stirling, Scotland.

Teachernet (2005) Schools Competition Developments: Bulletin 2, July 2005. Available at: www.teachernet.gov.uk/_doc/8773/Competition%20Managers%20 Bulletin%202.doc. Accessed 2 November 2005.

Tharp, R. G. and Gallimore, R. (1988) *Rousing minds to life: Teaching learning, and schooling in social context*. New York: Cambridge University Press.

Tharp, R. G. and Gallimore, R. (1991) 'Theories of teaching as assisted performance', in P. Light, P. Sheldon and M. Woodhead (eds), *Learning to think*, London: Routledge.

The International Council for Coach Education (n. d.) *About the ICCE*. Available at: www.icce.ws/about/index.htm. Accessed 1 June 2005.

Thorpe, R. (1997) *Game Sense: Developing thinking players* (video recording), Belconnen, ACT: Australian Sports Commission.

Thorpe, R., Bunker, D. and Almond, L. (eds) (1986) *Rethinking games teaching*, Department of PE and Sports Science, University of Loughborough.

Tinning, R. (1988) 'Student teaching and the pedagogy of necessity', *Journal of Teaching in Physical Education*, 7(2): 82–89.

Tinning, R. (1997) 'Performance and participation discourses in human movement: Toward a socially critical physical education', in J. M. Fernandez-Balboa (ed.), *Critical postmodernism in human movement, physical education, and sport*, Albany, NY: State University of New York.

Tinning, R., Kirk, D. and Evans, J. (1993) *Learning to teach physical education*, London: Prentice Hall.

Toole, J.C. and Seashore Louis, K. (2002) 'The role of professional learning communities in international education', in K. Leithwood and P. Hallinger (eds), *Second international handbook of educational leadership and administration*, London: Kluwer Publishers.

Trudel, P. (1987) 'Validation d'une stratégie de formation pour des entraîneurs bénévoles au hockey mineur [Validation of a strategy for training volunteer minor hockey coaches]', Doctoral dissertation, Université Laval, Québec, Canada.

Trudel, P. and Gilbert, W. (1995) 'Research on coaches' behaviors: Looking beyond the refereed journals', *Avante*, 2: 94–106.

Trudel, P. and Gilbert, W. (2004) 'Communities of practice as an approach to foster ice hockey coach development', in D. J. Pearsall and A. B. Ashare (eds), *Safety in ice hockey: Fourth volume*, ASTM STP 1446, West Conshohoken, PA: ASTM International.

Trudel, P., Côté, J. and Bernard, D. (1996) 'Systematic observation of youth ice hockey coaches during games', *Journal of Sport Behavior*, 19: 50–66.

Trudel, P., Bernard, D., Boileau, R. and Marcotte, G. (2000) 'Effects of an intervention strategy on body checking, penalties, and injuries in ice hockey', in A. B. Ashare (ed.) *Safety in ice hockey: Third volume*, West Conshohocken, PA, ASTM.

Van Manen, M. (1991) 'Reflectivity and the pedagogical moment: The normativity of pedagogical thinking and acting', *Journal of Curriculum Studies*, 23: 507–536.

Vygotsky, L. S. (1978) *Mind and society*, Cambridge MA: MIT Press.

Vygotsky, L. S. (1981) 'The genesis of higher mental functions', in J. V. Wertch (ed.), *The concept of activity in Soviet psychology*, Armonk, NY: Sharpe.

Vygotsky, L. S. (1987) *The collected works of L.S. Vygotsky. Vol. 1: The problems of general psychology*, including the volume *Thinking and Speech*, in R. W. Rieber and A. S. Carton (eds), N. Minick (trans.), New York: Plenum Press.

Waddock, S. A. (1999) 'Paradigm shift: Toward a community-university-community community of practice', *International Journal of Organizational Analysis*, 7: 244–302.

Wallace, M. (1996) 'A crisis of identity: School merger and cultural transition', *British Educational Research Journal*, 22(4): 459–472.

Wallace, M. (2001) 'Sharing leadership of schools through teamwork: A justifiable risk?', *Educational Management and Administration*, 29(2): 153–167.

Wallace, M. (2003) 'Managing the unmanageable? Coping with complex educational change', (Inaugural professorial lecture, University of Bath) *Educational Management and Administration*, 31: 9–29.

Wallace, M. and Hall, V. (1994) *Inside the SMT: Teamwork in secondary school management*, London: Paul Chapman.

Wallace, M. and Pocklington, K. (2002) *Managing complex educational change: Large scale reorganisation of schools*, London: Routledge.

Wells, G. (1999) *Dialogic inquiry: Towards a sociocultural practice and theory of education*, Cambridge: Cambridge University Press.

Wenger, E. (1998) *Communities of practice: Learning, meaning, and identity*, Cambridge University Press.

Wenger, E. (2000) 'Communities of practice and social learning systems', *Organization*, 7: 225–246.

Wenger, E., McDermott, R. and Snyder, W. M. (2002) *Cultivating communities of practice: A guide to managing knowledge*, Boston, MA: Harvard Business School Press.

Werstch, J. (1991) *Voices of the mind*, Cambridge, MA: Harvard University Press.

White, R. T. (1988) *Learning Science*, London: Blackwell.

Wilcox, S. and Trudel, P. (1998) 'Constructing the coaching principles and beliefs of a youth ice hockey coach', *Avante*, 4(3): 39–67.

Wink, J. and Putney, L. (2002) *A vision of Vygotsky*, London: Allyn & Bacon.

Wolff, R. P. (1970) *In defense of anarchism*, New York: Harper Row.

Wood, D. (1998) *How children think and learn* (2nd edn), Oxford: Blackwell.

Wood, E. J., Bruner, J. S. and Ross, G. (1976) 'The role of tutoring in problem solving', *Journal of Child Psychology and Psychiatry*, 17: 89–100.

Wooden, J. (2004) *They call me coach*, Chicago, IL: Contemporary Books.

Wooden, J. and Jamison, S. (1997) *Wooden: A lifetime of observations and reflections on and off the court*, Chicago, IL: Contemporary Books.

Woodman, L. (1993) 'Coaching: A science, an art, an emerging profession', *Sport Science Review*, 2: 1–13.

Woorons, S. (2001) 'An analysis of expert and novice tennis instructors' perceptual capacities', unpublished doctoral dissertation, Athens, GA: University of Georgia.

Wright, S. C. (1997) 'Induction issues for physical educators in Singapore'. Paper presented at the AIESEP Singapore World Conference, Republic of Singapore.

Wright, S. C. and Smith, D. E. (2000) 'A case for formalised mentoring', *Quest*, 52(2): 200–213.

Wright, T., Trudel, P. and Culver, D. (in press) 'Learning how to coach: The different learning situations reported by youth ice hockey coaches', *Physical Education and Sport Pedagogy*.

Young, M. F. D. (1998) *The curriculum of the future: From the 'New Sociology of Education' to a critical theory of learning*, London: Falmer Press.

Youth Sport Trust (2002) *Best practice in sports colleges: A guide to school improvement*, Loughborough: YST.

Zeichner, K. M. and Liston, D. P. (1996) *Reflective teaching: An introduction*, Mahwah, NJ: Lawrence Erlbaum.

Index

Lightning Source UK Ltd.
Milton Keynes UK
UKOW05f0215160515

251666UK00005B/66/P